Poverty and state support

SOCIAL POLICY IN MODERN BRITAIN

General Editor: Jo Campling

POVERTY AND STATE SUPPORT

Pete Alcock

LONGMAN
London and New York

LONGMAN GROUP UK LIMITED,
Longman House, Burnt Mill, Harlow,
Essex CM20 2JE, England
and Associated Companies throughout the world

*Published in the United States of America
by Longman Inc., New York*

First published 1987

BRITISH LIBRARY CATALOGUING IN PUBLICATION DATA

Alcock, Pete
  Poverty and state support.——(Social
  policy in modern Britain)
  1. Social security——Great Britain
  I. Title   II. Series
  368.4′00941   HD7165

ISBN 0-582-29652-8

LIBRARY OF CONGRESS CATALOGING IN PUBLICATION DATA

Alcock, Peter, 1951–
  Poverty and state support.
  (Social policy in modern Britain)
  Bibliography: p.
  Includes index.
  1. Social security——Great Britain.
2. Great Britain——Social Policy.   I. Title.
II. Series.
HD7165.A77   1987   368.4′00941   86-27857
ISBN 0-582-29652-8

Set in 10/11 Comp/Edit 6400 Plantin
Produced by Longman Singapore Publishers (Pte) Ltd.
Printed in Singapore.

CONTENTS

EDITOR'S PREFACE

This series, written by practising teachers in universities and polytechnics, is produced for students who are required to study social policy and administration, either as social science undergraduates or on various professional courses. The books provide studies focusing on essential topics in social policy and include new areas of discussion and research, to give students the opportunity to explore ideas and act as a basis of seminar work and further study. Each book combines an analysis of the selected theme, a critical narrative of the main developments and an assessment putting the topic into perspective as defined in the title. The supporting documents are an important aspect of the series. A number in square brackets, preceded by 'doc.', e.g. [doc. 1] refers the reader to the corresponding item in the section of documents which follows the main text.

Poverty and State Support has been written not only for students of social policy, social administration, social studies and social work but also for the increasing number of professionals whose work involves the understanding of complex social security issues. It provides a clear and easy to read introduction to social security in post-war Britain. The book not only deals with the detailed history and structure of social security policy, but also includes examination of the problems experienced within benefit provision, of attempts to overcome these in practice, and of the possibilities and prospects for reform of the system itself. It thus includes much which will be of interest to all those concerned with the operation of social security policy in Britain at both a practical and political level. The book has been written without footnotes or detailed references, and, as much as is possible without jargon or specialist knowledge. For those wishing to pursue particular aspects of theory, law or practice in more detail, references to other materials are provided throughout the text, and listed in the references section at the end.

The book opens with a theoretical discussion of the meaning of poverty and the role of state support, and develops a critical perspective towards previous material in this area, which is used to inform the analysis of social security policy pursued later in the book. The opening section also includes consideration of the gender dimension within state support, which it is argued is crucial in structuring the nature of welfare policy in Britain. In the second section there is a description of the development of social security policy in post-war Britain, focusing upon the changes in the politics and principles of benefit provision. This is followed by a more detailed analysis of benefit policies in the 1980s, providing a simple, but comprehensive, coverage of the major features of existing social security provision and including examination of the changes flowing from the reviews of social security in 1985 and planned to be introduced in April 1988. The final assessment section contains discussion of the problems and contradictions of benefit policy, a brief review of strategies for working within the welfare system, and analysis of alternative proposals for reform of social security provision. In this last section, in particular, the book provides readers with perspectives on welfare not normally covered in introductory books and thus offers a unique contribution to the study of social security policy in modern Britain, which will remain of value for many years to come.

Jo Campling

ACKNOWLEDGEMENTS

The attempt to write a comprehensive, and yet comprehensible, introduction to social security policy in Britain has not been an easy one. Especially so because it was begun before the most 'substantial examination' of the system since Beveridge, and finished after it. I had to make adjustments both to detail, and to principle, almost up to the last minute. The ideas and the analysis which inform the book have not quite been so hurriedly constructed, however. They are the result of discussion over a number of years with colleagues active in the promotion of social security reform, and to all of them I owe a debt for the criticisms and the insights which they have provided. I believe that it is only through such collective work that we are able to develop our ideas, and ultimately our policies too. Although, of course, for the errors and the inconsistencies which still remain, I am happy to be personally responsible.

I owe particular debts, however, to a number of people without whose personal support and assistance the book would never have been written. Jo Campling was throughout the period of its construction a constant source of support and encouragement. Sue Lonsdale encouraged me to begin the project, and then read through drafts and manuscript providing invaluable ideas and comments. Finally Jane Shepherd provided comments and advice throughout, and support without which I might never have got through at all.

Pete Alcock
August 1986

We are grateful to the following for permission to reproduce copyright material:

Basil Blackwell Ltd for an extract and Document Sixteen; the Editor for Document Eight; Gower Publishing Co Ltd for Document Six; the Controller of Her Majesty's Stationery Office for Documents 3, 4, 5, 7, 9, 10, 11, 12, 14, 15, 18 and various extracts from Crown Copyright material; New Left Books Ltd for Document Twenty Three; Oxford University Press for Document Twenty One; Sheffield City Council for Document Seventeen; the Adam Smith Institute for Document Nineteen; the Society of Civil & Public Servants for Document Twenty Two.

LIST OF ABBREVIATIONS

CBI	Confederation of British Industry
CDP	Community Development Project
CPAG	Child Poverty Action Group
DHSS	Department of Health and Social Security
EOC	Equal Opportunities Commission
FC	Family Credit
FIS	Family Income Supplement
HB	Housing Benefit
ICA	Invalid Care Allowance
IFS	Institute for Fiscal Studies
IS	Income Support
LEA	Local Education Authority
LRO	Liable Relative Officer
NAB	National Assistance Board
NCC	National Consumer Council
NCVO	National Council for Voluntary Organisations
NHS	National Health Service
NI	National Insurance
NIT	Negative Income Tax
SB	Supplementary Benefit
SBC	Supplementary Benefits Commission
SCPS	Society of Civil and Public Servants
SDA	Severe Disablement Allowance
SERPS	State Earnings-Related Pension Scheme
SSAC	Social Security Advisory Committee
SSAT	Social Security Appeal Tribunal
TUC	Trades Union Congress
URO	Unemployment Review Officer

Part one
DEFINING THE PROBLEM

Chapter one
POVERTY

WHAT IS POVERTY?

The title of this book suggests that social security policy in Britain is concerned with state provision of support for the poor, or the tackling of the problem of poverty through collective provision. In simple terms this is clearly correct – social security expenditure is money collected by the state in the form of taxes and contributions, and paid, for the most part, to those who are poor because they have no income of their own or because such income as they do have is inadequate to meet their needs. However, anyone with any experience of the social security scheme in Britain, especially from the receiving end as a claimant, will know that this collective provision is riddled with complications and qualifications, and that in spite of the existence of a so-called *welfare state* in modern Britain, there is no guarantee that state support will provide adequately for those in poverty, as almost all studies of poverty have found out [doc. 1].

These complications and qualifications are, however, deeply embedded within the structure of the social security scheme. They are not the unfortunate product of poorly organised policy decision-making, but are the reflections of more fundamental complications and contradictions within the concept of poverty itself and the development of policies for state support. In this first section of the book we will examine some of these fundamental problems, before proceeding to a discussion of their effects within current social security policy and the prospects for alternatives to them. This will involve us questioning first of all the very notion of poverty itself as the focus of state policy and also the assumption that state support is a product of collective benevolence towards the poor.

In spite of the development of the welfare state in Britain there is still widespread agreement that problems of poverty persist in our relatively affluent society. Studies by Abel Smith and Townsend (1965) in the 1950s and 1960s and Mack and Lansley (1985) in the 1980s found harsh and grinding poverty still a daily experience for millions of people in affluent Britain. However, both were at pains to point out that the issue of how the problem of poverty was defined was central to assessment of its scope and its persistence. And how the problem should be defined is in practice a matter of some dispute.

Townsend's (1979) major study of poverty in the United Kingdom opens with a discussion of the concepts of poverty and deprivation, and Holman's (1978) book on poverty has a first chapter on the meaning of poverty. Both conclude that different definitions of poverty are used for different purposes and, not surprisingly, that these can lead to different priorities for study and reform. Perhaps the most commonly discussed difference, however, is that between absolute and relative poverty.

ABSOLUTE POVERTY

Absolute poverty, sometimes called subsistence poverty, is the idea that being in poverty is being without the minimum necessary requirements for life or subsistence within life. If we do not eat, we starve, therefore those without the resources to acquire food fall below the absolute standard for life, and, unless they can escape this state, by theft or begging, they will starve. Absolute poverty is the most unacceptable face of any social order, and with the development of capitalist prosperity in nineteenth-century Britain there was a widespread assumption amongst those in power that it had largely been removed from the country by the end of the century.

However, towards the end of the nineteenth century social surveys were carried out which suggested that this may not be the case. Booth's (1889) work was the first to appear. It contained a definition of poverty as living under a struggle to find the necessities of life. He fixed this, somewhat arbitrarily, at an income of 18s. to 21s. (90p to 105p) a week (above the incomes of many who were in full-time work) and according to him over a third of Londoners were living in poverty. Inspired to some extent by Booth's work, Seebohm Rowntree set out to discover if poverty was more widespread than the Metropolis and carried out a detailed study in his home town of York in 1899 (Rowntree 1901).

Rowntree's definition of poverty was more complex than Booth's. He used the work of nutritionists to calculate a basic diet and priced the items for such a diet in shops in York. He then made a distinction between *primary poverty*, which was where total earnings of a family unit were insufficient for the maintenance of physical efficiency, and *secondary poverty*, which was where total earnings were sufficient but physical efficiency was not reached because the money was being spent on non-essentials. Having made this distinction, Rowntree in fact paid little attention to secondary poverty and, concentrating on the former, found that 15.6 per cent of wage-earners in York were living in primary poverty – 9.19 per cent of the population as a whole.

The impact of both studies was great because the numbers of those in poverty were somewhat higher than complacent official opinion of the time had been content to assume, though they were really only further confirmation of increasing awareness in some quarters of other indicators of deprivation, such as the poor physical condition of recruits for the Boer War. Rowntree repeated his study in 1936, and again in 1950, and in these later studies he extended the definition of subsistence to include expenses such as trade union dues and the cost of a daily newspaper. Under this measure in 1936 31.1 per cent of the working class of York were in poverty – 17.7 per cent of the population as a whole (Rowntree 1941; Rowntree & Lavers 1951).

What was most important about Rowntree's work for our purposes, however, was that in attempting to demonstrate the persistence of poverty within British capitalism he introduced a measure of *absolute poverty* which became very influential. If subsistence needs could be measured and they were not being met, then the task of social policy, and social security policy in particular, was to eliminate poverty by providing for these subsistence needs.

State provision for poverty appeared to accept such a measure. Under the Poor Law local administrators were supposed to assess the 'needs' of applicants before deciding whether assistance should be given. And under the Unemployment Assistance, introduced in 1934 to provide a national replacement for the Poor Law, a rigorous and intrusive investigation into means was made to ensure that no more than the minimum provision was made from state funds. This means test continued in the Supplementary Benefit (SB) scheme. The provision for subsistence was also central to the proposals for social insurance in the Beveridge Report (1942). Beveridge relied directly on Rowntree's calculations of subsistence needs as the basis for fixing the insurance benefit levels recommended in the report; and (somewhat reduced!) these subsequently became the basis of National Insurance (NI) benefits.

However, there are serious flaws in this subsistence measure, and indeed in the whole notion of an absolute measure of poverty. For a start the rigidity of the measure ignored the varying needs of families of different sizes and workers with different jobs, and yet the calculations were supposed to be based upon real needs. Furthermore the inflexibility of the calculation of the basic diet, for instance the assumption that bread would be baked at home, took no account of the actual eating habits and life-styles of people living in poverty or of the value of domestic labour carried out in the home. People did not organise their lives and their resources to meet Rowntree's minimum standard of efficiency. They had, and continue to have, needs and *desires* beyond the provision of basic food, clothing and shelter. Rowntree's inclusion of the new elements in the measure of poverty in 1936, whilst still endeavouring to cling to the notion of subsistence, in effect implicitly recognised this.

Of course Rowntree was adding new elements because expectations about what was a minimum standard for sufficiency had changed between 1899 and 1936, and so the definition of poverty had to reflect this. But this immediately raises certain important questions. If expectations can change, then presumably minimum standards can change. And if minimum standards can change, then what is the status of the supposed absolute measure of poverty? As we shall see, policies for benefit provision have continued to be based upon attempts to meet only subsistence needs; but whether these have any rational basis is doubtful.

RELATIVE POVERTY

The notion of relative poverty has appeared more recently in academic and political discussion of the problem of poverty, most notably since the *rediscovery of poverty* in Britain in the early 1960s. It was discussed in the important studies of poverty by Abel Smith and Townsend (1965) and Runciman (1966), and formed the basis of Townsend's own massive study of poverty in the 1970s (Townsend 1979).

Taking up the problem of the inflexibility of the absolute measure and the changing expectations of minimum standards, the notion of relative poverty is based on the idea that the measure of poverty, and consequently the numbers of people deemed to be living in poverty, can only be determined in relation to the standard of living of all members of any particular society. Thus people should be considered poor in Britain if they cannot afford to heat their accommodation adequately in winter, or if they cannot afford to maintain a stock of clothing when some is old or worn out, or even if they cannot afford to enjoy the advantages of advancing technology such as refrigerators and televisions which the vast majority of us take for granted.

The standards used to measure poverty in this case are derived not from a calculation of minimum needs, but from a comparison with the general level of affluence within society. It is thus a changing standard which will be different for different societies and different within one society over time – or, to put it more cynically, if the standards of the rest of the society move up we might expect the poor to be better off, but not, of course, better off relative to everyone else.

This does, of course, then raise the question of how to arrive at an objective measurement of a relative standard of poverty and of what aspects of wealth or affluence to include within the measure. Abel Smith and Townsend's (1965) seminal study of relative poverty in the 1950s and 1960s used as a measure the level of assistance benefits provided by the state (although of course as we mentioned above this level is at least in part based on an attempt to provide for a subsistence notion of poverty) in order to demonstrate that relative to nationally fixed standards many were still in poverty, in spite of increasing levels of affluence in society.

A more directly relative measure, however, would be to take a proportion of average earnings, say 75 per cent, and regard all those with an income below this figure as being in poverty. Although commonly used in studies of low wages, such a measure has not often been used in studies of poverty, and in any event there remains the problem of comparing individual income and household expenditure given the varied composition of different households.

However, if we do measure poverty relatively against levels of benefits or wages, the results are striking and rather depressing. According to Bradshaw (1982, p. 98), flat-rate NI Unemployment Benefit has remained static at around 19 per cent of average male manual earnings since 1948. And according to Department of Employment figures quoted in Pond and Winyard (1983, p. 5), the weekly earnings of the lowest 10 per cent of full-time male manual workers as a percentage of median weekly earnings did not change significantly from 1886 (when it was 68.6 per cent) to 1982 (when it was 68.3 per cent) (see also Routh 1980). Thus if we look at the incomes of the working and non-working poor on a relative basis their situation does not seem to have been significantly improved by the growing affluence of British society.

In 1985 Mack and Lansley attempted to measure the extent of relative poverty in Britain by asking respondents to a questionnaire what they considered to be necessary items of expenditure to maintain a minimum standard of living. They then calculated the numbers living in poverty relative to their ability to afford this. It was an attempt to arrive at an objective measure directly based upon relative judgements of affluence, and it revealed 7.5 million people living in relative poverty in the 1980s.

This should perhaps not be too surprising, for with a *relative* definition of poverty we could never hope to eliminate poverty without changing the relative standards of others in society too – some would have to get less in order for the poor to get more. This has seemingly not happened in Britain thus far, and has led some to argue that it means that poverty will always be with us. However, it would be possible to fix a level in relation to average wages, say 75 per cent, and ensure that all received at least this level. In a sense this would then eliminate a certain level of relative poverty.

Such a policy would mean, however, that provision for poverty would have to be directly related to the level of affluence within society, thus tying social policy more closely to economic policy within the political arena. This is a political issue, as was demonstrated in 1980 when the recently elected Conservative Government engaged in cuts in public expenditure and changed the basis upon which NI pension rates were increased – from moving up in line with wage or price inflation (at least in part a relative measure) to moving up in line with prices only (in theory an absolute measure). This meant that in a period of more rapidly increasing wages pensioners were relatively worse off. The aim of this was to 'save' money in order to reduce taxation levels on those with high levels of pay. It was a social and economic policy for redistribution though at the cost, not for the benefit, of a section of the poor.

Recognising a relative notion of poverty therefore raises a fundamental question about the relative distribution of resources within society between the poor *and* the rich. Within any society the problem of poverty is thus also the problem of inequality, with *the poor* merely being those receiving the smallest share. Affluence and poverty are different aspects of the same question of the distribution of resources, and in this context we perhaps need to widen the scope of our discussion of resources beyond the limitations of cash incomes, for many of the trappings of affluence in British society do not just come in a weekly or monthly pay-packet.

RELATIVE DEPRIVATION

In his study of poverty in the 1970s Townsend (1979) argued that in defining poverty he was using a concept of relative deprivation. This was necessary, he claimed, in order to take account of the fact that any measure of a relative standard of living of people in Britain would have to include more than just monetary wealth.

For a start there are the additions that employers can give their employees on top of monetary income, such fringe benefits as meals, expense accounts, company cars, long holidays, occupational pensions, and so on. These can mean that some workers are much better off than others even though their cash income may not be that different. There are also other forms of wealth beyond wages or benefits, such as savings and investments or capital assets. One immensely important capital asset in Britain in the 1980s is owner-occupied housing – over 60 per cent of the population (generally the top 60 per cent) own their own houses. As well as giving them greater freedom and security in their home this gives them an appreciating asset which can be cashed in or passed on on their death. Owner-occupation gives house owners greater control over their homes; ownership of other capital assets, for instance in a company, also provides control and thus power over the use of resources within that company. Such forms of wealth can be enjoyed through the power they confer as well as through the cash they represent.

As well as income and capital-related holdings there are also benefits in kind which can be enjoyed. These could be privately distributed and received such as produce from a small farm or gifts from family members; or they could be distributed publically by the state either locally or nationally, such as health services, social services or education. Benefits such as these obviously make a significant difference to the standard of living of people in Britain (they are sometimes referred to as the *social wage*). And if some benefit from them more than others they can be a major source of inequality. There is evidence to suggest that it is the wealthier middle classes who do benefit more from existing state services such as health and education (Le Grand 1981).

The distribution of assets and services affecting poverty and affluence is a direct product of social policies pursued by the state. Owner-occupied housing, for example, has been indirectly supported by all governments since the 1960s via the tax relief allowed on mortgage interest payments, and was openly encouraged after 1980 by the conferring of the right to buy on council tenants. Tax relief is also given on payments for life insurance and payments into occupational pension schemes. By the mid 1980s these counted together for almost £15 billion in forgone revenue, mostly from better-off members of society. This is significant redistribution of resources flowing directly from policy decisions taken within the state. As early as 1958 Titmus argued that these policy decisions were as much state welfare as was social security expenditure, although they were being used to compound and not to relieve relative poverty.

When we include possession of assets and access to services in an assessment of poverty both the definition and the scope of the problem become broader and more complex. As well as financial hardship, lack of assets can lead to loss of control and insecurity in other aspects of one's life, for instance over one's home. As Holman argued in 1978, unequal use of services can also lead to deprivation relative to the standards enjoyed by others. In spite of universal education some children fare much better at school than do others, and often those doing badly are concentrated in poor schools with inadequate resources. Some people also experience more frequent and more serious ill health than others, and often this is associated with working in bad conditions and for low wages (see Townsend & Davidson 1982).

Unequal access to services and benefits is also overlain by racist divisions within British society. Black people in Britain are more likely than white people to be unemployed or in insecure and poorly paid jobs. Their children are also less likely to do well at school. And they are likely to be excluded from services such as the National Health Service (NHS) as a result of suspicion and control of illegal immigration (see Brown 1984; Gordon 1983). Already experiencing insecurity because of the effects of immigration control, black people are thus further relatively deprived of the broader state support which makes full participation in British society possible.

Insecure housing, under-resourced schools and chronic ill health all contribute to the experience of relative deprivation. As well as being disproportionately experienced by black people these can also frequently be found concentrated in certain geographical areas, notably in run-down inner cities. Here the problems of poverty, standard of living, distribution of resources and the impact of state policies can become merely different aspects of the same problem. Thus we can no longer restrict the notion of poverty to one of simple needs or even the relative levels of cash income, it is a part of the wider question of the structure and distribution of resources in society and the power to control and use these. It also concerns the role of the state in controlling, regulating or supporting this structure. The question is that of inequality and power in British society, as it is indeed in any social order.

INEQUALITY

Most of the political and academic discussion of absolute and relative poverty in Britain has been conducted within a Fabian or social democratic framework, which has not related it to a broader discussion of the economic structure of society or of the role of government policy within this (see Taylor Gooby & Dale 1981; Lee & Raban 1987). Within such an approach poverty is seen as the basis for state intervention, and the more general causes of inequality within which poverty is based, including the policies of the state itself, are not discussed.

Once the issue of inequality, rather than poverty, is addressed then the question of the economic structure of power and resources becomes central to analysis. As Kincaid (1964), Gough (1979) and Ginsburg (1979) have argued, this means situating inequality within the structure of Britain's capitalist economy. Such analysis concludes that inequality is an inevitable product of the operation of a capitalist mode of production, and that state intervention to support the poor which does not *challenge* capitalist priorities will inevitably operate to *support* existing economic structures and may have the effect of *compounding* poverty and inequality, as we shall discuss later. This leads us on to a rather different perception of the problem of poverty and of its relation to policies of state support, and one which will be crucial to the perspective adopted throughout this book.

In a capitalist mode of production the necessarily unequal distribution of economic wealth and power is based upon a separation between different social classes. Classes are basically determined by their relationship to the mode of production, and there may be a number of classes within any society, in particular where, as in Britain, capitalism has been modified by state intervention. In spite of variations, however, there is a fundamental separation between the capitalist class (who own the means of production) and the working class (who do not).

Workers are paid wages out of the proceeds of their labour, which is employed in production and controlled by capitalists. Thus in very simple terms the lower the wages of the workers the higher the profit, or wealth, of the capitalists [doc. 2]. Consequently there is an inevitable tendency for workers to be forced into low-paid jobs. Obviously with changes in the economy and the structure of the workforce this will affect different groups of workers differently at different times (see Lonsdale 1985). However, it is likely to be the case for some even if the overall standards of society rise, which perhaps partly explains why the relative position of the poorly paid workers has not changed much since the nineteenth century.

Furthermore, at any given time there may be many workers who are ill-suited to labour because of age or disability or who are not required for labour because the forces of production are already at full capacity or because the products produced cannot be sold in a competitive market. These workers in effect constitute a reserve army of labour, some more likely to be chosen than others, who can be employed by capital if circumstances encourage profits but who otherwise will remain outside the wage relationship. As Beechey (1977) has argued, women occupy a particular position within this reserve because of their position of dependency within the family, and when they do enter work their wages are therefore on average lower. In all cases, however, those without wages will certainly be in poverty unless they can be supported by family members or friends, or by social security payments from the state.

Obviously individual capitalist economies like Britain are more complex than the simple model, and contain a number of classes in intermediate positions of wealth and power, such as the self-employed or those employed by the state. The state is now a major employer in British society, but its role is more extensive than that of employer alone. Gough (1979) discusses the welfare role of the state in capitalism in some detail. He argues that it operates to a large extent for the support and benefit of capital. In particular by providing some support for the poor it helps to ensure the social stability and control required for investment and the realisation of profit to continue. But of course such support is also of benefit to workers and non-workers – a contradiction of benefit and control to which we will return in Chapter 2.

It is arguable, therefore, that within a basically capitalist economy it is possible for poverty to be alleviated, through improved social support, whilst at the same time inequalities are preserved or accentuated. To remove poverty, however, would require a change in the relative position of the poor and thus an attack on inequality via a fundamental shift of power and resources. And this would require a change in the economic structure which produces that inequality. This is not to say, however, that any attempt to tackle poverty through a redistribution of resources must wait until after an economic 'revolution', but rather that all welfare measures are inevitably a compromise between greater provision to prevent absolute poverty and moves to reduce inequalities for all. And that if inequality is to be reduced then intervention must be made into the economic structures which produce it – the pattern of wages and investment – an issue to which we will return in more concrete terms in Part Four.

IDEOLOGY

How far concessions for the poor or redistribution of resources and power can be achieved within capitalist society without fundamental transformation of the mode of production itself is a political question which can only be determined by political action. In spite of improved living standards for poor people in Britain in the late twentieth century, in terms of relative deprivation, as we have discussed, little has been achieved. Part of the reason for this is that social policies are not just a product of economic forces and political action, but also of ideology. Ideological perceptions of what poverty is also structure explanations of how it is caused and what could or should be done about it.

As we have already implied, the notion of poverty as a problem of absolute need is based upon an assumption that it is caused by lack of access to basic essentials and will be removed by state support to provide these. It is thus a minimal and relatively easily 'solved' problem. Relative notions of poverty raise more complex questions about judgements of what constitutes the level of poverty and why some members of a relatively affluent society are not able to take advantage of its wealth.

Apart from Mack and Lansley's (1985) attempt to measure objectively perceptions of poverty, much discussion of relative deprivation is subjective. And as Runciman demonstrated in 1966, relative deprivation is perhaps not surprisingly *experienced* relatively. Those at the bottom of the social ladder by and large aspire to reach the relatively better position of those just above them, rather than to subvert the whole ladder by removing those at the top. Much of the real wealth in our society is not that conspicuous, and for those living in poor, run-down inner-city areas the deprivation experienced is by comparison with those just 'down the road'.

In addition those only marginally up the bottom of the ladder are frequently most conscious of their being *above* the bottom – especially where this position has been 'won' by hard work in an unrewarding and poorly remunerated job – rather than *below* the top. As Golding and Middleton (1982) found in their study of attitudes towards social security claimants, it was often the low-paid and unskilled workers who had the harshest views of the supposedly 'comfortable' life experienced on the dole. Even amongst the better paid the circuitous issue of *relativities* (maintaining one's position as better paid than someone else) has frequently been a more prominent feature of workers' struggles than the attempt to improve the position of the low-paid or unemployed.

Relative judgements of poverty also lead to judgemental views about its causes and solution. If a minority of people within an affluent society are unable to take advantage of the opportunities and services provided in order to alleviate poverty, this may be a product of their own inadequacy rather than deficiencies in state support itself. Perhaps the most influential version of such views is the *cycles of deprivation* thesis propounded by Keith Joseph, Secretary of State for Social Services, in 1972. Drawing indirectly on the work of American writers like Oscar Lewis (1968), he argued that the continued experience of poverty in Britain in the 1960s and 1970s was not a product of the failure of social and economic policies, which had provided opportunities and services for all, but of the failure of the poor to avail themselves of these. This was because they were trapped in a *culture of poverty* characterised by dependency and inadequacy, which was visited upon future generations via inadequate upbringing and education.

This is a *pathological* view of poverty which lays the blame for the problem firmly at the door of the poor themselves. It is also frequently overlain with racist assumptions about the inability of black people, in particular, to avail themselves of benefits and services, leading to their more acute relative deprivation discussed earlier, which it is assumed is caused by cultural or language problems within the black community rather than inadequacies in state provision itself.

It has, however, been widely criticised (see Holman 1978), and the notion of cyclical deprivation, in particular, has been shown to be of little empirical value (Rutter & Madge 1976). Nevertheless the pathological perception of the problem of relative poverty has been very important in shaping policies for state support.

It was such an ideological conception, and in particular its racist overtones, which informed the urban anti-poverty programmes which were established in the United States in the 1960s, and were followed in Britain by the Educational Priority Area, Urban Aid and Community Development Project (CDP) initiatives of the late 1960s and 1970s (Berthoud *et al.* 1981, and see Alcock 1986). Under these, state resources were targeted on to particular inner-city areas (especially those with large black populations) where high levels of relative deprivation were assumed to exist, not in order to redistribute resources to the poor themselves, but for the employment of professional social and community workers to encourage and assist the poor to escape from their poverty through their own efforts alone.

As most commentators on the anti-poverty programmes have demonstrated, they had remarkably little success in removing or reducing the poverty experienced in inner cities (Higgins 1978; Higgins *et al.* 1983). Indeed, as the seminal study of the US programmes by Piven and Cloward (1972) argued, they were not primarily directed at relieving poverty anyway but at meeting and containing the *political* threat posed by the (black) urban poor. And they could be contained through welfare programmes more easily than through economic and social reform.

What many of those professionals who worked in the anti-poverty programmes, especially the CDPs, found was that poverty was not a product of the inadequacies of the poor, but of fundamental inequalities of wealth and power within capitalist society. And that rather than reducing these, many state policies, notably industrial policy, were compounding and deepening them (Loney 1983).

The CDP workers thus became aware of fundamental contradictions in ideological perceptions of relative poverty which did not take account of wider economic structures and the role of state policy. The assumption that their work could help the poor to escape from their own poverty, and thus that support should be directed towards anti-poverty programmes rather than changes in benefit policy, wage levels or industrial development, was a direct product, however, of the ideological framework within which the problem of relative poverty was perceived. And it is a framework which, in spite of their challenge, remains remarkably influential in determining policies for state support, because it is broadly shared by many of those holding political power within the British state, and because it provides no fundamental challenge to political and economic structure. As we shall see in the next chapter, it is these factors which have largely determined the development of state policy on poverty.

THEORIES OF THE STATE

In the last chapter we questioned the nature of poverty as a basis of policies for state support. There is no clear problem of poverty which can be used to explain why policies of income support exist, for poverty is merely a feature of the broader inequalities of capitalist society. The state itself is a part of this society and thus is involved in the reproduction of the conditions which gave rise to this inequality. Policies of state support are the product of political decisions taken within the state. What policies these decisions represent and what effect they have on inequality and poverty will depend upon how we view the nature and role of the state itself and the processes of policy formulation and implementation within it.

To put this another way, since we cannot assume that income maintenance policies are based upon a desire to eliminate poverty, because poverty is an intrinsic part of the inequality of our social structure, we also cannot assume that such policies will automatically be designed to reduce or undermine the consequences of inequality. In an unequal society the state might be as concerned to maintain the structures of inequality as to change them. Thus we can only assess state policies if we have some appreciation of what we mean by the state and state policy, and this will depend upon theoretical questions about social structure.

We do not have the space, however, to discuss such issues in any depth here. Jessop (1982) examines some theories of state and state structure, and Gough (1979) provides a theoretical analysis of the welfare state in modern Britain, based largely on a Marxist theoretical background, which we will draw on throughout this book. Before going on to examine this in a little more detail, however, we will briefly look at two other approaches which have been very influential in much discussion of social policy, but which lead to important divergences in the analysis of policy within the state.

FUNCTIONALIST THEORIES OF THE STATE

Functionalism is a theoretical perspective which sees the different elements of society as integrated parts of an overall functioning whole. It is best exemplified in the theoretical work of Parsons (1949), and it has been a dominant theme in much writing about the state, especially in the United States. A lot of functionalist work on the state is descriptive rather than theoretical, but the assumptions inherent in a functionalist approach underlie much empirical work on social policy and thus give it a widespread influence.

Within such an approach the state is seen as the formal organising body of any advanced social system, providing the framework for functions which require national co-ordination. The state thus consists of the bodies charged with implementing these, and operates independently of the pressures or conflicts within any particular area. This is often represented in notions of the national interest, of the state being responsible for all citizens, or of the neutral state.

In this sense the state has an *objective* role in society, determined by the particular needs of that society and the need for central co-ordination. As advanced industrial societies have similar needs it is not surprising that the state should take similar forms within them. In the case of social security policy, the state is clearly responding to the need to provide for those in poverty who cannot support themselves in any other way. Of course this raises the questions of what is poverty and what are the needs of the poor; and, as we discussed before, there are different answers to them – which go to the heart of any analysis of the role of the state.

For a start, even if we accept that state policies are serving social functions, we can see that these policies have changed over time, and functionalists cannot readily account for this. It could be that the needs of society have changed. But arguably the basic needs of the poor are pretty constant, and they could hardly account for the fluctuations in social security policy we will discuss later. More frequently changes are said to occur as the state itself becomes better able to discharge its functions, for instance more by way of social policy through the state can be provided as the growth and modernisation of the economy permit.

Neither of these can really work as explanations of change, however. Changing notions of poverty are a product of changing *perceptions* of the problem, not changes in the nature of deprivation itself. And the problem of poverty is a product of the inequality which the state itself reproduces. It is not the case that poverty exists first and then the state comes along to solve or alleviate it. The notion of gradual improvement and modernisation is a more seductive explanation as it suggests that changes are somehow determined by events outside of state control, and that even if things are not perfect as they are they can only be changed if external forces permit. However, changes do not always follow a pattern of gradual improvement; and, of course, it is really the judgements of those in power within the state which determine what *is* an improvement and *when* economic and social conditions can permit it.

To say that the state functions to provide certain services within society is in a sense therefore little more than a truism. When we ask why these services at this time and in this form? And why do they change? A functionalist approach cannot provide any answer, except by referring to changing needs and conditions outside society which themselves cannot be explained. Clearly a theory of state policy must address these questions, in particular if we want to make any assessment of the prospects for *future* changes in policy.

If state policy is not a product of social needs and external constraints, then it must be produced by the activities of people within society and by the decisions of particular individuals or groups operating within the state at particular times. Some approaches to analysis of state policy recognise clearly the role of individuals and groups in the creation of social organisation, and rather than assuming that such organisation must take a certain form they concentrate upon policy decisions as the outcome of specific processes of struggle and agreement.

PLURALIST THEORIES OF THE STATE

Rather than starting with the assumption of particular roles for the state, a pluralist approach starts from the recognition that the state has a differing and changing character, and that this character is the product of the decisions taken by groups and individuals involved in the decision-making processes within it. State policy is determined by the aggregation of these decisions, and the state itself is the product of their implementation within the agencies of regulation and control.

Obviously the activities of the major political parties, and in particular the government, operating through Parliament and determining the constitution of the major state departments, are the primary example of the way in which the decisions of individuals and groups determine state policy. However, they themselves are also subject to the influences of their own organisational structures, which may put pressure on them to pursue particular policies, and to the influence of other groups outside of the party organisation such as the Confederation of British Industry (CBI) or the Trades Union Congress (TUC). In addition to this there are smaller groups who may be concerned only with particular areas of social policy, such as the Child Poverty Action Group (CPAG) campaigning in the social security area, or concerned with one issue only such as groups opposing the building of a new motorway.

Of course the numbers of individuals and groups involved in particular aspects of the state will vary, depending upon the issues and the organisations in different areas. The linchpin of the pluralist approach is that one cannot specify in advance what the outcome of any particular decision will be, because it depends entirely upon the nature of those involved and the relative power they are able to wield. Most pluralist studies of the state thus concentrate on particular areas of policy and often specific state institutions or policy decisions, and examine the influence exercised by those involved in making the decisions which have determined the character of policy.

One example of a pluralist discussion of the role of the state in the social security area is the study of the introduction of the SB scheme in 1966, as a product of the changes in Labour Party policy on benefits and the relations between the government and the civil service (Hall *et al.* 1975, Ch. 14). Though of course the Beveridge Report itself is a classic example of the influence on state policy which even an individual may be able to wield in some circumstances. What both of these demonstrate, however, is that state policies and state institutions are not a product of some predefined social needs but of the activities of individuals and groups struggling to implement their views and priorities at particular points in time. This involves not only the question of which policies to pursue but also the definition of social needs which are used as the basis for policies, for the protagonists of different policies base their arguments upon different definitions of need to which they then argue the state must respond. The changing influence of definitions of absolute and relative poverty in social security policy is an obvious example of this.

Thus pluralist accounts of the state and state policy recognise that these are a result of negotiation and decision-making, and decisions are based not only upon competing notions of how to provide services for needs but also competing notions of what such needs are. They have been very influential in more recent studies and accounts of the development of social security policy in Britain. And changes in social security in recent years have obviously been a product of political pressure and political decisions. Donnison (1982), writing about the Supplementary Benefits Commission (SBC), and Field (1982), writing about the CPAG, have demonstrated the roles that groups both inside and outside the formal state organisation can have on policy formulation. The campaigning work of the CPAG is itself based upon an attempt to use pressure-group strategies to influence the determination of state policy through the courts and through the Parliamentary process.

However, there are some serious shortcomings within pluralist approaches to state policy and some important questions to which there seem to be no answers. Changes within state policy are recognised within pluralism and are explained in terms of the role of individuals and groups within the political process. However, explanation remains at this subjective level and is always *ex post facto*, looking back at past events rather than forward to the future context in which state policy might develop. In fact the context of political events is generally rather absent from pluralist accounts, which tend to *describe* rather than *analyse* the political process. Fairly obvious questions are thus overlooked. Why do individuals *and* governments hold the views on policy that they do, and how and why do these change? Why are some groups more powerful than others? And are there any limits to influence that particular groups might have? Pluralist approaches cannot answer these questions because they concentrate upon the outcome of political pressure alone as the source of all policies and thus of the state itself.

However, pressure groups are operating within a given state structure and a given distribution of political and economic power. Their ability to achieve policy change is always constrained by this, as the CPAG have constantly found out. The existing structure of the state and its historical development provide an overriding influence upon the political activities and achievements of all individuals and groups. But by concentrating upon specific policy decisions or the activities of particular groups at particular periods of time little attention is paid to this in most pluralist accounts.

State policies are produced within particular political, economic and ideological constraints, and within British society policies clearly operate more to the benefit of some sections than others. This is also true of the state formation of other similar societies. The similarities between different state formations and the greater benefit which some sections of society gain from state policies cannot be explained merely by studying the political activities of individuals or groups. This does not mean, as functionalists assume, that the structure of the state is an external, pre-given entity. But there is nevertheless *some* structure there; and an adequate analysis of the state must be able to explain why the state is structured in this way and why in attempting to change it some groups have more influence and success than others.

MARXIST THEORIES OF THE STATE

Although Marx himself did not write much directly on the state in capitalist society, his main work in the area being a discussion of the nineteenth-century French state (Marx 1970), many writers since, drawing directly or indirectly on Marx's theoretical work (including Engels 1970), have argued that the role of the state in capitalist society must be understood in the context of changes in the economic structure of society and the activities of the antagonistic social classes which flow from these. However, disagreements run deep even amongst Marxists about the relative importance of economic forces, class struggle and political formation, and these in turn give rise to disagreements about the nature and role of the state. We cannot discuss all these differences here. Jessop (1982) discusses the state in Marxist theory and contrasts some of the major arguments about it, and Gough (1979) provides a Marxist analysis of the role of welfare within the capitalist state.

In spite of differences, however, there is overall consensus that the importance of a Marxist approach to the state is that it situates state formation within the broader framework of social structure. Social structure means that society should be understood as more than a mere collection of individuals and groups, because the need to reproduce these individuals within some social order and mutual dependence over time will pose limitations upon the freedom of action of all. These limitations will in general be a product of the requirements of the economy and the reproduction of society's material needs as these have developed over time.

Marx talks of this as the *mode of production*, the means by which material needs are met, and argues that modes of production will change over time as new and more sophisticated material processes develop and people struggle to control and exploit these. This leads in many cases to the development of antagonistic social classes, based on divisions between those who control the means of production and those who do not. This antagonism is based on the different economic

Longman is committed to publishing only the finest texts in your field and your comments are invaluable to us. After you have examined this text, please take a few moments to complete this form. Thank you.

Author _____

Title of Text _____

Name _____

Department _____

Institution _____

Telephone ( ) _____ Office Hrs. _____

Name of course _____ Enrollment _____

Present text _____

Is the Longman text applicable to the course you teach?
☐ Yes ☐ No

How would it be used?
☐ Main Text ☐ Supp. Text ☐ Recommended

Do you plan to adopt this text?
☐ Yes When? _____ ☐ No ☐ Undecided

Comments _____
_____
_____
_____
_____
_____

May we quote you?
☐ Yes ☐ No

Longman

position of classes and will lead to struggle between them, which provides a constant pressure to change the mode of production and thus other aspects of the social structure too.

Marxist theory thus emphasises *both* the structural constraints of society in general *and* the changing nature of that society as a result of the struggles of its members to change or control that structure. There is constant change, but within structural limits; and this applies to all aspects of society including struggles within the state. Indeed the state *itself* is a product of such struggles. It is not predetermined from outside of the social structure but is produced through struggles between classes within the constraints imposed by economic forces and by the existing power of the class or classes in positions of greater control of it.

This is not to say that the state is merely an 'instrument of oppression' used by the class with economic power. It also reflects struggles by other social classes to change this, and the difficulty of maintaining political power in a complex society makes outright oppression impossible. However, we must also not assume that the state can be subject to change merely as a result of members of the lower classes taking up the issue of change, for the existing power structures and economic forces may prevent them from achieving the sort of changes they want.

The state is thus *both* of these things at the same time. It is subject to constant change as the result of political struggle by classes or groups within classes, but it is also the product of a particular capitalist society with certain economic priorities and political power structures. It has both a structural and a historical dimension. We cannot assume that it will remain unchanged in the future, but we can assess the consequences and the likelihood of different changes based upon a knowledge of past struggles and existing structures. This is true for social and welfare policies within the state as much as for the more directly economic aspects of state policy.

Ginsburg (1979, p. 13) discusses this *dual character* of the state, and Gough (1979, p. 11) explores in some depth the *contradictions* of a state which both controls and oppresses certain social classes and yet is open to change through the struggles of those controlled, either against or within the state. In the case of social security, gains can be made to improve the state support for poorer members of the lower classes, but only within existing structures of economic and political power, and this means that along with the gains go further elements of control.

Thus Marxist theories of the state do not imply that everything is determined directly by economic needs, and that welfare policy and even the state itself are merely reflections of economic forces. It is the struggles of social classes within this economic structure which determine the state and welfare policy, and ultimately the economic structure too. But at any particular time these struggles must be waged within existing economic and political circumstances and (as we shall discuss later) under the influence of existing ideological notions of desirable and possible reform. Political change within and through the state, however, is not restricted to the struggle of social classes *per se*. Classes are the major economic groupings within society and the political parties that represent classes are the most powerful organisations within the state; but political pressure can be used by other groups representing particular interests which may cut across classes, such as community groups campaigning on environmental issues. The pluralist studies of the influence of such groups are not invalid, the problem is that they fail to discuss the economic and political context of the state which restricts the ability of many groups to campaign and to succeed.

Thus the state can be subjected to change as a result of political struggle. But change will be constrained by the economic structure of the mode of production and the existing political power which social classes wield because of this. This will continue to be so unless the economy itself can be changed. However, economic change can be made through political action within the state, for instance the nationalisation programmes of some Labour governments, and this can lead to a change in the economic position of social classes. But at the same time the framework of the capitalist economy will militate against major economic change; for instance, nationalised industries have generally become subservient to private enterprise. And the pressure to minimise change and preserve the existing balance of power can be keenly felt within the political arena of the state – as many who have worked within or against it will know.

From this perspective, policies for state support for the poor are *both* a state response to the political pressure of advocates for better provision for those in poverty *and*, at the same time, a form of state control over the unemployed and other groups within the lower classes. And political pressure to change this is thus often side-tracked into struggles to make minor improvements to existing benefits, which are already operating to divide and discipline the very people who are campaigning for change. The history of social security policy in Britain is a catalogue of such pressures and such contradictions, and we will now turn to look briefly at this history, before concentrating in later chapters on current policies and future prospects.

SOCIAL SECURITY POLICY IN BRITAIN

State-organised support for the relief and control of poverty dates back to the earliest days of capitalist development in Britain, and the time when central state planning was beginning to become important for the new economy (Anderson 1974). From 1601 the Poor Law declared that relief should be made available to those suffering from destitution in the country through funds collected and distributed at a parish level. It was a national provision but contradictions between this and its local administration and financing led to wide variety in the standards and levels of relief. Nevertheless in most places some distinction was made between beggars and vagrants (who were seen as personally responsible for their poverty through idleness or fecklessness and for whom relief should contain a punitive element) and the needy poor such as the disabled (for whom relief was provided on less conditional terms). This early distinction between the *deserving* and the *undeserving* poor signalled a division in state policy which had the effect not only of controlling the unemployed and enforcing labour discipline but also of dividing the poor amongst themselves through the creation of false ideological notions of desert.

When the uneven and haphazard Poor Law provision was reformed at the beginning of the nineteenth century these divisions were accentuated and incorporated directly into the ideological rationale of state support. The development of a capitalist economy was by this time in full flow in Britain, and the 1834 Poor Law Amendment Act was a clear attempt to ally social security policy to the needs of capital, through the state. Local expenditure on social security was controlled by the placing of restrictions upon the amount of relief provided – an early example of public expenditure control. Social control of the 'surplus population' outside the organisation and order of the labour market was introduced via penalties for vagrancy and, when indirect forms of control failed, via the use of institutionalised provision in the *workhouse*. Control over gender relationships and the position of women was also enforced through the assumption of family dependency and stricter state control of marriage and cohabitation in the Marriage Act 1836.

The control exercised through policies for state support made support conditional upon the *individual* circumstances of poor people, and was based upon the divisive notion of *less eligibility*. This meant that state provision was restricted to a minimum, below the level of wages, to encourage those dependent on the state to look for a better life in paid employment – or for women in family dependency. Less eligibility also enhanced the control exercised over the surplus population through its ideological impact in devaluing dependency on state welfare: in the eyes of recipients, because of the unpleasantness of life at subsistence level; and in the eyes of workers, because of the implication that those on benefits were really not standing on their own feet. This ideological dimension of state provision in the nineteenth century should not be underestimated, and it is perpetuated in twentieth-century fears of *scrounging* on the welfare state.

As well as reinforcing labour discipline, the ideological attack also weakened the political potential of benefit claimants by creating a separation of interests between them and the employed working class, and by limiting the possibility of alliances because of the negative connotations of claimants' status. Undeserving, inadequate and dependent claimants would be unlikely to see themselves, or be seen by others, as the basis of political struggles for social justice. For women within the family their devalued position was further reinforced by gender role expectations.

Of course the spectre of the workhouse did *not* encourage everyone to find jobs, *nor* did it contain all discontent. Jobs were not dependent upon workers' individual efforts but upon capital's needs, and as pay was often low in any case they did not prevent great hardship. The practice did also not always match up to the principles of the new state provision for poverty. Local Poor Law authorities varied a great deal in their treatment of claimants, some continuing to provide cash support (see Thane 1982, p. 12). And by the 1870s economic crisis brought social unrest which could not be contained by the impact of social policy alone (see Stedman Jones 1971). However, the limitations of state policy only led to further accentuation of the divisions and differences between the deserving and the undeserving; for instance, Booth in his study of the London poor found support only for provision for the minority of elderly and disabled claimants and a punitive attitude towards other undeserving categories (see Thane 1982, p. 15). By the end of the nineteenth century the *punitive tradition* had become a central feature of state provisions for poverty.

The punitive tradition also contained an important racist dimension. One aim of the vagrancy laws had always been to prevent persons arriving in a local area from claiming local support. When immigration into the country itself was first controlled in the twentieth century by the Aliens Act 1905, the power was included in the legislation to refuse entry to 'undesirables', who appeared unlikely to be able to support themselves. This effectively excluded poor aliens from Britain and linked policies of state support to those of immigration control. This link has remained throughout the twentieth century, and has resulted in benefit policies operating as a form of *internal control* over black people in Britain, who are constantly under suspicion of being illegal entrants and refused benefits as a result (see Gordon & Newnham 1985).

In the early part of the twentieth century there were new developments in state provision with the establishment of old-age pensions and compulsory state insurance for ill health and unemployment organised quite separately from the punitive traditions of the Poor Law. The early years of the century were a period of considerable social conflict and unrest both in Britain and abroad as the labour movement began to grow in power. They were also a period in which there was some official criticism of state provision for poverty, notably by the Royal Commission on the Poor Laws (see Thane 1982, p. 88). The new provisions thus contained some major gains.

The old-age pension of 5s. (25p) a week from 1908 was a direct state payment not tied to the vagaries of the Poor Law – its popularity at the time even extended to Lloyd George, the Cabinet Minister responsible for introducing it. Nevertheless it was less than the weekly income which Rowntree (1901) had calculated was necessary for subsistence, it was subject to a means test which excluded those with incomes from any other source from receiving it, and it initially contained moral restrictions too such as the exclusion of those who had been imprisoned in the previous ten years.

Insurance benefits for the unemployed (supported by William Beveridge, then at the Board of Trade) were introduced in 1912 and were also an improvement on the old Poor Law provision, giving those unemployed who were looking for another job the right to a benefit which they themselves had paid for through insurance contributions. In fact the idea of insurance for unemployment was not new; friendly societies and insurance companies had been organising it on an *ad hoc* basis amongst the working class for some time, and in many ways the new scheme was merely a nationalisation of existing private provision. However, the scheme *also* confirmed and extended aspects of state control of the unemployed and ideologies of division and dependency.

Though it was later extended to all, initially the scheme only covered skilled workers. The idea of insurance as the basis for protection also incorporated into state welfare notions of self-sufficiency and thrift amongst the poor. This was part of the ethos of the independent friendly societies and when taken into state provision it restricted dependency to rights guaranteed by one's own position and ability to pay. In effect this forestalled any demands that state provision for the unemployed should be paid for out of direct taxation as a redistribution of resources from the better paid to the poor. Indeed one of the intentions, and achievements, of the new scheme was to introduce provision without extra cost to the taxpayer.

By the 1920s unemployment was beginning to increase dramatically due to the onset of economic depression, and the insurance principle was quickly abandoned in the face of economic expediency, although only at the price of the increased enforcement of labour discipline. The Unemployment Insurance Act of 1922 'extended' insurance benefits to those not covered by the original scheme, but only if they were *genuinely* seeking full-time employment, a test based largely on character judgements by labour exchange officers which many, not surprisingly, failed. In 1922 a means test was also introduced to remove from benefit those with other incomes.

With the deepening of the recession the pressure on Unemployment Benefit increased and eventually in government and civil service circles this was turned into pressure to *cut* benefit rates. This was a direct attack on welfare provision – making the poor pay for the cost of economic decline. It also demonstrated the broader economic and ideological impact of welfare provision within a capitalist economy for it created a pressure to drive down wages by providing, through the state, a lower minimum acceptable standard of living, forcing those in the dole queue into poorly paid jobs. In 1931 the National Government, under ex-Labour Prime Minister Ramsay MacDonald, reduced the level of Unemployment Benefit by 10 per cent.

In 1933 the government restructured state benefits to consolidate some of the trends of recent changes. The insurance scheme was passed to the control of the *Unemployment Insurance Statutory Committee* and benefits were restored to a strict ratio based on contributions, reinstating the insurance principle. At the same time the *Unemployment Assistance Board* was also established to provide a national administration for the means-tested aspect of unemployment provision which had effectively replaced Poor Law provision for large numbers of the unemployed. Prior to this, Public Assistance Committees had been administering benefits under the state scheme at a local level in a similar fashion to Poor Relief, and with similar ideological overtones. The intention behind the new board was to establish a national pattern of provision and uniformity of treatment. Initially, however, the national scales were lower than many local rates and caused uproar in some areas – 300,000 demonstrated in South Wales alone (Deacon & Bradshaw 1983, p. 23).

The national scheme was thus unpopular when it was introduced and it effectively institutionalised the separation between insurance benefits, administered by one body, for the deserving who had paid, and means-tested benefits, administered by another body, for the undeserving who had not paid and were thus all potential scroungers. The administration of the schemes and claimants' experience of them confirmed and strengthened this ideological distinction. One thing that Public Assistance did achieve, however, was the gradual demise of the Poor Law itself and the dissipation of its functions, though most of these were incorporated into the new state social security provisions. Both assistance and insurance benefit levels were kept low to retain the principle of less eligibility and the incentive to find remunerated employment – although in fact there was little evidence to support the view that wages were falling below benefit levels or that there were jobs to be had for those that wanted them.

During the Second World War rapidly changing economic and political circumstances gave rise to some official commitment to a rationalisation of social security provision and the removal of some of the more unpopular aspects. The commitment was exemplified by the publication of the Beveridge Report (1942) and the widespread support it appeared to attract. In many ways, however, as we shall see, the report and the reforms which followed it have maintained the major contradictions of previous provisions, continuing divisions and dependency into the post-war welfare state.

CONTRADICTIONS IN THE WELFARE STATE

Social security policy over the last eighty years has resulted in the introduction of improved benefits for claimants and yet, as we saw in Chapter 1, their relative position within society has changed very little. Within a capitalist society this is a predictable development of state policy. Gains can be made by the lower classes; but without fundamentally challenging the priorities of the economy those gains will not transform existing balances of wealth and power. And, however severe the plight of the unemployed and other benefit claimants relative to the rest of society, political pressure has not been able to deflect other economic priorities.

In the case of social security policy, the failure to press the issue of redistribution further is partly a product of *economic* constraints. On the one hand a limited purchasing power for claimants is essential to the economy; but on the other the relative growth of this purchasing power must be limited due to the fear that too many resources in these hands would mean removing them from others and undermining the incentive to work. Social security provision is based upon state control over wage levels and labour discipline as well as support for the poor. Although to some extent contradictory, both are integral aspects of welfare policy, and they have political and ideological, as well as economic, dimensions.

Political debates and struggles over social security reflect and emphasise *different* aspects of the contradictory positions at *different* times and in *different* circumstances. Those putting pressure on the state to provide better welfare services have always stressed the obligations within the state to provide for the poor, and the continuing inadequacy of existing provision has been a constant source of criticism from campaigners such as the Webbs in the early twentieth century to the CPAG today. Yet in times of greatest hardship in the 1930s and in the 1980s benefit rates have been cut by the government. From a functionalist perspective this could only be explained as a failure by the state to fulfil its proper functions; or from a pluralist perspective as a failure of the campaigners to organise their political pressure effectively. From a Marxist perspective, however, it is only to be expected that political demands will be mediated by economic priorities.

Although social security policy can be seen as a contradictory product of the demands of a capitalist economy and the struggles of classes and groups within the state, it does not necessarily *appear* as this to those involved in struggles over it. As Townsend (1979) found in his study of poverty, this can include the poor themselves, many of whom had come to conclude that poverty did not exist or else believed that it was 'individually caused, through a mixture of ill-luck, indolence and mismanagement, rather than being a collective condition induced by institutional forces' (p. 431).

In the early 1980s the Conservative Government attempted to popularise the view that the state could not afford even the existing levels of support for the poor, and that there was widespread abuse of social security provision. This was not a new development, however, for it was obviously based on the broader ideological framework discussed in Chapter 1 which presents poverty as a product of individual failure rather than social structure and which occupies a predominant position within ideologies of welfare. The influence of *ideology* in the formulation of social policy and its implementation is not restricted to the Conservative Government of the 1980s, however. Ideologies structure the way in which all of us perceive and think about social events and they are as important in determining the form of policy as are economic demands or political struggles.

Golding and Middleton (1982) discuss how certain ideological perceptions of poverty, its causes and its consequences, have become dominant in Britain through the activities of the media and of prominent politicians, for instance the growth of the mythology of the benefit scrounger. Such perceptions *do* have consequences for the shape of social security policy; for instance in the 1970s and 1980s there was an increased concentration within the Department of Health and Social Security (DHSS) on the detection and discouragement of abuse. What the greater concentration on scrounging inevitably led to, however, was the identification and investigation of more scroungers, who were also given more publicity because of the policy. The framework of expectations thus created its own reality and *raison d'être*, and the ideology itself operated to structure social policy provision.

Such ideologies are not restricted either to politicians or the media. As the above excerpt from Townsend demonstrates, similar views have also penetrated the working class and even claimants themselves, who have little to achieve from such a structuring of policy. Taxpayers and NI contributors are very aware that they are paying for benefits which others receive. The divisive nature of the distinctions between those who pay and those who receive, and those who deserve and those who do not, are very much a part of popular knowledge about the benefit system, and have been a central feature of the construction of rights to benefit in the post-war period.

British social security is therefore not just *presented* in propaganda terms in a divisive way (though of course this does happen), the ideological framework both structures the provision and is also a consequence of it, thus reproducing itself. Social security policy *is* divisive both in terms of the forms of provision and the impact of these. It is, therefore, a difficult task to counter the structuring effect of this divisive framework, for any opposition must take on not only the perceptions of social security but the fact that the provisions themselves reflect and reproduce particular notions of poverty, inequality and the role of the state.

However, having said earlier that social security policy is a *contradictory* product of economic demands and political struggles, these contradictions must extend to ideologies of social security too. Whilst clearly these are dominant views about the form of policy, they are *dominant* and not *monolithic* ones, and even within them there are contradictions.

Post-war social security provision in Britain has been based largely, in principle at least, on the Beveridge Plan. Although this was by and large the expression of the view of one man, it was hardly an idiosyncratic fancy. Beveridge was a supporter of the Liberal Party and a close friend and follower of the economist Keynes. His view was that the government should intervene through the state to protect the poor, but only in ways which preserved incentives to work, to save, and to provide for oneself. This view, and his proposals, were not entirely accepted by Conservative elements of the government at the time and, as we shall see, they have never been fully implemented, in particular where they would have involved increases in state expenditure. And by the 1980s Beveridge's NI plan had been almost completely subverted in favour of benefits based on means tests.

Many disagree with either the insurance or the means-tested basis of benefit provision, but both are contained within the British social security scheme. And their coexistence produces contradictory tensions within the ideological framework which structures state support, carrying the contradictions of economic and political struggle into this level too. Any struggle to change or influence provisions must struggle to combat and exploit these ideological tensions, as well as political and economic ones.

We must also take account, however, of the fact that these positions are part of broader ideological frameworks concerning the role of welfare in capitalist society, and that these frameworks themselves are influenced by economic demands and political priorities. Thus whilst ideologies of welfare are an important part of the structure of social security provision, and a part which cannot be ignored in analysis or struggle, they are *only* a *part*.

Therefore whilst social security policy is about state support for the poor, it cannot be taken for granted that such support will be an inevitable product of a modern state. Nor can such support be measured either absolutely or relatively to determine its adequacy, so that if inadequate it can automatically, or following political pressure, be extended or improved, as functionalist or pluralist notions of the state might suggest.

That state support exists is a product of political struggle, restricted and directed by economic priorities, and constructed within particular ideological frameworks. This support serves the needs of a capitalist economy, yet at the same time it provides a platform for struggle to change the priority of these needs. In this struggle genuine gains can be made for the poor and for the broader working class – but without a fundamental change in the economic structure itself these gains will be contradictory in their form and their effect. In practice this is because the continued demands of the economy, the restrictions of political struggle and the impact of ideologies of welfare provision will mean that gains made will be provided within systems which continue to oppress, divide and control both the poor and their political supporters.

Chapter three
GENDER INEQUALITY

WOMEN'S SOCIAL POSITION

There are common assumptions in most social policy studies of class and inequality which ignore the question of gender and the position of women. It is predominantly assumed that the family is the unit of analysis or measurement and a woman's class position or social status is determined by that of her husband. Working-class women are thus the wives of working-class men and poor women the wives of low-paid or unemployed men – never the working or poor wives of middle-class men. This assumption runs so deep that frequently we do not even notice it and yet it is crucial in structuring analysis of women (and ultimately of all individuals) in British society *and* in determining the pattern of social provision. In doing this, of course, the assumption creates the conditions for its realisation and, as we shall see, state policy thus contributes to a situation in which women are forced into a secondary status in society unable to escape from dependency upon men.

As feminists such as Delphy (1984) have vehemently argued, there are no justifiable grounds for basing our assessment of women's social and economic position on that of their husbands and assuming that their dependency upon the men they live with is non-problematic. Delphy argues that the relationship between men and women in marriage is essentially and fundamentally one of economic exploitation which puts them in situations analogous to those of dominant and oppressed classes. To base women's position on that of their husband, therefore, is to ignore completely this relationship of difference and conflict. There is much debate amongst feminists over the question of whether women's oppression is a product of economic exploitation within marriage *per se*, or a product also of other social forces (see Barrett 1980). But all would agree that the marital relationship is one of potential or actual conflict in which it cannot be assumed that dependency leads to harmony or symmetry – or to a satisfactory standard of living for women.

For a start women's position is frequently that of workers themselves. Now over half of married women are in paid work and, as Land (1976) has discussed, this has always been an important source of financial support for their families. Most women who are not in paid work also do a significant amount of unpaid work in the home, in particular in child care and the care of dependent relatives. This work is of social importance whatever the class or social position of their husbands. However, the payment of wages or benefits to men on behalf of their wives and families, no matter how generous these are, is no guarantee that money will be equally distributed to reward women adequately and ensure that wives receive a sufficient income. Even where there is no overt conflict within a marital relationship, there may frequently be inequality.

It is not unusual in these circumstances for men to retain control over the family income, giving their wives only a *housekeeping allowance* to provide for food and other necessites. As Pahl (1980) and Barrett and McIntosh (1982) have pointed out, there is increasing evidence that sharing of the family income is not automatic, and that even where this income is not significantly low women may have a life-style much below that of their husbands. Some women have found that after leaving their husbands and claiming SB in their own right they were better off than they had been during marriage (Binney *et al.* 1981, Ch. 1).

The socio-economic position of women, including their relative wealth or poverty, cannot be judged therefore by their husband's social status and the wages or benefits for the family which he receives. Indeed it is just this assumption which creates the dependency of women on men and the inequality to which this leads. And, as we shall see, policies for state support in Britain have consistently reinforced this relationship.

THE HISTORY (OR HERSTORY) OF INEQUALITY

One of the intentions, and the effects, of the Poor Law amendments in the nineteenth century was to curtail separate support for men and women and encourage family dependency – or rather the dependence of women and their children upon men's wages. The spectre of the workhouse was expected to coerce women with young children into seeking private support. Female single parents were only given relief during confinement and nursing and after that would have to leave their children in the workhouse if they could not fend for themselves. And as this was unlikely to come through adequate wages at work it usually meant dependency upon a man. Widows generally received better treatment, reinforcing notions of deserving and undeserving single women.

It is perhaps not surprising that in this climate trade unions representing primarily male workers should seek to ensure that men were paid a *family wage*, enough to support a wife and children. As Humphries (1977) argued, in the political struggle of the labour market such a wage was a way of protecting the living standards of the working class. However, as we have already suggested, family wages do not always guarantee an adequate income to women, and as Barrett and McIntosh (1981) have argued, the price for increasing working-class income in this way was increasing control for men and increasing dependency for women.

By the end of the century the expectation of married women's dependency was a well-established plank of social planning. From it flowed the assumption that the needs of women for state support were different from those of men, primarily because men would provide for women on a private basis, and only where this could not be assumed, for instance in the case of childless single women, would there be a need for state help. The health and unemployment schemes of the early twentieth century, although in theory based on entitlement in return for contributions, in practice incorporated the assumption of married women's assumed dependency and different needs into the new provisions for state support.

Women paid slightly lower contributions than men and received lower benefits, usually about 80 per cent of the full rate, married women receiving even less than single women. As Land (1976) discussed, this was supposedly based on actuarial principles: women, especially married women, suffered more from sickness than men and would therefore be a disproportionate drain on the insurance fund. Of course this disproportionate 'malingering' was for many women largely connected with suffering related to childbirth and hardly constituted a justification for worse treatment within the benefit system. But in any event the rationale does not tally with the failure to apply the same principle to differential sickness rates elsewhere in the scheme, or with the lower level of unemployment benefit for women where arguably they were a lesser risk.

Of course the underlying assumption was that women would need less state support anyway because they could always rely on their husbands. This expectation turned into statutory principle in the Anomalies Act 1931, introduced to prevent women who were 'not really unemployed' from drawing unemployment benefit merely to enhance married life. Quite what the anomaly was in such situations might now be subject to reinterpretation(!) and the rule was withdrawn in the post-war reforms.

In the Unemployment Assistance scheme of the 1930s, designed to provide support for those not covered by the insurance schemes (a situation in which married women not in full-time work were more likely than most to find themselves), the assumption of dependency was an integral part of the determination of entitlement to support. All claimants had to undergo a household means test, which carried over some of the worst features of the enforced dependency of the Poor Law (see Deacon & Bradshaw 1983, Ch. 2). This meant that married women could have no independent claim for benefit and were required to rely on their husbands, and even single women could be regarded as part of another household such as that of their parents. The justification for this was to ensure that support went only to those who were in 'genuine' need; but it ignored completely the problem that women's needs might be different and separate from those of other members of their household.

The special position of women as child-bearers has received only limited and contradictory recognition within the development of benefit provision. Maternity Benefit, a cash payment on the birth of a child, was included in the early insurance scheme, but it was not very generous and hardly reflected the costs of child care at birth. After birth there was no support at all for the costs of child care, the assumption being that the man's family wage would cater for these as well as for his dependent wife. Of course many men did not, and could not, provide adequately for dependents in this way, and family wages have always had to be supplemented by women's paid work. The notion of the male breadwinner has always been a myth.

After the First World War campaigners such as Eleanor Rathbone began to argue for the payment of cash allowances to all families to provide for the costs of child care. This demand for *Family Allowances* did not initially meet with much official sympathy, partly because it was seen as undermining private family responsibility (see Hall *et al.* 1975, Ch. 9; MacNicol 1980). Eventually, however, the idea was taken up by Beveridge and incorporated into his proposals for social security reform. The reason for this support, though, was not so much a recognition of the financial needs of children and child carers as a desire to encourage childbirth because of fears of the effect on the post-war economy of the falling birth-rate experienced during the war, and a realisation that large families, with a potentially large entitlement to insurance benefits, might be better off claiming these than relying on the income of a man on low wages. A direct payment, related to family size, and paid to all would therefore help keep families together, encourage women to have children and stay at home to care for them, and ensure that there was an incentive for men to work.

In fact the Family Allowances which were introduced after the war were an inadequate compromise with the principle of direct benefits to cover the costs of child care. They were too low to reflect the real costs of care and provided no benefit for the first child, encouraging women to have more children, and nearly halving the cost of the scheme. The assumption behind state support for children was thus that mothers would be dependent upon their husbands and that benefits were an addition to family income, not a reflection of the costs of child care itself.

This assumption can be seen more generally in the discussion of women's role in the Beveridge Report (1942) itself. Beveridge argued that married women had a special status as housewives and that this should be recognised within social security provision. The married woman was thus different from her single sister, 'she has other duties' (p. 51), and must look for support first to her husband. This was presented not as dependency but as sharing: 'Taken as a whole, the Plan for Social Security puts a premium upon marriage instead of penalising it. The position of housewives is recognised ... by treating them, not as dependants of their husbands, but as partners sharing benefits and pension when there are no earnings for them to share' (p. 52). But it was a sharing, with the exception of the Family Allowance, of money paid to the man. The consequence of this special, and supposedly newly exalted, role for women was a continuation and confirmation of their inferior status within the NI scheme. It was not so much the case that married women needed less insurance benefit than men, rather they did not really need any at all as the benefits paid to their husbands would cover their needs too.

Thus married women were exempt from paying full contributions when they were in paid work in return for giving up their right to claim benefits in their own right when they were not. Even where they did pay and establish an entitlement to benefit, Beveridge recommended that they should receive lower rates (two-thirds of the full rate) except for maternity when they should receive more – a further inducement to engage in childbirth. As if this were not enough, however, Beveridge also proposed to encourage marriage directly and recommended the payment of a Marriage Grant (a single cash payment on marriage) and the provision of benefits or allowances on separation or divorce, in order to protect dependent women.

These latter two recommendations were never acted upon; indeed the final one was seen as an inducement to marital breakdown, not a support for married women. However, Beveridge also proposed a Widow's Benefit to support married women on their husband's death. It was to be a relatively generous benefit to cushion women against the loss of their breadwinner and was included in the post-war reforms, providing a benefit for women specifically based upon their assumed financial dependency.

As we have discussed, Beveridge's report was widely supported when it was published. His recommendations concerning women were also welcomed by many women's groups (Price 1979, and see Dale & Foster 1986, Ch. 1). It must not be forgotten that his proposals, although recommending a confirmation of women's dependent status, were nevertheless a significant improvement on what had been the position of married women before the war. And to a large extent support reflected the lack of any feminist perspective dominant within organisations at the time, and the fact that the assumption of dependency within marriage was by then already a deeply rooted feature of the ideology of state support. None the less, the proposals were not without their critics, notably the Women's Freedom League (Abbot & Bompas 1943), who pointed out that Beveridge's special position for married women was in effect a denial of the status of individual persons.

Beveridge's proposals for National Assistance were intended only as a temporary measure, although as we shall see, this has not proved to be the case. As with the insurance proposals, they were based upon the family unit, with a dependent wife. Thus married women could not claim benefit in their own right and were *aggregated* into the needs and entitlement of their husbands. In such circumstances women might be encouraged to remain unmarried in order to preserve an entitlement to benefit in their own right. This would lead to a situation in which unmarried and cohabiting women were treated more favourably than their married sisters. In order to avoid this, and the threat to the sanctity of marriage which it posed, unmarried women who were judged to be cohabiting with a man were regarded as dependent upon him whether or not financial support was in fact received. Immorality was to be no escape from enforced dependency in the post-war welfare state.

UNEQUAL TREATMENT

The social security scheme of post-war Britain is based by and large upon the insurance and assistance proposals of the Beveridge Report and contains their assumptions of a secondary position for married women, and as a consequence of this for single women too. Many features of the benefit system thus discriminate directly or indirectly against women. Much of this discrimination would be unlawful under the Sex Discrimination Act 1975 but for the fact that statutory provisions are excluded from the impact of the legislation. Some of it was also in breach of EEC directive 79/7 which requires equal treatment to be given to men and women in social security, however; and as we shall see, changes have had to be made as a result of this.

Within the NI scheme itself the option of the reduced rate of contributions for married women was withdrawn in the Social Security Act 1975, and new contributors now pay at the full rate and receive full benefits. Those who were paying at the reduced rate before, however, had the opportunity to continue doing so, which about a half of the 6 million working wives opted to do, although these contributions still do not entitle them to any benefits. The assumption, of course, is that married women will be entitled to benefits through their husbands' contributions.

In the case of Widow's Benefits this leads to an element of beneficial unequal treatment for widows who, because of their dependent status, are presumed to be without support on their husband's death. In such a situation they can claim a benefit based on their husbands' contribution record. In similar circumstances a widower is not entitled to benefit, even if he was dependent upon a wife paying full contributions. Widow's Allowance is a generous weekly flat-rate benefit paid for the first six months of widowhood. After six months widows are presumably expected to have found another husband, and in the 1988 changes this arbitrary period is to be replaced with entitlement to a lump sum on widowhood. Women over forty and those with dependent children, however (perhaps a less marriageable proposition), are entitled to a lower Widow's Pension or Widowed Mother's Allowance, until retirement or until the children grow up. These both cease, however, on remarriage and are suspended on cohabitation, when of course it is expected that dependency upon another man will have been secured.

Married women's dependency upon their husbands and their husband's contribution records are also a central feature of NI pension provision. The predominant assumption underlying pensions is that married women beyond pension age will continue to depend upon their husbands. Thus where married women have no pension contribution record of their own, they may retire, at between sixty and sixty-five, but will continue to be dependent upon their husbands. When the husband retires at sixty-five his pension will then include a dependants' addition for his wife. After their husbands' death retired married women can continue to receive a pension based on his contribution record, a right that is not accorded to married women who are divorced from their husbands before retirement age – another example of division between deserving and undeserving claimants.

The problems caused for women in establishing entitlement to NI pensions, because of their assumed or actual financial dependence upon their husbands during their working life and the different ages of retirement for men and women, are frequently complex (see Groves 1983, and Masson 1985). Without challenging and changing the assumption of dependency itself, however, equality can only be achieved by formally extending similar rights of dependency to married men (see Abel Smith 1983).

Married women in paid work paying contributions can establish their own right to NI pensions independent of their husbands. When the State Earnings-Related Pension Scheme (SERPS) is in full maturity this may provide a more adequate independent state support in retirement for married women, especially as up to twenty years spent caring for children or dependent relatives can be discounted from the working life for contribution purposes. However, married women are less likely to be in the well-paid, secure jobs which will guarantee them high earnings-related additions, and this will be exacerbated after the 1988 changes under which earnings-related additions will be reduced and will no longer be based only on contributions paid during the best-paid twenty years of a working life (White Paper 1985, p. 13). This is likely to continue effective unequal treatment into retirement even where women have established their own right to a pension, maintaining for many the need to depend on their husbands. That such dependency is not regarded as problematic for women needing support, however, extends beyond Beveridge's special status for married women in the insurance scheme.

This assumption has operated most harshly in the provision (or non-provision) of non-contributory benefits related to disability. In the case of the, now abolished, Non-Contributory Invalidity Pension it used to have the effect of denying married women this meagre benefit unless they were incapable of doing housework for their husbands. This has now been replaced by the Severe Disablement

Allowance (SDA). However, entitlement to this is restricted in a way which continues to discriminate against married and cohabiting women. To get the allowance claimants must prove that they are unfit for work *and* severely disabled – though this latter test is not applied to those entitled before the age of twenty (primarily the congenitally disabled). Of course those who have been in paid work before becoming disabled will be likely to have contribution records and be entitled to the more generous NI Invalidity Pension; and thus those becoming disabled later in life and unlikely to have adequate contribution records who will have to satisfy the severe disability test will primarily be married and cohabiting women who have been engaged in unpaid housework or who have opted for reduced contributions. Thus although formally not discriminatory, SDA is a benefit which provides in effect unequal treatment for women by imposing criteria which, as a result of their social position, they are less able to meet.

In the case of the Invalid Care Allowance (ICA) overt discrimination remained until a case brought before the European Court in 1986 under the EEC directive on equal treatment forced the government to extend entitlement to women. Invalid Care Allowance is a weekly benefit paid to adults who are out of work and caring at home for a disabled person receiving an Attendance Allowance. It is so small that without other income it would leave the claimant below SB level; but prior to 1986 it was nevertheless not paid to married or cohabiting women. The clear implication of this was that it was women's job to care for dependants anyway and that they should not expect to get paid or receive benefit for this if they were living with a man, because in these circumstances the man would support them. In spite of this refusal the pressure on individual women to care for dependent relatives, whatever the cost, has always been great and is strongly overlaid with moral expectations, as one woman interviewed in an EOC (1981) study revealed: 'My position is do I give up work and everything I have worked for, from paying full stamp to getting a pension in my own right, or do I let my husband spend the rest of his life in hospital? I know most wives are like me, they love their husbands and will take care of them' (p. 19).

What is clear from this is that discrimination and unequal treatment within social security are part of a broader ideology of family responsibility and women's role, in which differential treatment is expected to be accepted as part of a *natural* social order. However, overt discrimination contradicts the EEC directive, and in 1985 the non-payment of ICA to married or cohabiting women was challenged in the European Court in a case supported by the CPAG. In 1986 the court ruled that non-payment was a breach of the directive; but before the judgement had been delivered the government announced plans to extend payment to women carers, estimated to be in the region of 70,000. The problem of backdating payment was not conceded, however, and, although the legal victory was an important one, the benefit remains a derisory contribution towards the real costs of care.

The EEC directive also forced the government to make changes in entitlement to NI and means-tested benefits, which were introduced in November 1983. In the case of NI benefits, this means that either party in a couple can now claim an addition for a dependent adult if the latter is not receiving any benefit. In the case of SB, the effect of the change is more complex. The family unit is still the basis of entitlement and the resources of men and women are still aggregated, but now in certain circumstances either partner can claim on behalf of the couple. It is up to the couple to choose who is to claim, and this can only be changed at twelve-monthly intervals. However, restrictions were maintained on who could claim and these are more likely to exclude women as they require the establishment of some recent connection with the labour market. They are costly and time-consuming to administer, however, and the 1988 changes will remove them and permit either partner to claim at any time.

The equal treatment provisions also apply to Family Income Supplement (FIS), so that either male or female breadwinners can claim this. Although, of course, in most cases this will continue to mean that it is the man who claims, and in recognition of this it was originally intended in the 1988 reforms to pay the new Family Credit (FC), which would replace FIS, in with the breadwinner's wage rather than directly to the child carer. The effect of this would have been to deprive women at home of a significant, if limited, source of independent income; and this received much opposition from women's groups and the poverty lobby – as well as from employers, who did not want the extra burden of administering the payment. And, when the 1986 Bill was being debated in the Lords, the government announced their intention to abandon the change in the method of payment.

In spite of this concession, however, FIS and FC are hardly an independent income for mothers. Though they provide valuable cash for women at home with children they *are* based upon an attempt to supplement men's low household wages rather than to provide state support for women. In this context the transfer of the payment into the wage packet was in a sense a logical move, and that it would have contributed further to women's dependency would have been no real departure from existing policy. Indeed it is the ideological notion of dependency within existing benefit structures, rather than the issue of equal treatment in claiming benefits which is the root cause of gender inequality in social security. And, in spite of the moves towards more formal equal treatment in the 1980s, the fundamental structuring role of this ideology has not been undermined.

REPRODUCING IDEOLOGIES OF GENDER

Social security provision is by and large based upon the assumption that poor people live in 'family units'. Benefit entitlement is thus restricted to such units, forcing women into a dependent role. However, this is not just an indirect consequence of the structure of benefits, it is a direct effect of the operation of the scheme, for it requires the DHSS to determine family status in order to establish entitlement. In doing this they must investigate women's living arrangements and make judgements about how these are organised. And these judgements are then enforced because they determine entitlement (or not) to state support.

It is up to the DHSS to decide whether a man and woman are 'living together as man and wife', leading to the notorious *cohabitation rule*. There is no definition of this relationship in social security regulations or family law, although a DHSS leaflet gives guidelines to be taken into account by officers [doc. 3]. The presence or absence of any sexual relationship has traditionally been used as the basis for assuming financial dependency. This has overtones of prostitution, however, and is no longer claimed to be conclusive evidence. The criterion frequently used by DHSS investigators is whether a single woman has a regular male visitor staying overnight or regularly visits a man on such a basis. It is hardly surprising that these investigators have acquired the name of *sex snoopers*. When the relationship with a man does not involve financial support the effect of the rule in the withdrawal of the women's benefit will be either to enforce dependency or destroy the relationship – a high price for some to pay.

The assumption of dependency also continues after relationships have ended, especially where children are involved. Divorced or separated wives can claim maintenance for themselves and their children from ex-husbands, and the mothers of illegitimate children can claim for the children within three years of birth. Furthermore the DHSS have the right under ss. 18 and 19 of the Supplementary Benefit Act 1976 to recover from such *liable relatives* money paid out in

SB to women. They can even bring a criminal prosecution for persistent failure to maintain under s. 25, though this power is rarely used.

Specialist Liable Relative Officers (LROs) are now employed by DHSS offices to pursue maintenance payments. They can advise women of their rights to claim maintenance and the advantages of so doing. This advice can, of course, be turned down by women who would rather claim SB – it is certainly a more reliable source of income. However, as any maintenance paid is deducted from women's SB entitlement, the pressure put on women to claim whilst ostensibly offering them advice can be great, especially as it can be arranged for the DHSS to pursue and receive the money direct – few men can afford to pay enough maintenance to exhaust women's entitlement to SB altogether.

In these circumstances maintenance is of no benefit to women at all, and merely serves to reduce the overall cost of SB. Whether this is the best way to spread the cost of child care across the sexes is indeed an open question. It is certainly an arbitrary way, and the price paid by harassed and cajoled individual women can be high. In situations where the breakdown of the relationship has included violence against women, the enforcement of maintenance can be downright dangerous.

As we have suggested, the status of dependency in social security carries with it connotations of incapacity and stigma. It is also isolating and divides those who claim from those who finance their dependency willingly or unwillingly. Dependency is thus a negative status, and this negative status extends particularly harshly to women within social security because of their doubly dependent status. It is in the reproduction of this general climate rather than in the individual examples of unequal treatment that the policy is at its most significant in creating gender inequality, and where gender inequality runs deepest within it. The consequences of this are also far-reaching ideologically, politically and economically.

Ideologically the negative status of dependency means that in effect women are being denied the rights of citizenship. Married and cohabiting women's status is subsumed within that of their partners. In the case of single women, especially single mothers, this dependency is assumed in any relationship with a man. The climate is one of suspicion and disbelief overlain with assumptions about women's proper place.

Political consequences flow from this isolation and suspicion. Within their individual 'family units' women do not have the basis for organising to campaign against their assumed dependency; and such a challenge may in any case put them into conflict with their male partners and the male-dominated organisations of political struggle in the trade union and labour movement which have by and large supported men's supposedly predominant role as the breadwinner. The only apparently successful campaign for benefits organised specifically around the position of women was the inter-war Family Allowance campaign, and the appearance here was deceptive because the allowances eventually introduced were in effect a reinforcement of women's role rather than a challenge to it.

Suggestions have been made more recently for extension of the Family Allowance principle to recognise and support the unpaid work which women carers do in the home by the payment of a *home responsibilty allowance* to women in these circumstances. Although this would recognise and reward such work more directly and fairly than the assumption that men will automatically provide adequately for their wives, it would at the same time reinforce this as women's role and continue to encourage men to shun caring responsibilities in favour of the status of breadwinner, in spite of the fact that many cannot adequately fulfil this in any case.

Some feminists, for instance McIntosh (1981) and Bennett (1983), have argued that if women's position within the benefit system is ever to be changed significantly then a political challenge must be made to the male breadwinner myth and the assumption of female dependency. This would require a demand for the *disaggregation* of benefit entitlement and the payment of individual benefits direct to all those not in paid work whatever their marital status or the situation of their spouse. This is a political challenge to which we will return later.

Not surprisingly, however, it is the *economic* consequences of dependency which most seriously restrict women's social position and are likely to prove most difficult to change. Unemployed claimants constitute a reserve pool of labour for industry, who will be taken on only when economic circumstances favour employment, and whose generally low wages help to depress the wage demands of all. As Beechey (1977) has argued, this 'reserve army of labour' status applies particularly and peculiarly to women. They are more likely to be forced into the secondary labour market of low-paid and insecure employment because of expectations of their domestic role and their presumed dependency within the family. As dependants, women's benefit entitlement is lower due to aggregation and the presumption that they will be supported by a man can thus be used to justify lower wage levels for them – it is only *pin money*. Despite the Equal Pay Act 1970 women's average pay is still below 70 per cent of men's, and the choices which individual women, and men, have to make about the allocation of caring responsibilities in the home are likely to be influenced by such harsh economic facts.

Of course, the ideological, political and economic consequences of dependency are interlocking in their effects on the reproduction of gender inequality within the principles of the social security scheme and through its operation in practice. Low wages for women reinforce the expectation of dependency and stifle the political organisation to combat this, at the same time forcing women into a choice between paid employment, or care and dependency. Though in practice, of course, many women must choose both. Social security provisions are based upon such a structure and in responding to it they also reproduce it by failing to provide alternative forms of support for women. This aspect of social security is as central to its impact in society as the divisions between the poor and the rich, the deserving and the undeserving, or the contributors and the non-contributors, and must inform analysis of current benefit provisions and proposals for change.

Part two
THE POST-WAR SCHEME

Chapter four
THE BEVERIDGE PLAN

THE POST-WAR WELFARE CONSENSUS

The post-war British social security scheme has largely been based upon the reforms introduced after the Second World War by the Labour Government following the recommendations of the Beveridge Report of 1942. In fact, as we shall see, what Beveridge recommended was a rationalisation rather than a revolution in benefit policy. But the political climate in which they were introduced and the wide scope of the reforms made marked a turning-point in the development of policies for state support in Britain.

The post-war period has frequently been discussed as a period of political consensus over the necessity and desirability of social policy reforms, carried out by the state but without a fundamental challenge to economic structures (Crosland 1956; Gilmour 1978; MacMillan 1938; and see Raban 1986). The growth of collectivist and nationalist ideologies during the war had provided, it was claimed, a favourable climate for public provision which all political parties found it easy to invoke and difficult to resist. It was argued that the state had a new role to play in preventing the worst inequities of capitalism whilst maintaining its advantages through the guarantee of a minimum standard of care and support for all – the role of a *welfare state*.

Support for this new welfare state was presumed to cross party lines and was thus sometimes referred to as *Butskellism*, a mixture of the policies of the Conservative Butler and Labour's Gaitskell. Crucial to the supposed consensus, however, was support for, and belief in, the economic policies of Keynes, and an interventionist role for the state in a capitalist economy to ensure economic growth and full employment. In the first decade or so after the war it was perhaps possible to believe that such policies could both maintain a capitalist economy and permit the growth of welfare. However, contradictions and unrest were never far below the surface of 'never had it so good' Britain, most notably in the 'race' riots of 1958. And when Keynesian economic growth faltered in the 1960s and 1970s the façade of the political consensus and the support for the welfare state began to break up. By the 1980s it was under direct attack.

The widespread popularity of Beveridge's proposals for social security reform was the outstanding example of the appearance of the welfare consensus. They symbolised a commitment for the state to enter into a partnership with its citizens to prevent poverty and ensure that there was no return to the conflict and depression of the 1930s. However, they were neither revolutionary nor socialist in design. Beveridge was a Liberal and his aim was to draw on the liberal values of thrift and self-support organised through the state as a means of providing a basic standard of living for all, beyond which it was up to individuals to provide for themselves. He hoped the adoption of his recommendations would carry social security outside of party politics as a permanent social provision, indeed the proposed basis for the funding of the social insurance scheme was supposedly a mechanism for removing the determination of benefit levels from the vagaries of the economic policies of different governments. In the Parliamentary debate on the Beveridge Report there were those on the right who doubted the feasibility and desirability of the comprehensive proposals [doc. 4]. However, there was quite a wide-ranging inter-party support for the major principles of the scheme. And since then changes made have adapted rather than challenged the framework of provision and have generally been accepted by the governments of different parties.

Since the introduction of the post-war reforms, however, the supposed political consensus of support for the framework of the social security scheme has resulted in social security being seen less and less as a political issue on a mass or a campaigning scale. The initial hope that the welfare state would eliminate poverty was questioned with the *rediscovery of poverty* in the 1960s, but this did not lead to political challenge to the welfare state or the basis of the social security scheme. Campaigns, including the rediscovery of poverty, were largely led by academics who saw their role as expert critics of social policy providing advice to the government and the civil service on how to improve provision for the poor – a technical rather than a political approach to the solution of any continuing problem of poverty. And in their advice there was generally no suggestion of a need for major political change, rather they stressed the importance of building upon existing political achievements and agreements to ensure incremental improvement and not wholesale reform of state support.

The domination of policy-making by technical concerns with existing benefits was made all the more unassailable by the incredible and increasing complexity of social security. The Beveridge scheme itself was complex enough, but with piecemeal changes and developments to it it became a mammoth task to follow the details of its principles and its workings. In such circumstances the role of experts was bound to become influential indeed.

In preventing poverty and inequality becoming issues for broader political concern in post-war Britain, however, the increasing technicism of debate about social security served to disguise the fact that benefit provisions, and changes and additions to them, were the product of particular ideologies and particular political forces. And that far from being for the general good of claimants, they might be serving only to further the control and oppression within the scheme. As we have discussed, these negative features are an inherent and contradictory feature of state provision within capitalism which the political supposed consensus over the welfare state could only paper over.

Beneath the surface of all-party support for the establishment and gradual improvement of the welfare state were important ideological, political and economic differences about the extent of provision and the nature of state support itself. The changes in benefit provision since implementation of Beveridge represent the entrenchment or weakening of these different positions, even though they may appear as part of a general improvement. At root the differences are about whether social security is a minimum provision for the prevention of absolute poverty or part of a general attack upon inequality. In social security policy, however, the issue has most frequently turned on the difference in emphasis between *selective* and *universal* benefits (see Deacon & Bradshaw 1983, Chs 3 & 4; MacGregor 1981, Ch. 5).

In simple terms selectivists argue that the role of state provision should be restricted to the elimination of absolute poverty, and the limited public resources that can be afforded for state support should go only to those most in need. Sometimes called *targeting* benefits, this basically means that social security provision should be means-tested and proof of individual (or family) need should be the basis of entitlement. Means-testing was supposed to have a minimal role in the Beveridge Plan; but it has remained a central and growing feature of the post-war scheme.

Universalists, on the other hand, point out that means tests can operate to stigmatise and discourage benefit claimants and are based upon an unjustifiable notion of absolute poverty. Social security provision should therefore seek to minimise means-testing as much as possible by providing universal benefits for categories of claimants based on social status alone. They argue that state support should be used to provide protection from the inequalities of the economy or (in more socialist versions) should be used to attack those inequalities through a redistribution of resources to those receiving state support.

Extreme versions of either position have rarely been influential in post-war social security policy. Indeed the NI scheme itself was something of a compromise between replacing means-testing with an automatic entitlement to benefit and restricting the extent of that entitlement and its threat to the existing distribution of wealth by requiring those claiming to have first paid contributions into the scheme. And, as we shall see, the major disagreement since then has centred around the question of how far it is desirable or possible to minimise the numbers of those dependent upon means-tested assistance by extending or adapting NI benefits. Labour governments have generally tried to minimise such dependency and extended insurance, though with very little success. Conservative governments have permitted or encouraged the gradual extension of means testing, without any direct threat to the NI scheme itself. It is such developments which have contributed to the appearance of consensus and have also led to the incredible complexity of benefit provision. In the 1980s, however, the return to power of a more right-wing Conservative Government led to questions being asked about this increasing complexity, and to a more direct reassessment of the political and economic priorities for state support, and to a questioning of the Beveridge Plan itself.

THE BEVERIDGE PLAN

The Beveridge Report of 1942 was the culmination of a review of the whole of social security provision in Britain commissioned by the wartime National Government. Beveridge and his team of civil servants were asked 'To undertake, with special reference to the inter-relation of the schemes, a survey of the existing national schemes of social insurance and allied services, including workmen's compensation, and to make recommendations' (p. 1). Certainly the heavy demand on state support in the 1930s had revealed that the piecemeal development of provision had left a confusing and overlapping series of benefit schemes which, though broadly under the aegis of the state, still maintained the role of private insurance and friendly societies in the administration of social insurance. Furthermore the widespread receipt of benefits in the recession, in particular means-tested social assistance, had created much unrest and antagonism to state welfare (see Deacon & Bradshaw 1983, Ch. 2).

Published only days after the Battle of Alamein, the report touched an optimistic belief in what could be achieved after the war. It received widespread popular acclaim and became an instant best-seller. It also received the approval of the wartime Coalition Cabinet, although many in the Conservative Party and in Whitehall had severe reservations about some of its more far-reaching implications. The Prime Minister, Churchill, although not openly opposing the report made it clear that, in spite of Beveridge's hopes, it could not be implemented until after the war.

Some of the implications of the basic conclusion of the report, that a subsistence benefit for all should be provided through an NI scheme, were likely to have significant effects on the structure of provision; and the civil servants who had worked with Beveridge were instructed not to sign the report lest the impression be given that their ministries had endorsed the proposed changes. In practice, however, the report was far from revolutionary in nature. Beveridge had been closely involved with the development of insurance provisions before the war, and what he proposed was largely an attempt to use existing principles of state support through insurance in order to provide a more rational and effective form of subsistence benefit and minimise the role of means-testing. This involved a clear role for the state in providing welfare, but one restricted to a minimal, organisational level.

Beveridge's report optimistically, and perhaps naïvely, appealed to an assumed consensus over the basic goals of social planning and social policy, linked to the economic policies of his close friend Keynes. He identified five *giants* of social evil which the organisation of the state must be enlisted to attack: disease, ignorance, squalor, idleness and want. His remit, he claimed, was the latter. Thus his proposals were for a plan to eliminate want. Other measures would be needed in the other areas. And Beveridge clearly envisaged social planning on a broad scale, for he said that his proposals would only be viable if assumptions that he made about provision in other areas were proved to be correct.

He made *three* central assumptions: that Family Allowances would be paid for children; that a comprehensive health service would be introduced to cater for physical needs; and that virtually full employment would be maintained (for men). It was no major insight to realise that social security policy could not be separated from broader political and economic developments, though since then supporters of Beveridge have often overlooked the integration of his proposals with economic policy. There was a general labour shortage in Britain for the first two decades after the war, but since then unemployment levels have continued to grow, rendering essential features of his proposed plan unworkable.

Beveridge claimed that he was working within certain guiding principles. These included the need to attack want, the need for revolutionary thinking(!), and the need for a partnership between the state and the individual. The individual he had in mind of course was the male head of a dependent family, who would wish to provide for himself and his family in cases of need over and above the provisions of state support, and should be encouraged to do this through private insurance. Public support was thus seen as a stimulus not an alternative to private relief.

The recommendations in the report were more than just a series of proposals for change. Beveridge had taken seriously the requirement for a thorough review of the structure of provision and presented his report as a complete *Plan for Social Security* [doc. 5].

The plan was to provide income support from the state for periods of interruption of normal earnings from the labour market. Support was to last for as long as the period of interruption. In the case of pensioners and the disabled this would be permanently, but the expectation was that interruptions would normally only be temporary as employment would be available for those who were available for it. Beveridge therefore proposed that Unemployment Benefit should be conditional upon availability for work and that training should be made available, on a compulsory basis, for those who had been unemployed for more than a certain period. As with previous benefit schemes therefore, state support was to be a complement not a challenge to the labour market, although this did not extend to married women who were expected to be outside of both the labour market and the social security scheme.

There were three methods of support in Beveridge's plan: *first*, social insurance, which was to be the basis of the scheme; *second*, national assistance, for those not covered by the insurance scheme who were expected to be a small and declining number; and *third*, voluntary insurance on the private market, for those who wanted, and could afford, greater support than the state minimum.

Social insurance was intended as an extension of the existing insurance measures to provide a comprehensive, national scheme for all. It would cover those who had been excluded from previous schemes and would replace the insurance companies and friendly societies with central state administration. Beveridge was adamant that insurance should be retained as the basis of state support because it was what people wanted: 'The capacity and desire of British people to contribute for security are among the most certain and impressive social facts of today' (p. 119). Individuals would feel that they had a right to claim benefits because they had paid for them and were getting them 'not as a charity but a right'. Contributions would be paid on a weekly flat-rate basis by all those in work, including the self-employed, so that all would feel that they had paid on an equal basis. There would also be a contribution from employers; and a contribution from the exchequer out of general taxation. These contributions would then constitute the Insurance Fund, which would be independent of the Treasury and would be maintained at a level sufficient to meet all future benefit claims on it. In this way the insurance scheme would be a provision *for* the people *by* the people, with the state merely handling administration and payment of benefit.

Clearly Beveridge's plan did not include any proposals for redistributing resources from the rich to the poor, indeed the fact that the scheme would be largely self-financing, with a regressive effect on those on low incomes as compared with direct taxation, was seen as one of its great attractions to people, not one of its drawbacks.

Benefit levels were also not fixed with redistribution in mind. Beveridge intended these to be *flat rate* and fixed at *subsistence* level. He recognised that the actual level of such benefits would obviously be affected by price levels at any particular time; but his intention was that they should provide only for basic needs, which he based on Rowntree's calculations of essential needs. This led to much disagreement at the time due to the impossibility of defining absolute needs. There was also the problem of rents, which fluctuated widely throughout the country. Some Conservative MPs argued that subsistence benefits including rents could end up being too generous, because the Insurance Fund would not be able to pay the rents for all. And in the event the average figure which was compromised upon was far too low for many, and over the subsequent forty years has fallen further and further behind the subsistence level exclusive of rent in the means-tested assistance scheme, contributing to a problem of serious overlap to which we shall return shortly.

The insurance scheme was intended to be comprehensive, with benefits to cover all possible cases of need. Beveridge proposed *four* different forms of benefit to do this: *benefits*, short-term weekly payments; *pensions*, long-term weekly payments; *allowances*, weekly additions for dependents; and *grants*, single payments for particular needs. He also identified *eight* different cases of need (excluding industrial injury which he considered separately): unemployment, disability, loss of livelihood, retirement, marriage (at its formation and its dissolution), funeral costs, childhood, and disease or incapacity. And he proposed that insurance payments be made for each of these. This should, in theory, have covered all cases of need. However, if there were still some not provided for, Beveridge recommended that means-tested assistance payments be retained as a safety net.

The retention of *National Assistance*, in spite of Beveridge's recognition of the unpopularity and undesirability of means-testing, was seen as a temporary expedient with a limited role within the overall plan. It was to be a subsistence payment for those with no insurance benefit and no other resources to rely on. By implication, therefore, there was no right to benefit as in the insurance scheme; and although the hated household means test of the 1930s was 'reduced' to a family means test, the degradation and stigmatisation of means-testing were to remain. Indeed Beveridge was quite clear that the receipt of assistance was not supposed to be a pleasant experience and suggested that, 'It must be felt to be something less desirable than insurance benefit' (p. 141), in order to maintain the popularity of the latter. It was also to be financed out of general taxation, rather than the Insurance Fund, and would therefore be more likely to be subject to direct political control, and to the accusation that those dependent on it were 'scrounging' at the taxpayers' expense.

Voluntary insurance was an essential part of Beveridge's plan, not only as a supplement to (and additional justification for) state subsistence benefits, but also as some compensation to the insurance companies and friendly societies who were to be excluded from the social insurance scheme. Thrift and self-help were felt to be generally good for the economy and were essential ideological features of the whole thrust of the report. This 'partnership' between the state and private insurance was part of the logic of the Beveridge Plan and not a subsequent modification of it.

The Beveridge Report also included proposals for the *administration* of benefits. It was Beveridge's intention that social security administration should acquire a more prominent and co-ordinated role within the state. This would require the creation of a Ministry of Social Security under the control of a Cabinet Minister responsible for the whole range of benefit provision, including administration of Unemployment Benefit which was then covered by the Ministry of Labour. This hoped-for co-ordination has never been fulfilled. As we shall see however, it is not the only feature of the Beveridge Plan to have come to grief in the real world of post-war Britain.

IMPLEMENTING BEVERIDGE

Although Beveridge's plan was a comprehensive set of proposals for a social security scheme and received much acclaim as such, it was not in the end implemented in its entirety. There were disagreements over the extent of insurance benefits and their levels, particularly in the report of a committee of Ministry of Labour officials which appeared shortly after (see Deacon & Bradshaw 1983, p. 43). In 1944 the government produced a *White Paper* outlining their proposals for the implementation of Beveridge's recommendations. The overall structure of the insurance scheme and the assumptions on which it was based were largely accepted, as was the range of benefits proposed, with the significant exception of Marriage Grants and benefits payable on marital breakdown (leaving most divorced women without insurance cover).

The White Paper included specific contribution rates and conditions for entitlement. For short-term benefits these were 26 weekly contributions paid in any one year and 50 paid or excused in the last full year before claiming; and for long-term pensions an average of 50 paid over the whole working life. Benefit rates were also included: 24s. (£1.20) a week Unemployment and Sickness Benefit, 20s. (£1.00) Unemployment Benefit for married women, and 36s. (£1.80) Maternity and Widow's Benefit.

In spite of Beveridge's proposal that benefit entitlement should last as long as need remained, limitations on payment were proposed. After a year those still on Sickness Benefit would go on to a lower invalidity pension, Maternity and Widow's Benefit would last for thirteen weeks, and most significantly Unemployment Benefit would cease after thirty weeks in order to avoid 'abuse'.

The funding of the scheme was to be on the tripartite basis advocated by Beveridge, administered by a new Ministry of Social Insurance. The National Assistance scheme, providing means-tested benefits outside of the insurance plan, was to be funded out of taxation and administered separately, under the aegis of the new Ministry. The role of friendly societies and other approved bodies within the scheme was to be terminated.

After the war the Coalition Government was disbanded and the ensuing election won by the Labour Party, with a manifesto based on the introduction of far-reaching changes in social policy. In fact the Labour Government adopted almost entirely the proposals in the White Paper, though they did slightly raise the benefit rates to reflect a rise in the cost of living. Unemployment Benefit went up from 24s. (£1.20) to 26s. (£1.30) a week, inclusive of rent.

It was Family Allowances which were introduced first in 1945: 5s. (25p) a week payable for second and subsequent children only. In 1946 the insurance measures, now called National Insurance, were introduced, including a separate industrial injuries scheme. In theory pensioners would not have been able to establish entitlement to NI pensions until some years after the introduction of the scheme, because of the need to build up contribution records. However, this would have immediately excluded from the insurance scheme large numbers of the 'deserving' poor and thus they were all given entitlement via fictitious contribution records. This led to a major contradiction within the supposedly self-financing insurance scheme, to which we will return in Chapter 6; but in the short term it led to a significant reduction in the numbers of people dependent upon means-tested benefits and appeared to confirm initial optimism in the potential achievements of the Beveridge Plan.

However, the optimism was relatively short-lived. In 1948 the National Assistance proposals were enacted, and the seeds of major structural problems within the schemes began to be revealed. The main difficulty was that assistance benefits were supposed to be a safety net for those falling through the insurance scheme. Their level, therefore, was fixed at a minimum to provide for basic needs, with discretionary additions for those with needs above these. However, these basic needs did not include rent, which was to be paid on top of benefit. Because insurance rates had been kept at a subsistence level too, yet inclusive of rent, the assistance rates announced in 1948 (24s. (£1.20) a week for a single person) were effectively higher than insurance benefits for large numbers of claimants who had no other income available. This meant that in 1948 675,000 claimants were having their insurance benefits 'topped up' by assistance benefits, and by 1951 the number had risen to a million.

As we shall see, the problem of the overlap between two different, subsistence, benefit schemes has never been resolved, although in practice many may have been deterred from claiming under both because of the degradation associated with the means test in the assistance scheme. It was operated independently of the Ministry of National Insurance by the *National Assistance Board* (NAB) with any extra needs over and above the weekly rate being subject to the discretionary judgement of NAB officers. From its first introduction the procedure for claiming must have smacked of a kind of begging off the state.

To make matters worse, however, the government was worried in case those on assistance were better off than they would have been had they been in full-time work, thus undermining the commitment to full employment and posing a threat to labour discipline. They therefore refused entitlement where the head of the household was in full-time work, and where *he* was not, entitlement for the whole family was subject to a *wage stop*. Under this benefit entitlement was restricted to the amount of wages available in full-time employment, even if these (hypothetical) wages were below the family's weekly National Assistance needs. Whether the wage stop acted as an incentive to seek employment is impossible to prove, though it is just as likely that it operated as a disincentive to claim assistance where there was already some income for the family from NI benefit, even though this was below subsistence level, further underlining the second-class nature of the assistance scheme.

In spite of its contradictions and compromises, however, by 1950 Britain had a more comprehensive social security system than ever before, based on the ideals of Beveridge and hailed as an integral part of the new welfare state. Even though it was less than the watershed envisaged by Beveridge himself, it was nevertheless a high-water mark from which both the principles and the practice of benefit provision have since retreated. Drifts in benefit rates, amendments to the original scheme and piecemeal additions have undermined even the limited principles of the Beveridge Plan and left a system much less adequate in preventing poverty than that intended and yet immensely more complicated and confusing. Underneath both the post-war achievements and the subsequent retreats, however, the fundamental contradictions between subsistence and redistribution remain.

Chapter five
ABANDONING BEVERIDGE

THE DECLINE OF INSURANCE

With the defeat of the Labour Government in the second general election in 1951 power was taken over by the Conservatives and retained for the next thirteen years. For the most part the view of the new government was that an adequate social security scheme had now been introduced in the country and that further major changes were not needed. Their expectation was that economic growth and not social policy would now provide for social needs.

They thus retained the major features of the insurance and assistance schemes, making only minor amendments to remove some anomalies, notably the differential benefit rates for married women. Throughout the 1950s benefit rates were increased sufficiently to keep them in pace with price and wage increases. In a period of economic expansion this meant that in absolute terms levels were improved, but relative to increases in average earnings they showed no change. The effect of this was that National Assistance benefits with rent paid in addition remained generally higher than insurance benefits; and despite the fact that many were probably not taking up their entitlement to assistance the numbers dependent upon it gradually expanded.

With unemployment levels generally low the large majority of these were pensioners, whose NI pensions were not sufficient for their needs. Their dependence upon means-tested provision was potentially a source of embarrassment to the government, but their major commitment was to encourage the growth of private pension schemes to provide for pensions above NI level rather than reform the insurance scheme itself. Private pension provision did grow during the 1950s with many millions of workers joining *superannuation* schemes run by their employers, though of course the majority of these were middle-class employees in secure jobs, and in any event they provided for *future* retirement, not the needs of current pensioners.

The plight of pensioners on assistance thus remained an unresolved problem, and in 1957 the Labour Party proposed significant changes in state pension provision to deal with it. Their plan was to introduce a *national* superannuation scheme run by the state into which all would contribute and from which earnings-related payments would be made on a weekly basis after retirement. The proposal would have involved major changes in the state insurance principle, and yet like the private schemes would provide for future not present pensioners. It was never implemented because the Conservative Government remained in power, but it was to provide the basis for future proposals to attempt to reduce the scope of means-testing by raising the incomes of some NI claimants with additions based on previous earnings.

This became much more of a political issue in the 1960s, fuelled to some extent by the rediscovery of poverty arguments of critics of the assistance scheme and their emphasis upon the need to respond not just to subsistence needs but also to the problem of relative poverty.

Relative poverty was an ambiguous concept, however. It meant poverty relative to the standard of living enjoyed by others in society; but it could also mean poverty relative to the standard of living recently enjoyed by those now on benefits. In other words, a drop from reasonable wages on to subsistence benefits on unemployment or sickness was, relatively speaking, a drop into poverty. In an article entitled '*Beveridge II: another viewpoint*' published in 1963, Abel Smith argued that it was this that was now the major problem with the social security scheme and that Beveridge's flat-rate benefits, although appropriate for the hungry 1930s, were out of step with the demands of the affluent 1960s. What people wanted, he claimed, were wage-related benefits provided by the state, both in retirement and in situations of unemployment and sickness.

In the early 1960s the Labour Party took up the challenge of the persistence of poverty within the welfare state and the need to reform social security. They published a programme of reforms called *New Frontiers for Social Security* (Labour Party 1963), proposing earnings-related benefits in return for earnings-related contributions in NI and a minimum income guarantee to lift existing pensioners immediately off the assistance scheme. However, they also accepted the commitment to economic growth as a means of paying for such 'improvements' in the benefit system. And after gaining power in 1964 they were unable to achieve the levels of growth which had been experienced in the boom years of the 1950s, leading to a dilemma in the policies for social security reform.

The Beveridge Plan, of course, had never envisaged social security provision as a challenge to economic priorities. However, the decision to subvert demands for social security reform in favour of policies to encourage economic growth in the 1960s meant that the reforms made to social security, rather than ironing out some of the persistent failings of the post-war insurance scheme, in fact tended to exacerbate and accentuate these. They also began a process in which reforms were to be seen less and less as improvements to the original Beveridge Plan and more and more as economically expedient, short-term reactions to contradictions and crises within the existing benefit system. In practice this meant an increasingly rapid drift towards means-testing.

In 1966 changes were made to the NI scheme, partly as a response to the relative poverty arguments, and partly as a contribution towards the government's strategy for stimulating growth by making short-term unemployment more acceptable. In return for slightly extended earnings-related contributions, an earnings-related addition was paid to short-term NI benefits, such as Unemployment and Sickness Benefit, lasting for the first six months of entitlement. After that benefit reverted to the flat-rate level, and after a year Unemployment Benefit ceased altogether. The earnings-related pension scheme was delayed, however, and disappeared when the party lost power in 1970. It was eventually reintroduced by the subsequent Labour Government in 1975, however, and as SERPS began to come into operation in 1978.

The failure to introduce reformed NI pensions in the 1960s, however, made the income guarantee for pensioners all the more important. Yet this too was abandoned and instead the government decided to reform the assistance scheme upon which so many pensioners depended, in spite of their own previous opposition to tinkering reforms of means-testing. In the Ministry of Social Security Act 1966 a new Ministry was created with overall control of most social security, including the assistance scheme, which was renamed Supplementary Benefit and placed under the direction of a new body, the *Supplementary Benefits Commission*. The idea was to create a new image for the scheme by renaming it and making entitlement to weekly SB a legal right, thus removing the stigma and degradation associated with assistance. In reality, however, the change was nothing more than window-dressing as nearly all of the degrading and undesirable aspects of means-testing were retained. Indeed without the commitment to more fundamental reform it is difficult to see how they could not have been.

In fact for many the stigma of means-testing was made considerably worse by the introduction of the notorious *four-week rule*. It primarily affected unmarried, unskilled male claimants aged under forty-five, whose entitlement to SB was stopped in circumstances where it was judged that there were good local employment prospects and would not be reinstated unless they reapplied for benefit and convinced a social security officer that they were 'genuinely seeking work'. There was an extension to the rule for skilled and married men, and women, under the age of forty-five who, after three months on SB, would be called in for interview and then may be subject to loss of benefit after four weeks; and a further extension for those over forty-five or not fully fit who may be subject to the rule after six months.

Although it was ostensibly aimed at reinforcing labour discipline, the main effect of the rule, which remained in force until 1973, was to fuel official and unofficial suspicion that significant numbers of unemployed men were choosing a life on means-tested benefits, as Meacher (1974) called it *Scrounging on the Welfare*. This was of course an unsubstantiated, and unsubstantiable claim, but it heralded a heightening of concern within social security over the so-called abuse of benefits, which in the 1970s and 1980s became the cause for a major call for increasingly divisive and punitive measures towards benefit claimants.

What the measures also signified, however, was a new emphasis on the increasing dependency on means-tested benefits, and thus a further drift away from the post-war ideal of insurance for all. Apart from the earnings-related supplements to short-term benefits little was done in the 1960s to plug the widening gaps in insurance provision. Indeed with the further encouragement of means-tested local authority benefits for rents and school meals and clothing it seemed to be being increasingly recognised that NI could not be expected to provide for all. In the next decade this extended role for means-testing continued apace.

THE EXPANSION OF MEANS-TESTING

The election of a Conservative Government in 1970 began a period of much more rapid development of a range of measures for state support primarily designed to meet the specific needs of the poor as opposed to the general prevention of poverty. Most notably this was done through the extension of specialised, means-tested benefit.

These included the introduction of FIS to supplement the low wages of family breadwinners, the creation of national rent and rate rebate schemes for low-income householders, the extension of means-tested education benefits such as free school milk, and the growth of means-tested health service benefits to cushion the poor against the effects of increasing charges for services. The growth was quite phenomenal and by 1976 the National Consumer Council (NCC) had calculated that there were forty-five different means-tested benefits operating in Britain.

In the case of the Conservative Government of the early 1970s this clearly exemplified a commitment to selective rather than universal social provision. Universal measures were reduced and withdrawn via reductions of state support for housing, health and education; and in their place means-tested provisions were introduced in an attempt to ensure that the very poorest were not entirely excluded from these services by their inability to pay. Of course this placed an increasing demand on the poor to identify and ensure their own entitlement to these benefits, which with means-tested provision is, as we shall see, always likely to leave many without. It also added further support to pathological perceptions of the problem of poverty as being due to the inadequacy and incompetence of the poor themselves rather than the limitations and failures of policies for state support.

The replacement of the Conservatives with a Labour Government in the mid 1970s did little to reverse this trend. The new means-tested benefits were largely retained by Labour. They also introduced some non-means-tested specialist benefits for the disabled, notably Non-Contributory Invalidity Pension, Mobility Allowance and ICA. And in 1975 they introduced Child Benefit.

Child Benefit was a new universal benefit for those caring for all children replacing the previous Family Allowances and child tax allowances, and it had widespread support amongst the poverty lobby. It did not come fully into force until 1977, however, and then only after heated debate and plans within the Cabinet to abandon it altogether, which were leaked to the press [doc. 6] and later reversed.

The Labour Government also made some changes to the NI scheme, mainly to accommodate the new earnings-related pensions scheme (SERPS), which was to be phased into full maturity over twenty years from 1978 to 1998. This meant replacing the flat-rate NI stamp with earnings-related contributions and the phasing out of the married woman's reduced rate contribution for new contributors.

Of course earnings-related contributions were a major departure from Beveridge's flat-rate insurance scheme in which all were equal contributors to, and beneficiaries from, the NI fund. As we shall see, however, they hardly put contributions on to a progressive taxation basis. Nor did the reforms do very much to prevent the continuing decline in importance of the NI scheme as more and more claimants found that NI benefits were either unavailable or inadequate for their needs. By the mid 1970s 4 million were dependent upon SB and this rose to 5 million by 1979.

However, the 1966 reforms had done little to improve the image or the operation of the major means-tested provision, SB, and by the mid 1970s even the SBC itself, under its chair David Donnison, was publishing reports calling for review and reform of the scheme to meet the increasingly mass role with which it was now operating (SBC 1978; and see Donnison 1982).

In 1976 a review of the scheme was commissioned by the government, to be undertaken on an internal basis by officials of the DHSS [doc. 7]. Significantly, however, it was restricted to recommending changes which could be made on a zero-cost basis, because the Treasury had ruled that the country's poor economic performance could not support any improvement in benefits – a fatal, though by then familiar, blow to any hopes for major reform. The review was published as a discussion document, *DHSS, Social Assistance*, in 1978 as part of a gesture towards more open policy debate, and it received widespread criticism and condemnation (Lister 1978; and see Walker 1983), including from the SBC itself (SBC 1979).

The basic recommendation was that the increasing confusion and complexity of the SB scheme should be tackled by the replacement of discretionary entitlement to additions under the guidance of the SBC with regulations outlining clear and simple legal rights. As we shall see, the new regulations when eventually introduced singularly failed to achieve the hoped-for clarification. However, the recommendations in the review were initially sat on by an embarrassed Labour Government and it was only after the 1979 election had been won by a new Conservative Government that the changes were made. By then they signalled the start of a new period of social security reform in which commitment to the gradual adaptation of the post-war benefit system was subject to open questioning and challenge.

REVIEWS, REFORMS AND THE RETREAT FROM WELFARE

As we discussed in Chapter 4, the supposed post-war consensus over the role and extent of social policy has always masked important ideological and political differences over the form of social security provision. By the 1970s it had become little more than a grudging support of existing structures fuelled primarily by a recognition of the immense difficulty of making any major change to the complex and unwieldy bureaucracy that benefits had become. In essence the consensus rested more on the generally shared assumption that the economy could not afford improved benefits than on any agreement that existing benefits were either adequate or appropriate. In the 1980s, however, even this consensus came under direct challenge from a government more openly committed to restricting the scope of welfare provision and claiming popular support for this departure from previous post-war social policy.

Whereas previous governments had argued that improvements in social security must await economic growth, the Conservative Government took this one stage further and claimed that it was over-expansive state provision itself which was inhibiting the economic growth that Britain clearly lacked by the 1980s. They thus advocated not just constraint and control, but a real reduction in state expenditure in order to permit resources to be redirected towards private capital to stimulate investment and promote growth (see Bull & Wilding 1983 and Loney 1986). In this new climate social security, by far the largest item of state expenditure, would have to take its share of the cuts.

In fact cutting social security proved no easy matter and expenditure on it continued to reach higher and higher levels every year in the early 1980s. The complex provisions proved as difficult to curtail as they had been to reform, and of course the government's economic policy of encouraging unemployment was creating greater and greater demand. Nevertheless cuts were made in benefits, the first direct cuts since the 1930s, and with them went a major extension of the ideological attack on claimants based on the myth that potentially large numbers of people were abusing and defrauding an inefficient and over-generous welfare state (see Loney 1986, Ch. 4).

Cuts were first made in 1980 when, along with the introduction of the reformed SB scheme, the government severed the link between pension rises and increases in earnings, so that like other benefits pensions would only have to be increased annually in line with prices, which with wage inflation running above price inflation had cost each pensioner around £3 a week by the mid 1980s.

Later in the same year direct cuts were made in most NI benefit rates, finally destroying Beveridge's hope that the scheme could protect these from economic priorities. Short-term NI benefits were increased at 5 per cent below the estimated inflation figure for the year, in lieu of a plan to make these benefits subject to tax which was introduced two years later, for Unemployment Benefit only. The earnings-related supplement to these benefits was also phased out over the two years up to 1982, a loss to those who would have been entitled to it of around £11 a week.

The 1980 legislation also introduced swingeing cuts in benefits paid to strikers. Those engaged in industrial action were not entitled to benefits in any event, but strikers' families could claim SB to cover their needs only. After 1980, however, an amount of assumed strike pay, initially £12, was deducted from their weekly benefit, regardless of whether or not strike pay was actually being received.

Taken together these cuts made initial savings of around £500 million in the social security budget, rising to over £2000 million by the mid 1980s. For most ordinary NI claimants, notably the growing number of unemployed, they also meant that NI benefit rates were below SB level. And in ever-increasing numbers claimants were forced to claim means-tested benefits in addition to the NI benefits to which they were entitled. By the mid 1980s this had increased to around 8 million the number of people dependent upon SB.

In 1982 further changes were introduced to Sickness Benefit and to rent and rate rebates. Provision for sickness was subject to a significant measure of privatisation with entitlement to NI benefit being withdrawn for the first eight weeks of sickness in any one year (extended in 1986 to twenty-eight weeks). In its place employers were put under an obligation to pay at least a minimum level of *sick pay* during this period. The minimum levels of sick pay were fixed by the government based upon previous average earnings, and for the low paid with dependent families could be below SB level, though this could then be claimed in addition by those who realised that they were entitled to it. Many employers did already pay sick pay and, to placate those who did not, they were permitted to deduct it from employers' NI contributions, as a compensation for taking over a major area of benefit administration from the state.

The transfer of the responsibility for administering Sickness Benefit from the state to private employers was continued in 1986 with the publication of plans to replace Maternity Benefit with maternity pay. Taken together these constitute a significant measure of *privatisation* of the social security provision envisaged in the Beveridge scheme, taking the role of private welfare beyond Beveridge's original complementary relationship to that of a replacement for state support. They also, of course, reduce the burden of benefit administration on the state, thus creating pressure to reduce public expenditure itself.

The creation of Housing Benefit (HB) to replace rent and rate rebates also shifted a significant burden of benefit administration from the DHSS, on this occasion to local authorities. As we shall discuss in more detail in Chapter 8, this was done very much at the expense of claimants, who failed to understand or benefit from the transfer of responsibility and then suffered cuts in entitlement the following year. And it only reduced state expenditure by transferring the cost of administration to local government, initially supported largely by a direct subsidy from the DHSS itself. In overall terms the cost of administering the new, decentralised HB scheme was greater than that previously borne by the DHSS alone, but this could now appear to be the responsibility of local councils rather than the government itself.

The cuts and restructuring in benefit provision were 'saving' the government over £2.5 billion a year in the social security budget by the mid 1980s (Manwaring & Sigler 1985), but in a budget of over £40 billion this was still a limited achievement. And it was not sufficient to meet government concern about the deleterious effect of benefit provision on the economy. So in 1984 Norman Fowler, Secretary of State for Health and Social Services, announced that there was to be a thorough review of social security policy and provision, conducted by four independent review teams taking evidence from the public and submitting reports to the government, who would then consider their suggestions and decide what to do. He called it 'the most substantial examination of the social security system since the Beveridge Report forty years ago'.

The review teams investigated four separate areas of provision: SB, benefits for children and young persons, HB, and pensions. Although they were supposedly independent, three were chaired by government ministers [doc. 8]; and although they took evidence from a wide range of sources it was clear that they had certain priorities in mind, most notably the desire to contain the growth in social security expenditure.

Their reports were not, with the exception of the HB team, separately published, however. Instead they were jointly presented in June 1985 as a government *Green Paper* on the *Reform of Social Security*, outling their commitment to a new approach towards social security and the needs for consequent reforms [doc. 9]. They received much hostility and criticism from the poverty lobby (CPAG 1985; NACAB 1985; NCC 1985), especially over the proposal to withdraw SERPS, only six years after its introduction with all-party support. However, they were followed by a *White Paper* (1985) later in the year, proposing legislation to introduce virtually all the changes outlined (with the exception of SERPS which was to be cut rather than withdrawn); and in 1986 legislation was introduced to enable the

Secretary of State to bring in the necessary legal changes, though the date set for implementation of the new scheme was put back to April 1988.

The decision to exclude NI from direct consideration in the review process was an indication that they were likely to be somewhat less comprehensive than the Beveridge Report with which they were initially compared. Apart from the changes to SERPS and a minor change to Widow's Benefit it was not proposed to alter the scheme, leaving it likely to continue to suffer from a gradual atrophy. The proposals for reform thus settled largely on the means-tested aspects of social security, which by the mid 1980s had come to dominate both claimants' and administrators' experience of the operation of state support.

The Green Paper concluded that the largely unplanned growth of means-tested benefits had resulted in a system plagued by confusion and complexity. The government was also concerned, however, to ensure that the planned limited resources available for state support should go to those most in need. The proposals thus concentrated upon a reform of the existing means-tested aspects of provision in order to simplify administration and entitlement and target benefits on the very poor (Alcock 1985b).

The major means-tested benefits are thus to be retained, but in a changed form: FIS is to be replaced with a similar family wage supplement FC, entitlement to which will be aligned with a (slimmed down) HB scheme; SB is to be replaced by Income Support (IS), a means-tested benefit for those not in full-time work, but with no entitlement to additional payments for special needs, merely a series of premiums to the weekly rates for certain categories of claimants, such as the elderly, the disabled and those with dependent children. As Berthoud (1985) argued, this will be likely to reproduce to some extent the existing distinction between the long- and short-term rates of SB, but without the extra payments some claimants will be likely to be significantly worse off unless the basic benefit rates are substantially improved. However, the indicative benefit figures published with the White Paper in December 1985 suggested that this is not likely to be the case.

We will discuss the details of the changes planned for 1988 in the next section. The important general point about them, however, was that they symbolised more clearly than ever before the intention of the Conservative Government of the 1980s to depart from the Beveridge Plan and the post-war consensus on welfare. They are proposals to move to centre stage the selective, means-testing aspects of state support and cut back as far as possible the universal and insurance aspects.

Unlike previous governments which had introduced means-tested benefits, almost apologetically, in attempts to shore up gaps in the Beveridge scheme, the Conservatives of the 1980s were quite open in their support for the principles of selectivity. They argued that the role of the state should be restricted (as it had been under the Poor Law) to the provision of minimal subsistence benefits to relieve established poverty, and that beyond that the distribution of wealth and resources should be subject only to the control of the free market, in which private insurance would be available to those who could afford it. This implied a significant privatisation of welfare provision, as discussed above; in his Parliamentary speech introducing the Green Paper Norman Fowler called it a 'better partnership' between the individual and the state.

That the proposed reforms did not go further in restricting Child Benefit and NI benefits is perhaps testimony to the enduring power of the post-war benefit system, at both a political and a bureaucratic level, however. And for all the talk of major examination, at the end of the day the changes planned for 1988 will not bring about any fundamental resolution of most of the problems and contradictions of the social security system. Indeed they largely represent a recipe for more of the same (though in real terms the same is likely to be less for many claimants).

However, what the review of social security in 1985 did do was to restore the question of policies for state support once more to the political agenda, reversing the effect of the technicism and gradualism of the post-war drift from Beveridge. This cast a more critical light on the intricacies and inequities of existing benefits and their contradictory effects, and brought a new publicity to proposals for more radical reform. After looking at some of the details of current provisions we will return to these questions in the final section.

Part three
SOCIAL SECURITY PROVISION

Chapter six
THE INSURANCE MYTH

THE INSURANCE PRINCIPLE

The insurance principle is common to state-controlled income support in a number of European countries (see Walker *et al.* 1984). Yet in spite of the fact that it has supposedly been the basis of social security provision in Britain too for the most part of the last century, it is doubtful whether insurance has in reality had the dominant role within state provision that official support for it might appear to suggest.

The principle of the insurance base for income maintenance is basically the same as insurance against any other occurrence. Premiums are paid into an insurance fund and if events covered by the scheme arise benefits are paid out to cover them. Thus only those who have paid into the scheme can claim benefits under it, and the premiums (or contributions) paid must be sufficient to meet all potential claims. The distinguishing features of the NI scheme are its compulsory nature and the intention to provide comprehensive cover for all cases of individual need from contributions paid by everyone whilst in paid work.

The scheme is predicated upon the assumption of paid work being available and of wages as the primary means of distributing income. As we shall see, this has had important consequences for the operation of the scheme in Britain since the war; however, for many of the supporters of NI within the state this has always been one of its major attractions. It does not commit the state to intervening directly in the existing distribution of income, and restricts state involvement in income support instead to that of the administration or organisation of self-support. The intention is that the scheme should be self-sufficient, merely providing the framework for those in work to provide for themselves in times of need. For those with large incomes and wealth the attraction of this is obvious; it removes any expectation that they should be required to provide for those less fortunate than themselves. For the working class and the poor the attraction is less obvious, yet it has frequently been claimed that there is widespread support for the insurance principle because self-support is what the bulk of the people want.

If such support has always existed, and most evidence that it has is based largely on assumptions and assertions about its appeal, then it must be seen in the context of the peculiar history of insurance-based state support in Britain and of the alternatives to which it has normally been counterposed, as much as any rational assessment of the viability or desirability of the idea of insurance itself. And the fact that throughout almost all of this history the insurance principle itself has not been rigidly adhered to within the scheme, ironically makes this appearance of support all the more understandable. Understandable, because since the harsh imposition of payment only to the fully paid up has not in practice been applied, then support could still be claimed for the principle of insurance without having to face up to all the undesirable consequences of it in practice. This contradiction, as we shall see later, is still very much a part of recent political support for NI, and may have contributed to the scheme's exemption from the 1984 reviews of social security provision.

THE DEVELOPMENT OF INSURANCE

The development of insurance in Britain must be seen in the context of other state policies for income support and the struggles to change or marginalise these, in particular the punitive tradition of the nineteenth-century Poor Law. The principle of less eligibility and the harsh regime of the Poor Law workhouse had made the receipt of state support in the nineteenth century an experience to be avoided if at all possible. And by the latter part of the century the more secure and better-paid sections of the working class had sought to do this via independent insurance schemes providing support for those who would otherwise be subject to the Poor Law. The insurance was provided by working-class organisations such as trade unions and friendly societies, providing self-help as an alternative to draconian state support, rather than a challenge to it.

Most insurance covered times of sickness, but many also covered old age, and by the end of the century large numbers of workers were covered by these private schemes (Thane (1982, p. 29) estimated 6 million in 1904). However, they were largely restricted to secure, respectable, *male* workers. And as Booth's (1889) study of London, with its large casual labour market, showed they had not prevented the continued existence of serious poverty and deprivation.

However, the fact that these insurance schemes had the apparent support of the respectable, and most powerful, sections of the working class made the possibility of their further extension a potentially attractive strategy for those in power who wished to stifle any demands for more progressive policies for poverty relief. And in Germany in 1884 it was such a calculation which persuaded Bismarck's government to introduce a compulsory, nationally administered scheme to cover sickness at work, which five years later was extended to cover retirement too (see Thane 1982, p. 108). Coverage did not extend to casual workers or to women, however, capitalising on and deepening divisions which, as in Britain, could already be found within the working class.

In the 1910s the British government, faced as Bismarck had been with increasing pressure for social reform, made a similar calculation, introducing compulsory state insurance for sickness, and later for unemployment and old age. Coverage was also restricted to the upper reaches of the working class, initially only 2.25 million workers in seven industries were covered (Gilbert 1966, p. 53) and only in 1920 was unemployment cover extended to all. In order to placate the interests of the trade unions and friendly societies, they were given an administrative role within the new scheme.

The central role which insurance provision acquired within policies for state support in twentieth-century Britain was therefore a product of the particular political configurations and priorities of this period of social reform, rather than any rational appraisal of the desirability of an insurance basis for social security in the country.

At a political level it met the need to make some concession through the state to the demands for greater social justice that a stronger and more vociferous working class were able to make after the turn of the century. And yet at the same time by drawing on existing private insurance provision, it permitted the state to build on, and to some extent incorporate, the interests and values of the most powerful sections of the working class without conceding radical changes to improve conditions for the most deprived. As in Germany this accentuated existing divisions within the working class, which since then have had an increasing influence upon the experience and operation of schemes for state support (see Mann 1986).

The divisive political strategy was related to an economic strategy to minimise any role for state taxation to support the poor, or any redistribution of resources from capital. The whole logic of the insurance scheme was that it was financed by the working class themselves, and being based upon contributions from wages, and benefits as a substitute for wages, was firmly predicated upon wage labour as the primary form of economic support.

Ideologically insurance was based on the friendly society notion that collective self-support was more desirable than punitive state provision. The introduction of compulsory insurance effectively transformed this into a belief that state support in return for contribution was preferable to redistribution of resources via benefits paid for out of general taxation. However, the popularity of this belief amongst the working class must be seen in the context of continued opposition to the less desirability of alternative means-tested support. In the 1930s this was maintained when the Poor Law was replaced by Unemployment Assistance, on which, because of the inadequate coverage of insurance, large numbers of unemployed claimants were forced to rely. Dependency on assistance was degrading and unpopular, creating divisive comparisons with the insurance scheme.

In fact there were three different insurance schemes operating between the wars (Unemployment, Health, and Widows and Pensions) with different administrative arrangements for each. It was this disparate framework which Beveridge sought to consolidate in his social insurance plan. He drew directly on the political and ideological support for the insurance schemes, intending that a more effective NI scheme would be able to provide self-financed support for all, and avoid the hated means test.

As we have already seen, however, Beveridge's scheme was doomed to failure. To operate as an insurance scheme for all it would have to ensure that contributions made would be invested to pay for future benefits. To be actuarially sound contributions would need to be sufficient to meet all anticipated needs – which the inter-war schemes had failed to do. To avoid existing contributions being unacceptably high (Beveridge intended flat-rate contributions equal for all) future provision would have to be low (Beveridge's proposed benefit rates were very low) – demand must not exceed anticipated supply. These requirements were unacceptable to the post-war government, and have remained unacceptable since. Consequently the strict insurance basis has not been adhered to. Governments have wanted to pay insurance benefits to all those supposedly within the scheme, without waiting for their contributions to build up a fund to pay for them. They have also wanted to do this without heavy subsidies to the fund from general taxation. The result has been a 'pay as you go' strategy towards insurance – meeting current benefit needs out of current contributions, and increasing contributions to pay for increased benefits when demand has risen.

Using contributions from today's workers to provide support for today's unemployed and retired pensioners is not necessarily an undesirable or irrational form of state support. But it is not a national insurance scheme. As Dilnot *et al.* (1984, p. 33) argue, the six 'fundamental principles' [doc. 5] of the Beveridge insurance plan have been departed from. The ideology of collective self-support through benefits in return for contributions has been retained, but the principle has never been operated in practice. The insurance scheme is a myth. And the resulting contradictions between myth and reality have led to complexity and confusion within the scheme, accentuated by changes introduced in attempts to respond to inadequacies within the original plan.

CHANGES TO THE INSURANCE SCHEME

By giving entitlement to the vast majority of pensioners on the introduction of the NI scheme the government departed from the insurance principle of benefits paid for by contributions, in order to avoid large numbers of claimants being excluded from the scheme. However, because NI benefits were fixed at such a low level, many of those who were covered by the scheme were nevertheless forced to rely on further support from the means-tested National Assistance scheme, contradicting the major intention of the Beveridge Plan.

To tackle this problem post-war governments have introduced changes to the basic NI scheme in attempts to *lift* or *float* claimants off dependency on means-testing. All these attempts have been pretty much unsuccessful in reducing dependency on assistance, but they have meant that NI has departed significantly from the Beveridge model.

The first major change came in 1958 with the introduction by the Conservative Government of the Graduated Pensions scheme. Under this contributors paid a limited earnings-related addition on top of the flat-rate stamp in return for an addition to basic pension after retirement. In fact the value of the additional benefit did not reflect the increased contributory element, and the major effect, and intention, of the scheme was to increase contributions in order to meet increasing current demands. But the principle adapting contribution and benefit rates had been established, and since then it has been taken much further.

In 1966 the Labour Government introduced the much more

substantial earnings-related supplement to short-term NI benefits. The intention of this was to cushion workers against the drop on to flat-rate benefits for short periods out of work. Its effect was to introduce the inequalities of the labour market into the insurance scheme, and initially based still on flat-rate contributions with a small earnings-related top-up.

The Labour Government also intended to introduce earnings-related additions to NI pensions but the plan to do this was lost with the 1970 election. The subsequent Conservative Government also planned to introduce pension reform, but this too fell with the government at the next election. Thus in 1975, when the Labour Government did eventually introduce their State Earnings-Related Pension Scheme, they sought to get all-party support for it in the hope that its long lead into full maturity, not planned to be reached until 1998, would not be used as an excuse by a subsequent government to reverse policy on pension reform once again.

In order to attract all-party support significant concessions were made in introducing SERPS, primarily towards the now extensive private pension provision. The state was to provide a guarantee for private pensions, and, providing minimum standards were met, private schemes could then *contract out* of SERPS with contributors giving up their right to the state earnings-related addition and paying reduced NI contributions in return. Indeed the effect, and the political attractiveness, of the new state scheme was that it provided something like a private pension for those who could not afford or were not in a position to acquire one.

What SERPS did intend to provide was an addition to basic pension roughly equivalent to a quarter of earnings over the lower contribution limit during the best twenty years of the claimant's working life. However, only contributions years after the scheme came into operation in 1978 were to count for this purpose, hence the long run-in to maturity. In comparison with private pensions the long wait for full entitlement was only to be expected. However, it contrasted starkly with the post-war, flat-rate pension to which contributors had been given immediate entitlement despite lack of contribution records and, as we shall see, left the scheme open to amendment before maturity was reached. In spite of delayed entitlement a new earnings-related basis for contributions was introduced immediately in 1978. It replaced the old weekly NI stamp with a contribution paid direct by employers based on a percentage of earnings between nationally determined lower and upper limits.

Though nowhere near as progressive in raising revenue as direct taxation, the new earnings-related contribution did signify a major departure from the Beveridge Plan of equal benefits for equal contributions which had always been claimed as one of the most important sources of popular support for the insurance principle. The hope was that the earnings-related element would eventually do for pensioners what the earnings-related addition was intended to do for the short-term unemployed and raise claimants' incomes enough to avoid the need to claim SB. Once again, however, this was basing the presumed desirability of insurance on its superiority over means-tested benefits rather than on the supposed positive values of the amended NI scheme itself. With increasing dependency on SB many claimants may have been unable to make the comparison, and this situation was accentuated after 1980.

The cuts to short-term NI benefits and the removal of the earnings-related supplement by the Conservative Government in 1980 exposed the myth that the insurance principle could protect benefits from the harsh world of monetary policy. They also destroyed some of the rationale for the new earnings-related contributions, which apart from their relevance to future pension entitlement were now being paid for flat-rate benefits. As the cost of paying benefits was also going up with escalating unemployment the government also had to increase revenue to meet benefit demands and so the level of contribution was increased on two occasions, permitting the Treasury supplement to the scheme to be reduced at the same time from 18 to 11 per cent of the total cost, a much lower level of taxation subsidy than the one-third originally envisaged by Beveridge.

In 1982 short-term Sickness Benefit was removed from the NI scheme to be replaced with Statutory Sick Pay, which in 1986 was extended to twenty-eight weeks, entirely replacing entitlement to Sickness Benefit for most employees. And in 1986 plans were also introduced to replace Maternity Benefit with maternity pay from employers. These removed two of the major causes of need identified by Beveridge from the NI scheme, replacing them with private provision, further undermining what was left of the supposedly comprehensive insurance plan. The lump sum payment in replacement for Widow's Benefit in 1988 will take this a stage further.

Although NI was largely excluded from the 1984 review of social security, pension provision generally was a specific focus of concern. And when the Green Paper was published in 1985 it recommended phased abolition of SERPS and its replacement with private pension provision. The ostensible reason for this rapid departure from the presumed consensus of political support for SERPS was the claim that the scheme would be incredibly expensive to operate when full maturity was reached at a time when demographic projections suggested that there would be relatively increased numbers of retired claimants. Ironically the combination of the 'pay as you go' NI approach and yet a long lead-in to entitlement to earnings-related additions was thus undermining rather than strengthening political support for insurance.

However, savings to be made in expenditure here would not of course be realised until the next century, and the government's much more immediate concern was the encouragement of private pensions for all. When a number of major private pension providers made it clear that they were not particularly interested in pension schemes for those in low-paid and insecure employment, the feasibility of this plan began to be in doubt. The government thus bowed to the pressure of opposition to the abolition of SERPS from the poverty lobby and the other political parties, and in the 1986 legislation included instead proposals to restrict future entitlement by reducing the proportion of earnings paid to 20 per cent and basing entitlement on a lifetime's earnings rather than the best twenty years.

The changes will reduce entitlement for some future claimants. They also undermined the supposed security of a national pension scheme based on insurance. By the mid 1980s, however, the security of the insurance scheme for state support was in any event under serious doubt. The scheme had departed significantly from the principles of Beveridge and in practice was no longer fulfilling any of his hopes. It was more complex and yet less comprehensive, and in its operation almost defied rational comprehension or control.

THE CONTRIBUTION CONDITION

The original form of insurance contribution was a stamp bought every week and stuck on to a card as a record of payments made. It gave the notion of contribution a sort of physical immediacy, but it was extremely laborious to operate. Since the 1975 reforms the process has been replaced by a system of direct debits paid by employers in the same way as PAYE income tax. Records of contributions are kept on computer at the central DHSS office in Newcastle.

There are in fact *four* different kinds of NI contributions: for employed persons, for the self-employed, for people voluntarily paying to complete an inadequate record, and for those paying from the profits of a business. Class One contributions from employed persons are the most important, they include contributions from employees and employers based on a proportion of earnings between a lower and upper earnings level fixed each year by the government. Contributors who are contracted out of SERPS pay a reduced rate of contribution and since 1985 those with incomes just above the lower level have also paid at a slightly reduced rate. In spite of this recent change, however, contributions continue to constitute a disproportionate burden on the lower paid. The lower earnings limit is well below the threshold for liability to income tax, and the upper limit (beyond which income is free of contributions) is only around one and a half times average earnings. This preserves the intention that NI should primarily be financed by ordinary workers rather than by redistribution from the more wealthy.

However, whether this regressive basis for funding state support is realised by the majority of low-wage contributors is doubtful. And if it was, it seems unlikely that they would see it as a major advantage of the NI scheme, as compared to the taxation basis for other benefit provision. Yet it has always been asserted that support for NI is based upon such a notion of self-financed support, and that for this reason contributions are paid more willingly than other direct taxation. If they guaranteed adequate benefits this might be a more plausible claim, but as we shall see even this is not the case.

Self-employed and other contributions are flat rate, but they do not entitle contributors to Unemployment Benefit and are only really of value in contributing to pension entitlement. Claimants are not expected to make contributions into the scheme, but if they are *signing on* as available for work they are given *credits* equivalent to the lower earnings limit to maintain their record for future entitlement after they have returned to work or retired.

Although it is a fundamental principle of the NI scheme that payment of contributions ensures entitlement to benefits, the relationship between contributions and entitlement is in fact a quite arbitrary and divisive one, in particular for short-term benefits such as Unemployment Benefit. In order to claim this claimants must satisfy *two* conditions: they must have paid Class One contributions equivalent to twenty-five times the weekly lower earnings limit in any one year of work, *and* they must have paid or been credited with contributions equivalent to fifty times the limit in the last full year before claiming.

The details of the conditions are more complex than this. For instance, for contribution purposes the year is the April-to-April tax year and yet for benefit purposes the year is the calendar year. This makes counting contributions simpler for administrators, but claiming benefits more confusing for claimants. The simplest guide to the details of the scheme is the CPAG's *Rights Guide to Non-means-tested Social Security Benefits* published annually; and the most authoritative discussion of the law is Ogus and Barendt (1982).

The contribution conditions thus operate to ensure that those claiming benefits have had some prior connection via contribution with the NI scheme. But the nature of that connection is really quite arbitrary. It does not guarantee that benefits received bear any relation to contributions made, and it excludes large numbers of claimants who may have made contributions but not at the right time (as well of course as excluding those who have not made any). Indeed apart from the fact that large numbers of civil servants are employed in maintaining them, the justification for maintaining contribution records for short-term NI benefits is hard to find in spite of their supposedly central role in the insurance plan [doc. 10].

For long-term benefits there is a more logical connection between contributions and benefit entitlement. The flat-rate pension is only paid at the full rate to those who have paid or been credited with the minimum level of contributions throughout 90 per cent of their working life, and earnings-related additions are paid for contributions above this level paid since 1978. However, the justification for the condition is still hard to find. It does not ensure that a full return on contributions is received, and lower-paid manual workers with lower life expectancies are likely to get less back than the more comfortably off in this respect. It also excludes many over retirement age who have not paid enough contributions, particularly women who, in spite of the fact that they can deduct up to twenty years in unpaid caring work from their working life, are less likely to have full contribution records and thus have to rely on their husbands' contributions. Since contributions are not in fact saved in the fund to pay for future pension entitlement the connection in any case is entirely fictitious and, as the 1980 cuts in pension rates demonstrated, is no guarantee that future entitlement will be ensured.

INSURANCE BENEFITS

The intention of the NI scheme was to provide income maintenance for all those unable to provide for themselves or depend on others. To do this categories of need were identified and benefits designed to meet those needs. However, the categories of benefit do not in fact provide for all needs because some were overlooked or not anticipated when the scheme was introduced, for instance single parents and the congenitally disabled. There were also assumptions made about gender roles, as we discussed in Chapter 3, which meant that certain benefits reinforced women's dependency and primary responsibility for child care by creating special benefits based on these, for instance Widow's Benefits and Maternity Benefit.

Apart from the restricted categories of provision, however, limitations are also imposed upon the receipt of NI benefits by a complex set of rules designed to ensure that benefits do not compete with paid work. Whether unemployed, sick or old the insurance scheme was concerned from the outset with the discouragement of malingerers. Thus the enforcement of labour discipline was as essential to benefit entitlement as the need to prevent want, and rules were developed to ensure that only the genuinely deserving received benefits.

The details of these rules are best covered in the annual CPAG guide and Ogus and Barendt (1982). For pensioners they take the form of the retirement rule and the earnings rule for those between pension age (sixty or sixty-five) and retirement age (sixty-five or seventy), who if they do not give up paid work are not entitled to pension if their earnings are above a fixed level. After retirement age pension is received irrespective of employment status.

The privatisation of support for short-term sickness has transferred the problem of enforcing labour discipline here to employers, who are likely to have a vested interest in conditions as stringent as possible. Though in the case of disputes the right of appeal to Social Security Appeal Tribunals (SSATs) has been retained. For those not in work and for those with long-term incapacity Sickness Benefit, or after six months the more generous Invalidity Benefit, remain. They are subject to stringent tests of incapacity to work. Claimants can be required to attend for medical inspection by DHSS-appointed doctors, and, if they are declared fit for work, benefit is withdrawn and claimants must go on to Unemployment Benefit or SB and sign on as available for work.

It is of course in Unemployment Benefit where most of the restrictions on entitlement can be found. Prior to the establishment of the NI scheme benefits had not been provided for those whom it was felt were able to get paid work, and thus claimants were frequently required to demonstrate that they were 'actively seeking work', for instance by getting certificates from employers to prove that they had presented themselves for work. Under the NI scheme there is no entitlement to Unemployment Benefit if claimants are not willing to take *any* suitable job, and if claimants leave employment voluntarily or refuse an offer of a job then benefit can be stopped for thirteen weeks (extended in October 1986 from six). At the inception of the NI scheme it was expected that jobs would be available for those who were unemployed, and for the long-term unemployed Beveridge had originally envisaged that training would be provided to equip them for new work. With the escalation of unemployment in the 1970s and 1980s, however, these ideals were abandoned, and it was no longer possible to offer suitable (or unsuitable) jobs to large numbers of the unemployed. Nevertheless Unemployment Review Officers (UROs), based in Social Security Offices, continued to offer advice and 'encouragement' to find work to long-term unemployed claimants, with remarkably little success. And in 1986 it was announced that such 'help' was to be withdrawn and replaced by the appointment of *claimant advisers* in Unemployment Benefit Offices, whose remit would more directly include checking whether unemployed claimants were either work-shy or *moonlighting* on the black economy.

In spite of the supposed attraction of the simplicity of the principle of benefits in return for contributions, the rules to determine entitlement to NI benefits have thus become incredibly complex. The HMSO publication on the regulations, *the Brown Book* (1976), runs to three volumes and there is a massive amount of case law. Disputes over entitlement are dealt with by *Social Security Appeal Tribunals*, with a right of appeal on a point of law to a *Social Security Commissioner* and then to the Court of Appeal. There is no legal aid for representation in SSATs and claimants who cannot secure support from any other source (as the vast majority cannot) are likely to be hopelessly lost in any appeal they do make. For those in these circumstances, and perhaps for the majority of NI claimants, principles of state insurance against want must seem a long way away from the practice of securing the benefits themselves.

THE DEMISE OF INSURANCE

In spite of the complex rules governing entitlement, the most important measure for ensuring that NI benefits do not interfere with incentives to undertake waged work has always been the maintenance of benefits at low, subsistence levels. Although there has been an increase in the absolute level of benefits, the basic rates have not risen at all relative to average wages since the war, though the earnings-related additions to short-term benefits in the 1960s and 1970s did raise them for some, for a while.

Whilst this may have prevented benefits from overlapping with low wages, it has not prevented them overlapping considerably with means-tested provision. And the dependency on means-tested benefits which was supposed to wither away as the comprehensive NI scheme came into operation has in practice grown greater and greater. As well as the expansion of minor means-tested benefits to which most NI claimants are entitled, the restriction of NI benefit levels, compounded by the removal of the earnings-related additions in the 1980s, has meant that the majority of claimants with no other source of income are entitled to SB to supplement their NI benefit, thus destroying the advantages of entitlement based on insurance.

This growing dependency on means-testing has in practice seen the demise of the insurance scheme as the central feature of state support in Britain. As we have seen, it is not anyway an insurance scheme in anything other than name, and in spite of intentions it is not comprehensive, initial defects and subsequent amendments leaving large categories of potential claimants uncovered. The relationship between contributions and benefits is a tenuous one, and it is now difficult to see contributions as anything other than a more regressive form of direct taxation, earmarked for social security.

Although NI was not directly covered by the 1984 reviews of social security, the changes following from the reviews are likely to further undermine its role by removing Maternity Benefit and Widow's Benefit from the scheme. This will continue the marginalisation of insurance within benefit provision, and, given the recognised inadequacies of NI provision and the concentration in the reviews on the desirability of means-testing, it is pertinent to ask why it was not considered feasible to abolish it altogether.

Critics have frequently argued that abolition has not been considered because of the enduring ideological support for the (mythical) notion of insurance and because the progressive elements of insurance provision still provide a basis for pragmatic reform of benefit provision without disturbing the whole framework of support (Creedy & Disney 1985). However, official support for insurance may in practice be based upon a more pragmatic, short-term desire to retain NI contributions as a source of government revenue. If they were openly merged with direct taxation then the basic tax rate would (appear) to rise around nine points – a hard political pill to swallow. That people are already paying this money under another guise is a powerful reason for leaving well alone. Whether it is a desirable means of funding and organising state support is a different question to which we will return in Chapter 11.

Chapter seven

FROM ASSISTANCE TO SUPPORT

THE MEANS TEST

In spite of the supposedly central role for insurance within British social security provision throughout most of this century, dependence upon means-tested benefits has remained a significant, and in recent years rapidly growing, feature of the benefit system. However, the principle of means-testing extends from before the insurance benefits of the twentieth-century welfare state, back to the Poor Law of early modern Britain. As Beltram (1984, p. 6) says, current provision is 'the lineal descendant of the Elizabethan and Victorian poor law, and bears significant traces of its ancestry'. Its aim is the relief of identified poverty, based on an absolute notion of need. It is redistributive, redistributing resources to the poor, but only up to strictly controlled subsistence levels.

Essential to means-tested provision is the notion of *less eligibility*, the attempt to ensure that benefit provision does not interfere with other forms of income distribution by discouraging and stigmatising dependency on benefits. Coupled with this is the need to ensure that benefits only go to those who are in need, which requires tests of means and needs and a constant attention to possible abuse of these tests by claimants who do not need state support. The stigmatisation of dependency and the constant fear of abuse are thus intrinsic features of means-tested provision, and they contribute significantly to the experience of distinctions within state support between the *deserving* (the old and infirm forced by external events on to benefit dependency) and the *undeserving* poor (the unemployed and feckless who could be expected to provide for themselves).

When the Poor Law was replaced by assistance in the 1930s these negative features of dependency were deliberately retained, and as we have seen they were also incorporated into the post-war National

Assistance scheme. In spite of growing dependency upon means-tested benefits the divisions and the suspicions have remained in more recent years, most notably in the *scroungerphobia* of the 1970s and 1980s. With the failure of the NI scheme they have increasingly come to occupy the centre stage of benefit provision and the plans to recast means-testing in the late 1980s are likely to confirm their now dominant role.

THE DEVELOPMENT OF ASSISTANCE

It was the failure of insurance-based Unemployment Benefit to cope with the rising numbers of the unemployed in the 1920s and 1930s which led to the introduction of means-tested benefits in their current form. After the cuts in insurance benefits following the economic crisis of 1931 a means test, administered by local Public Assistance Committees, was imposed upon claimants who had been dependent upon unemployment benefit for twenty-six weeks.

The local committees administered what was called a *household* means test, under which the resources of anyone in the same household would be assumed to be available to the claimant, harshly enforcing dependency relationships amongst the poor. It was an extremely unpopular measure and led to rioting and protests in a number of cities in 1932 (Deacon & Bradshaw 1983, Ch. 1). It was also open to a large amount of local discretion, leading to major discrepancies between provision in different areas. Thus in 1934 the local committees were replaced by the national Unemployment Assistance Board in an attempt to regularise and stabilise the scheme. In spite of this the harshness and unpopularity of the scheme remained, and in 1938 around a third of claimants had their assistance reduced because of the household test (Deacon & Bradshaw 1983, p. 25). In 1940 the scheme was extended to cover the elderly and the national body renamed the Assistance Board.

It was the intention of Beveridge's plan for social insurance that the need for means-tested assistance would gradually wither away. In the interim, however, assistance was retained in the post-war welfare reforms in the National Assistance Act 1948 which placed it under the control of the new *National Assistance Board*. There was a significant difference in the post-war assistance scheme, however, with the removal of the household means test and its replacement with the assumption of family dependency, which was likely to affect women much more than men.

As we have discussed, however, the hopes for a declining role for assistance have proved to be unfulfilled. Because of the gaps within the NI scheme and the low level of NI benefits there were already in 1948 large numbers of claimants dependent upon assistance. In the following seventeen years there were more upratings of assistance than there were of NI benefits, with the 1959 uprating leading to a significant increase in its value. Thus the numbers dependent on assistance rose rather than declined during this period, especially amongst pensioners [doc. 11]. Though with the negative connotations of assistance benefits no doubt still in people's minds it is probable that there were even more who would have been entitled to assistance but preferred to struggle by on their inadequate NI pension (Deacon & Bradshaw 1983, p. 103).

Those who did apply were not only subject to the test of their means, but also, in order to establish whether they were in poverty, their needs too had to be investigated. In different households these would obviously fluctuate quite widely, and the NAB officers were given the power to award payments on top of the ordinary weekly assistance to those with special needs. These payments depended upon officers' judgements and thus they introduced the somewhat arbitrary element of discretion into the scheme. Officers' judgements of what was necessary varied in different circumstances and between different groups of claimants, leading to discrimination within provision. But in general the role of additional payments expanded throughout the 1950s and early 1960s and by the end of the period over a half of claimants were receiving them (Berthoud 1984, F9).

The 1966 reform of assistance replaced the NAB with the SBC, responsible to the new Ministry of Social Security for the administration of assistance, now renamed SB. At the same time that these administrative changes were made the weekly benefit rates were made a legal entitlement (to encourage take-up) and the additional payments were consolidated into a weekly long-term addition (in effect a higher weekly rate) for pensioners, and other claimants who had been dependent upon SB for two years. In 1973 this addition was recast as a separate (higher) long-term scale rate, and in 1980 the qualifying period for non-pensioners was reduced to one year. However, unemployed claimants were never permitted to receive the long-term rate and had to remain on the lower ordinary benefit level no matter how long they were dependent upon SB. This was intended to prevent the higher benefits competing with alternative low-paid employment, which the unemployed should be encouraged to take; but its effect was to accentuate further the distinction between deserving and un-deserving claimants within the scheme and create the ground for widespread hardship as the number of unemployed claimants began to grow in the 1970s and 1980s.

Initially the 1966 reforms did lead to some increase in take-up, and simplification via a reduction in additional payments. These achievements were short-lived, however, and by the 1970s problems were once again becoming manifest, accentuated by the growing numbers of SB claimants. The growing numbers also represented a significant change in the nature of dependency on SB, as with rising unemployment and increased marital dissolution they included an expanding proportion of claimants with dependent children [doc. 11]. These claimants also contributed to the growing problems of the administration of the scheme because their means and needs were more complex and constantly changing than those of pensioner claimants.

The reduction in additional payments was dramatically reversed in the 1970s. In 1972 15 per cent were receiving additional weekly payments; by 1979 this had risen to 60 per cent. The rise in lump sum payments was equally staggering, from 580,000 in 1971 to 1.2 million in 1978 (Deacon & Bradshaw 1983, p. 110). Although the weekly rates were now an entitlement these additions were still based upon the discretion of officers, and the exercise of their judgement continued to fluctuate widely throughout the country, and even within individual DHSS offices (Beltram 1984, p. 30). In order to try and introduce some consistency to the exercise of discretion the SBC began to issue guidance to officers on when to make payments. However, the scope for discretion was so broad that the guidance had to be extensive. It was kept as a series of volumes of circulars issued by the SBC, known as the *A Code*, and was covered by the Official Secrets Act. Merely keeping it up to date added considerably to the burden on staff – a burden of which the SBC were increasingly aware, and warned in their 1975 annual report could lead to a breakdown of the scheme.

It was primarily in response to this pressure that the internal DHSS review of SB was established in 1976. As we have discussed, the remit of the review was extremely limited by its restriction to the SB scheme alone and its no-cost basis [doc. 7]. The consultative document, published in 1978, thus suggested organisational rather than structural reforms, admitting that ' . . . the most realistic aim is to fit the scheme to its mass role of coping with millions of claimants in known and readily definable categories for the foreseeable future' (*Social Assistance* 1978, p. 5). What was proposed was a pragmatic response to the dominant role within social security which assistance now found itself during economic recession. Within such constraints reforms could only be introduced in which some would lose (about 1.75 million) in order for others to gain (about 0.5 million).

When the changes proposed in 1978 were implemented by the Conservative Government in 1980 little work had been done on how to transfer a scheme dependent on large elements of discretion on to a regulated basis. In the end much of the old SBC guidance in the A Code was drafted into regulations and rushed, largely unexamined, through Parliament. The result was that the regulations were as complex and voluminous as the guidance had been. They were also fraught with errors and were almost immediately subject to a series of amendments. The replacement of discretion meant the end of the SBC, whose guidance was no longer needed. They were abolished and responsibility for the scheme transferred formally to the DHSS, with an advisory role being retained for a new *Social Security Advisory Committee* (SSAC).

The voluminous and complex regulations were published by the DHSS in the two-volume *Yellow Book* (1983), which ran to thousands of pages of almost impenetrable legal jargon. And rather than simplifying and clarifying entitlement the new rules only confused and alienated claimants all the more. The regulations were even too complex for DHSS officers to work from, and in spite of intentions they still left many areas open to interpretation and discretion. After a while the DHSS began to issue guidance on the interpretation of the new regulations through the office of the *Chief Adjudication Officer*. And this too was eventually collected into a two-volume procedure guide, called the *S Manual*, not dissimilar to the old A Code, although the manual is a public document and can be purchased from the DHSS.

On top of the confusion over the nature of the regulations the new SB scheme was implemented very rapidly in 1980, with little time for adequate publicity or staff training. It also took place at a time of a rapid increase in the number of claimants, who rose from 2.85 to 4.14 million between December 1979 and 1982, due in large part to the growing numbers of unemployed claimants who rose from 56,000 to 1.7 million in the same period (Deacon & Bradshaw 1983, p. 116). This meant that the hoped-for staffing cuts could not be made. Indeed there was increased pressure on staff, and the official error rate in DHSS offices went up from 10 to 14 per cent (Beltram 1984, p. 132). The increased pressure of work meant that DHSS officers were instructed not to advise claimants about potential entitlement but merely to respond to claims actually made. Interviews with claimants and home visits were also cut, and a self-completion claim form introduced to reduce the time taken in processing claims. In spite of these changes, however, pressure continued to mount, leading to industrial action over staffing levels in DHSS offices in Oxford and Birmingham in 1982.

The problems in the administration of the new SB scheme were felt most acutely, however, by claimants themselves. The notion of entitlement under the regulations was not readily understood or taken up by them, and in a major study of the scheme in 1982, commissioned by the DHSS (Berthoud 1984), it was revealed that only one in six claimants said they understood clearly how their ordinary benefit was worked out (A11). When it came to the new legal entitlement to weekly additions and lump sums, 76 and 83 per cent respectively said they had no idea at all how the system worked (A11). In fact the majority of claimants still thought these were based on discretion, only 12 per cent recognising that they were legal rights (A83). And more worrying still was the finding that a majority of claimants (56 per cent) had not even heard of the possibility of claiming lump sum payments.

The 1982 survey also revealed the continuation of discrepancies over entitlement in the administration of the new scheme. When questioned about entitlement via hypothetical claims a majority of DHSS officers gave incorrect answers (Working Paper B). Yet only a minority claimed to use regularly the Yellow Book or the S Manual, relying instead upon individual judgements about the 'worthiness' of claimants (Working Paper C). A separate study of a DHSS office in Northern Ireland also found that 'local practice (still) exhibits a significant moral complexion' (Howe 1985, p. 67) with a distinction being made between *deserving* claimants, who were quiet and well behaved, and *undeserving* claimants, who were demanding and insistent about their rights.

The distinction between deserving and undeserving claimants of SB also had an important racist dimension. There is much evidence that the take-up of means-tested benefits is lower amongst the black people than in the rest of the population, not the least reason for which, in the case of Asian people in particular, is the lack of adequate information and advice about entitlement in other languages (Gordon & Newnham 1985, Ch. 3). This is frequently compounded, however, by racist attitudes amongst DHSS officers that black claimants can always be supported by their community or are more likely to cause trouble in benefit offices. On occasions this can turn into outright hostility, as the observations of DHSS offices in the 1982 survey revealed (Working Paper C), even though this evidence was at first suppressed by the DHSS (Gordon & Newnham 1985, p. 64).

Thus the 1980 reforms did not simplify the SB scheme, nor did they remove the exercise of discretion or the experience of being subject to it. If they were intended to reduce reliance on additional payments and lump sums this too failed. By 1984 90 per cent of pensioner claimants and 45 per cent of others were receiving additional payments, primarily for heating costs; and after a brief initial decline the number of lump sum payments rose in 1984 to 3 million, an increase in cost over three years from £44 million to over £200 million (Green Paper 1985, Vol. 2, p. 15), in spite of the widespread ignorance of entitlement revealed in the 1982 survey. The hope that regulations might make it easier for DHSS officers to refuse speculative requests for extra payments (CPAG's commentary on the new scheme was called *We Don't Give Clothing Grants Any More*, Allbeson and Smith 1984) thus proved unfounded, and by 1984 entitlement to SB was more unwieldy and confusing than ever, leaving little opposition to Norman Fowler's call for a fundamental review.

SUPPLEMENTARY BENEFIT

Although the household means test was abolished in the post-war reform of assistance, the principle of determining entitlement to benefit has remained much the same within subsequent provisions. It is based upon family units, called *assessment units* in the 1980 SB scheme, and an assessment of means and needs, called *resources* and *requirements*, with entitlement being restricted to the extent to which the latter exceed the former. As we have discussed, however, the regulations governing this assessment are extremely complex, and we cannot go into them here. The simplest guide to them is the CPAG's annual *National Welfare Benefits Handbook*, and the most authoritative statement of the law Mesher's (1985) annotation of the regulations themselves. It is the principles upon which the regulations are based, however, that give rise to the more detailed problems within the scheme, and thus these require some brief examination.

Resources, or means, must be taken into account to ensure that those who do not need relief from poverty are not getting it. Thus those with over £3000 in savings, excluding a house and personal possessions, are not entitled to benefit under the 1980 scheme. This is an automatic cut-off from benefit, though after 1988 it is proposed to replace it with a gradual loss of benefit for those with savings over £3000 up to £6000. It may appear to be a relatively generous rule, but in fact it excludes significant numbers of potential claimants, punishing them for their thrift.

The assessment of earnings and other income is much harsher, however. There is no entitlement at all to SB for those in full-time work (over thirty hours a week, to be reduced in 1988 to twenty-four) – assistance has only ever been intended to provide for the non-working poor. Claimants are permitted to undertake part-time work, but disregarding expenses at work only the first £4 of earnings can be kept, the rest being deducted from benefit entitlement. This is hardly an encouragement to take part-time work, unless of course it is illegally concealed from the DHSS; and indirectly the rule may have contributed to a significant indirect incentive to such black economy work. The changes in 1988 are unlikely to make much difference to this, since it is planned merely to increase the amount of earnings which can be kept to £5 a week and to remove the disregard for work expenses.

Income other than earnings, such as maintenance from a former spouse, NI benefits or occupational pensions, are deducted entirely from benefit entitlement so that SB effectively becomes a supplement to them. The only exceptions to this are universal disability benefits such as Mobility and Attendance Allowance.

The main requirements, or needs, which claimants are assumed to have are the weekly scale rates fixed annually by the government. As we have already discussed, these include an ordinary and a long-term rate, with a difference of around £8 a week for a single person in the mid 1980s. In spite of recommendations to the contrary by the SBC and the SSAC, unemployed claimants have never been able to claim the long-term rate, suggesting that the difference between the two is not entirely based on need.

In addition to the weekly rates, however, claimants' special circumstances may entitle them to additional weekly payments. These cover fairly obvious needs such as additions for the blind and for extra heating costs for pensioners and children under five, but they also include less clear-cut requirements such as exceptional laundry costs, special diets and even the cost of extra baths if more than one a week is needed, for medical reasons. The scope for interpretation here is clearly quite broad.

Requirements also include housing costs where these are not met by the HB scheme. This primarily applies to owner-occupiers, who can claim a weekly amount to cover repairs plus the cost of paying off the interest on any mortgage debt, but not the repayment of capital. This can cause some problems for claimants with large mortgage debts inherited from a previous period in relatively well-paid employment. And this is likely to get much worse if the 1986 proposal to reduce entitlement to mortgage interest payments for the first six months of benefit is carried through, forcing some claimants to sell their homes in order to claim state support.

As well as the weekly additions SB also includes entitlement to lump sum payments for items not provided for in the weekly rates. Whatever claimants' needs, however, payments can only be made for items specified in the regulations for single payments, which include a hot water bottle for the elderly and infirm but exclude clothing and footwear (covered by the weekly rates) and 'luxuries' such as carpets and refrigerators. It is hardly surprising that the 1982 survey found widespread confusion amongst claimants about entitlement to such payments, and they have been a source of many frustrated claims and appeals. In spite of this, however, the number of payments rose substantially in the early 1980s. And as a result in 1986 the government introduced amending regulations to reduce entitlement and to cut the cost of single payments by removing payments for some items and severely restricting entitlement to others.

In cases of urgent need there is provision for immediate weekly or lump sum payments to be made to those whose entitlement to SB has still to be established. The normal rules do not apply to urgent payments, however, and they can only be made when the need cannot be met from any other source. This recalls elements of the household means test and is frequently administered in a similar way, with claimants being questioned about potential sources of loans or hand-outs.

Since entitlement to SB under the 1980 scheme is based upon legal rules appeals against refusal of benefit are legal hearings. Appeals can be made to *Social Security Appeal Tribunals*, as with appeals against refusal of NI benefits, and from here there is an appeal on a point of law to a *Social Security Commissioner* and then to the Court of Appeal. The decisions of Commissioners and the courts are legal interpretations of the regulations before them and thus constitute legal precedents which should determine entitlement in similar cases in the future; the most important ones are thus reported and published. As in NI cases, there is no entitlement to legal aid for representation before SSATs, and most claimants appear unrepresented and hopelessly lost in the face of the complex legal jargon of regulations and Commissioners' decisions.

For most claimants, therefore, entitlement is in practice determined by a DHSS officer in one of the 500 or so local offices which administer the SB scheme. As we have discussed, these offices began to come under increasing pressure in the 1980s as the number of claimants rose dramatically. Around 6 million claims and 20 million reviews were dealt with every year. And in spite of plans for computerisation this was still being done entirely by hand. The pressure has also increased the wide gulf of distrust and suspicion between claimants and officers, which can be most starkly witnessed in the plastic screens in DHSS offices, the uncomfortable chairs bolted to the floor, and the long and frustrated queues. It had ensured that by the mid 1980s the experience of living *on the social* was no more satisfying or satisfactory than it had been under the old assistance schemes. The proposal to change this in 1988, whilst retaining the core of the means-tested scheme in a streamlined form, may prove to be an unachievable goal.

INCOME SUPPORT

The plans for the reform of social security in 1988 are based on the assumption that means-tested support will remain the major feature of benefit provision for the majority of claimants and the recognition that the attempt to introduce a SB scheme based on legally defined tests of need in 1980 did not work. 'It cannot be right', concludes the Green Paper (Vol. 2, p. 18), 'to run a system which requires claimants to have such a detailed knowledge in order to get their entitlement.' Thus fairly drastic changes are proposed in order to simplify entitlement and administration. Of course these goals are hardly innovatory, in theory they were the aims of the 1966 and 1980 reforms of SB. The idea of a change of name in order to provide symbolic expression of a new start is not original either, but this too is planned with SB to be replaced by *Income Support* [doc. 12].

The IS scheme will be simpler than SB primarily because there will be no entitlement to extra weekly and lump sum payments for special needs. It is no longer intended 'to provide in detail for every variation in individual circumstances' (Vol. 2, p. 23). Instead there will be broad differences in the weekly rates of benefit for different groups of claimants by the payment to some of *premiums* on top of the basic rate.

There is one premium for pensioners over sixty, with a higher rate still for those over eighty. There is another for claimants with disabilities, equal to the higher-rate pension premium. There is also a premium for families (claimants with dependent children) in addition to the children's ordinary weekly rates, with an additional premium for lone parents. Certainly these are the groups who under the previous scheme were on average most likely to be in receipt of additional payments for things like heating, diet and laundry needs. But whether the new premiums will compensate adequately for the loss of these is extremely doubtful. The indicative benefit rates issued with the White Paper in December 1985 suggest that few will be better off. And if account is taken of the loss of entitlement to lump sum payments and the plan to require all claimants to pay their water rates and a proportion of their general rates out of weekly benefit (under SB additional payments are made for these), many are likely to be much worse off – including families, who it was argued were those most in need of the extra help that premiums would provide. Although transitional regulations will ensure that no claimants suffer a cut in the cash value of their weekly benefit when the new scheme is implemented.

In fact the rationale for the new premiums is far from as straightforward as it might appear from the government's justifications for reform. As Berthoud pointed out in an examination of the Green Paper and White Paper proposals (Berthoud 1985, 1986), in order to make broad distinctions between groups of claimants arbitrary dividing lines must be drawn, for instance between those with disabilities sufficient to qualify for the premium and those with less serious disability. The choice of the groups themselves is also rather arbitrary, for instance it is not clear why unemployed lone parents should have greater needs than unemployed two-parent families (though their position in the labour market may be weaker). Indeed the major reason for the proposed premiums appears to be to retain in another form the, supposedly abolished, distinction between the long-term and ordinary SB rates (Berthoud 1985, p. 36), with the continuing connotations of deserving and undeserving poor that this distinction creates.

Further division is to be created, however, by the plan to pay a lower rate of benefit to the single under twenty-fives. Within the SB scheme there is a lower rate of benefit for non-householders (because they are presumed to have no need to purchase household items). Many of those on this lower rate are young people living in someone else's household. The distinction between the two rates, however, has led to complex rules and quite arbitrary practice by DHSS officers. The new scheme will remove these problems by automatically paying a lower rate of benefit (equivalent to the non-householder rate) to all under twenty-fives and the full rate to all over twenty-fives, irrespective of household status. This will certainly simplify things; and since the new lower rate is exactly half the ordinary rate for a couple, it will also effectively remove the distinction between single and couple claimants for this group, so that the cohabitation rule will no longer have to be applied.

The reduced rate for the under twenty-fives is not merely a move to simplify the determination of entitlement for this group, however. It is also part of a policy to ensure that benefit levels do not compete with wages for low-paid jobs, for the government had made it clear for some time that young employees could not expect to command the wage levels which might be expected by older workers. And where such low-paid employment is not available then non-householder status and continued dependency upon parents is likely in effect to become compulsory for all young people. Single parents under twenty-five will not be subject to the lower rate, however – perhaps an inducement to enter parenthood to escape from home.

A major measure of simplification in the new IS scheme is the plan to do away with entitlement to single payment for special needs, though there is no intention to increase weekly rates to compensate for this. Berthoud (1985) has calculated that these payments are worth on average £1 a week to each claimant, though families receive more payments and for them the average loss will be nearer £3 (over half of the proposed family premium). As we have discussed, the SB regulations governing entitlement to items like hot water bottles are hopelessly inappropriate and unworkable. But this does not mean that the *need* for such items (most importantly household furniture) will disappear when the regulations are removed.

This is recognised in the plans for IS, and it is proposed to cater for such needs by means of discretionary loans from a new *Social Fund*. The fund will be a cash-limited account administered by local benefit offices under guidelines issued by the Secretary of State. It will make grants for maternity needs and funeral expenses, replacing the previous automatic grants for these. In the case of funeral expenses these will be recoverable from the deceased's estate. It will also make grants to support people leaving institutional care and re-establishing themselves in the community and to relieve the pressure on families providing *community care*.

The major role for the fund, however, will be in the provision (or not) of discretionary loans to claimants to purchase items which they cannot afford out of their weekly benefit. These will be subject to a minimum and maximum size and will not be payable to those with savings over £500, and whether a payment is made will depend upon whether it is judged reasonable to meet the need and how practical recovery will be. In most cases it is expected that recovery will be made by deduction from future benefit, and problems will thus arise if claimants cease to become dependent upon IS because of the receipt of a new form of income. The other criterion governing payment will presumably be the cash limit on the fund in the local office, though it is suggested that administration will be flexible enough to avoid offices simply running out of money – at least until the scheme is reasonably maturely established.

It is not expected that the guidelines will 'cover every conceivable' situation. Presumably this is in order to avoid a return to the old A Code. If they do not, however, then the role of the new specialist officers administering the fund will be extremely important. Their appointment is likely to imply a clearly delineated role for discretion within the new scheme, based on the existing role of Special Case Officers, who advise claimants with serious debt problems. This will create an expectation that loans will only be available to claimants who have got into financial difficulties – a much narrower provision than that in the previous SB scheme. It will also compound pathological notions of the inadequacy of the poor, as claimants will have to prove that their problems are too great for them to cope with in order to get a loan from the state.

As the Social Fund is to be operated on a discretionary basis there were no plans to permit appeals against refusals to make loans, though attempts were made when the legislation was in Parliament in 1986 to introduce a right of independent appeal. However, a reconsideration of the request by the DHSS office is all that will be available, with a general monitoring function to be exercised by a Social Fund Commissioner. Once again this underlines the fairly restricted role that it is intended for the fund to have. Whether this restriction will succeed in reducing the need for additional payments in a way that previous attempts at reform have not done, however, will probably largely turn not on demand but on how the new features, the cash limit and the recovery of loans, operate to reduce the cost of the scheme in practice.

The proposals for the replacement of SB with IS are thus quite radical and far-reaching. They were certainly presented as such. As we have discussed, however, changes in name and restrictions on entitlement should not too readily be taken as evidence of fundamental reform. The structure of IS remains firmly within the principles of SB and other assistance schemes. It is a means-tested benefit, paid on a family basis to those out of full-time work, operating alongside the NI scheme. Although as critics have pointed out (Lister *et al.* 1985), many claimants are likely to be worse off under the new scheme and, in the Social Fund in particular, there is likely to be an accentuation of judgemental attitudes towards claimants, there are clear links between IS and previous schemes for means-tested support – most notably because the scheme is still far from comprehensive and will have to operate alongside the numerous other forms of benefit provision for those out of and in work. We will turn to look at these in the next chapter.

Chapter eight
MORE AND MORE BENEFITS

EXPANDING BENEFIT PROVISION

In spite of Beveridge's intention for a comprehensive role for insurance within social security, and the increasingly dominant role of SB within the system in recent years, there has also been a dramatic growth in benefits outside of the NI and SB schemes, designed to meet both particular and general needs. Some of these such as free school meals predate the post-war reforms, others such as Family Allowances were an integral part of them, but most have grown up since then to fill the many gaps within the major benefit schemes or to compensate for inadequate or expensive services outside of the social security system.

Some of these benefits are *universal*, being paid to all those falling within the social category covered. These include Child Benefit, and a number of general benefits for people with disabilities. As we have already discussed, however, universality has not generally been a major feature of post-war social security provision, and these benefits have at times received only grudging support and have been restricted to relatively nominal levels of payment.

The majority of other benefits are therefore *selective*, providing means-tested support only for those with incomes below levels fixed within the particular scheme. They have largely been introduced in attempts to ensure that poor people have not suffered too harshly from policies to reduce general subsidised services in areas such as housing, health and education and replace these with charges or private provision, by providing exemption from charges or means-tested support for those unable to compete on the private market. By 1976 the NCC calculated that there were forty-five different means-tested benefits (including SB) operating in Britain administered either by central or local government, and since then the numbers have not declined. Generally speaking, the levels of means tests are different for each different scheme, contributing, as we shall see, to much confusion amongst claimants and the failure of many to realise their full entitlement under all.

CHILD BENEFIT

Child Benefit is the most widely known and widely claimed benefit outside the major NI and SB schemes. In the mid 1980s it was being paid for almost 12.5 million children at a cost of around £4.5 billion. Child Benefit came into operation in 1977 when it replaced Family Allowances and child tax allowances and has always commanded strong support from the poverty lobby because of its universal nature (McClelland 1982; Walsh & Lister 1985; Henwood & Wicks 1986).

As we have discussed, the history of the introduction of Family Allowances is a rather contradictory one. They were both support for child care and encouragement for women to remain at home and give birth. There was never any intention that they should cover the full costs of caring for children and throughout the 1950s and 1960s their level was allowed to fall against inflation. Although for those in paid work, this was mitigated to some extent by the effect of tax allowances for dependent children which reduced the amount of tax paid by the (usually male) breadwinner. In the late 1960s the government bowed to pressure from the poverty lobby and doubled Family Allowances, restoring them to around the 1948 level, and mitigated the overall cost of this by reducing the value of the tax allowances.

This link between benefits and tax allowances provided the springboard in the mid 1970s for a campaign to replace the two with a single universal benefit for all children, which would be of greater value to those poorer families who did not pay tax. As Field (1982) discusses, the poverty lobby as at the forefront of this campaign, in particular during the period in 1976 when the Cabinet having supported the passing of the Child Benefit Act 1975 tried to go back on the commitment to introduce the new benefit [doc. 6]. Although when the benefit was finally introduced in 1977 it was fixed at a level way below the real costs of child care (see Piachaud 1979) and little higher than the Family Allowance level of the 1940s.

Because of the universal nature of Child Benefit and the ease of identifying entitlement, there is virtually full take-up of it and no stigma attached to claiming. The opinion survey commissioned as part of the 1984 reviews of social security revealed widespread support for it (Green Paper, Vol. 3, p. 76). Because of its apparent high cost, however, government commitment to it has always been mixed, as the events of 1976 demonstrated. The changes planned for 1988 do not include any change in it, however. Although in 1985 its value was permitted to fall against inflation (unlike other benefits there is no requirement that its value be maintained), and its role is still likely to be restricted to one of providing only a contribution towards the costs of child care, with the expectation that families themselves will bear the major burden.

For single-parent families there is some recognition that there may be extra need for support and a single premium, *One-Parent Benefit*, is paid on top of Child Benefit. In fact this was something of a compromise with the more comprehensive proposals for separate benefits for single parents proposed by the *Finer Committee* in 1974, which were not taken up by the government. And although it was worth around £5 a week in the mid 1980s it was only claimed by around a half of those entitled.

This is primarily because, like Child Benefit itself, One-Parent Benefit is automatically set against entitlement to SB, which already includes weekly rates for all children. In effect this means that both are only of any real benefit to working parents or those dependent entirely on NI benefits (a minority). As we shall discuss later, this is to some extent the product of a deliberate policy to boost the incomes of families in work and thus create a gap between them and those on means-tested benefits in order to encourage paid employment. That this gap is therefore greater for single parents is due to the greater difficulty that they generally face in finding reasonably paid jobs because of the lack of collective child care facilities. However, as we shall see, it is not the only measure for supporting parents in low-paid work, and because of this the payment (or non-payment of benefit) can have contradictory consequences. In the case of most single parents, around a half of whom are dependent upon SB anyway, this means that Child Benefit and One-Parent Benefit are of no value, and thus the latter is frequently not claimed. We will return to some of the more general consequences later.

DISABILITY BENEFITS

Although the NI scheme was intended to provide for the needs of those with disabilities through Sickness and Invalidity Benefits, it has never been able to meet even the basic needs of most disabled people. The NI benefits are not significantly higher than those for able-bodied claimants and do not make any provision for the extra costs of living which many disabled people have to bear. They are also based upon the assumption that disability is a work-related contingency which could be provided for under the insurance scheme. Yet the most serious disabilities are frequently not caused by work, and many disabled people do not, *because* of their disability, have adequate contribution records. In recognition of some of these shortcomings within NI provision, specialist benefits for those with severe disabilities were introduced on a universal basis in the 1970s, to meet some of the extra costs experienced by disabled people and those living with them.

Attendance Allowance was the first to be introduced in 1971. After a six-month qualifying period it provided a flat-rate weekly payment to those requiring constant attention during the day or night for assistance with basic bodily functions. Although it was extended in 1975 the benefit was only worth a maximum of £30 a week in the mid 1980s, hardly enough to employ someone to provide care for twenty-four hours a day.

Mobility Allowance, a weekly payment for those unable or virtually unable to walk, was introduced in 1976, replacing the DHSS provision of special invalid vehicles. Like Attendance Allowance it is a payment for special needs and is thus an addition to any other benefit, including NI benefits or SB. However, in both cases qualifying need must first be established and here quite stringent tests apply to restrict entitlement only to those with the most severe physical conditions; for instance difficulty in walking because of *mental* handicap does not generally entitle claimants to Mobility Allowance.

In 1974 Non-contributory Invalidity Pension was introduced to provide a source of income for disabled people not entitled to NI benefit. It discriminated against married women, to whom it was not paid unless household duties could also not be carried out, and was replaced in 1984 by *Severe Disablement Allowance*. This is paid to all people disabled before their twentieth birthday or *severely* disabled after then who are not entitled to NI benefit. Severely disabled means 80 per cent disablement, though this automatically includes those receiving Mobility or Attendance Allowance. The SDA is a weekly payment, considerably below NI and SB levels. However, because it is intended for those with no other form of support it is deducted from SB if this too is being claimed. For many disabled people, therefore, it is irrelevant; and, as we discussed in Chapter 3, because of the relative exclusion of married women from more generous NI provision, it is still discriminatory in practice.

Invalid Care Allowance, introduced in 1976, is intended to provide a minimum income (equivalent to SDA) for those who have had to give up paid work to care for a disabled relative. Like SDA, it is intended for those with no other income and thus is deducted from SB if this is also claimed, although, as we discussed in Chapter 3, until 1986 it was not paid to married or cohabiting women.

In general, benefits for those with disabilities are restricted in scope, excluding many whose disability or circumstances do not quite match the rules for entitlement. They are also paid at very low levels. They are thus no substitute for the provision of services for the disabled and do not provide sufficient resources for these to be purchased on an individual basis on the private market. Given that most disabled people can have little prospect of obtaining decent paid work and will therefore have to survive on them indefinitely, this means that many live in extreme poverty and have to depend in addition on SB.

For some time, therefore, groups such as the Disability Alliance have been campaigning for a comprehensive disability payment to provide an adequate income for all people with disabilities. An attempt was made to introduce this in a partial form in the House of Lords' consideration of the 1986 legislation. However, it was eventually reduced by the government to an additional disability premium for a restricted category of disabled people already receiving IS. It will thus benefit few and is unlikely to provide even these with the money to purchase the range of services they may need to play a full role in society.

The only major provision of services for people with disabilities is that by local authorities under the Chronically Sick and Disabled Persons Act. This can cover the provision of special equipment in the home, payment for alterations to a house, and access to leisure and holiday facilities (see Topliss 1982). However, these are discretionary provisions. Consequently the level of services varies considerably from authority to authority and establishing *entitlement* to any particular provision is virtually impossible.

FAMILY INCOME SUPPLEMENT

Of the *selective* benefits introduced to deal with the growing problems in state support in the 1970s, FIS is perhaps the most important. This is not because it affects large numbers of people – only about 200,000 received it in the mid 1980s – but because it exemplifies most clearly the expanding role for means-tested benefits and the problems associated with this.

It was introduced by the Conservative Government in 1971 as something of a compromise measure in an attempt to resolve a number of contradictory problems with one single mechanism. It was an attempt to meet the needs of poor families caring for children without the expense of raising Family Allowances for all. It was an attempt to increase work incentives by raising the income of parents in low-paid work. And it was a step towards the integrated tax and benefit system, to which the government were on paper committed, by the introduction of a sort of tax credit for families with incomes below a prescribed level in the form of a direct cash payment in addition to wages. The Labour Opposition were highly critical of FIS, though Labour had themselves considered a similar measure in 1967, and when they returned to power in the mid 1970s they retained it and developed other means-tested benefits such as the electricity discount scheme which were dependent on it.

Basically, FIS is a supplement to low wages for people with dependent children. It can be claimed by anyone in full-time work (thirty or more hours a week, twenty-four for single parents) whose normal gross income is below the prescribed level in the scheme. The prescribed level includes an element for each child and is uprated in line with inflation every year. The FIS payment is equivalent to 50 per cent of the difference between gross income and the prescribed level, subject to a fixed maximum amount. Once entitlement has been established it is paid for twelve months irrespective of any change in financial circumstances. Payment is made not to the wage-earner but to the parent with major responsibility for child care, in most cases the mother.

On the face of it the twelve-month period is a rather crude, and generous, basis for the payment of a means-tested benefit. However, it is in part a recognition of sometimes rapidly fluctuating circumstances of low-wage earners, which otherwise would make administration of the scheme exceedingly time-consuming and expensive. It is also a recognition, though only a temporary delay, of a major problem with means-tested supplements to low wages. In order to avoid making payments to those above the fixed income levels benefits must be withdrawn if income rises. However, this acts to reduce the real increase received as a result of higher wages, and since FIS is a 50 per cent subsidy its withdrawal reduces this by 50 per cent. This is likely to act as a disincentive to work for higher wages, *or* to claim FIS in the first place. The twelve-month payment period acts as a cushion against this disincentive effect, but it cannot remove it and, as we shall see in Chapter 9, it is a major feature of one of the most problematic consequences of means-tested support – the *poverty trap*.

The disincentive to claim FIS may be real and may have a broader basis than the fear of future withdrawal. Means-tested benefits for those in full-time work attempt to cross the division between workers and claimants which, as we have seen, has always been a central ideological feature of state support. Those in full-time work, most of whom are also paying tax, may not welcome, or (more likely) realise, their potential dependency on state benefits and thus may not claim them. It is estimated that only about a half of those who are entitled to FIS do claim it, leading to another of the problems associated with means-tested benefits, that of *take-up*.

It was problems like these that were intended to be part of the focus of the 1984 reviews of social security. However, the reforms to be introduced in 1988 are unlikely to do much to improve them; FIS is to be formally abolished, but it is to be replaced with *Family Credit*, another means-tested supplement to low wages for those with dependent children. Unlike FIS, entitlement to FC will be based on *net* income set against prescribed levels based on those in the IS scheme, and on a twenty-four-hour working week. It will also only be paid for six-month periods. The shift to a net income basis will reduce the harshest effects of the poverty trap, but will spread high withdrawal rates over a wider proportion of the low paid. The six-month payment will also bring these into effect sooner. As we discussed in Chapter 3, it was also originally planned to pay FC directly into the wage-earner's pay-packet rather than to the person caring for the children; but this was abandoned when the legislation was in the House of Lords in 1986.

HOUSING BENEFIT

The problem of how to provide support for housing costs is one which has dogged all benefit schemes throughout the last century in Britain. Beveridge's social insurance proposals contained no clear strategy for dealing with them. And the ensuing post-war NI scheme contained a compromise, an average amount to cover rent being included in weekly benefit, which was too low to cover the costs of many householders, and which was in direct contradiction to provision in the National Assistance scheme of payment of full rent in addition to weekly benefit. The compromise and the contradiction have remained since.

One of the immediate effects of this was to make householders better off if they claimed assistance in addition to NI benefit, destroying the comprehensive aspirations of insurance. However, because housing costs fluctuated so widely between different parts of the country, different types of tenure and even, on occasions, different sides of the street, the impact of this was uneven.

In the 1950s and 1960s, however, housing costs rose quite dramatically, much more rapidly than benefits or wages. This meant that not only NI claimants, but also those on low wages might be better off claiming assistance and getting their rent met in full. Although this could be tackled by means of direct state support to keep the costs of housing down, the government did not favour such universal provision and by the late 1950s was encouraging selective support for those who could not afford their housing costs via local authority schemes to pay *rent rebates* to those with incomes below locally determined levels. In the 1960s these were extended and the Labour Government published a circular setting out a model scheme. However, it was not compulsory to follow this and a wide variety of provision remained (Reddin 1968).

In the early 1970s it was the policy of the Conservative Government to increase council rents and, as we have seen, to extend selective provision for the poor. Thus in 1972, when rents were increased, they introduced a mandatory national rent rebate scheme, and followed this in 1973 with *rent allowances* for private-sector tenants and *rate rebates* for all. However, although the schemes were planned nationally they were still administered by local authorities. Because of the need to base them on both wages levels and rents (the so-called *tapers*), they were also extremely complex, and in spite of increases in levels for entitlement, take-up generally remained low – as little as 10 per cent for rent allowances (Deacon & Bradshaw 1983, p. 87).

The complexity was compounded by the overlap between subsidies for housing costs via rebates and provision for full housing costs under SB. For those not in full-time work but receiving pensions, NI benefits or other income it created the nightmare of the *better-off* problem – the dilemma of whether to claim rebates or go on to SB. And critics argued that the complexity and overlap created an unanswerable case for reform. Most notable amongst these was David Donnison, Chair of the SBC, who argued that there should instead be a single, unified scheme for support for the housing costs of the poor (Donnison 1979, 1982). However, as Donnison himself realised, complex existing provision created complex vested interests which could not be overcome without the injection of significantly more resources into the schemes, and these were not forthcoming [doc. 13].

Nevertheless in 1982 the government decided to introduce a single unified scheme without the injection of more resources. It was called *Housing Benefit* and was to continue to be administered by the local authorities, no doubt in anticipation of the political backwash that Donnison had predicted. In fact the new scheme was not unified in anything other than name and the problems of complexity remained, as was admitted later by a senior civil servant in the DHSS; 'We found it impossible within the constraints that the government set of expenditure to devise a unified scheme of a kind which might have avoided the problems of the scheme which we now have' (quoted in Lister *et al.* 1985, p. 20).

The main change that was made was to transfer the administration of SB payments for rent and rates from the DHSS to local authorities. This was now to be called *Certificated HB* and once a certificate confirming that the claimant was on SB had been sent from the DHSS local authorities either paid claimants their rent money or issued nil demands for rent and rates, recovering the cost back from the DHSS. Owner-occupiers' housing costs other than rates, however, continued to be met directly by the DHSS.

The rebates scheme was retitled *Standard HB* and the tapers slightly adjusted. The basic principles of entitlement, however, remained intact (for a detailed guide to entitlement see CPAG's *National Welfare Benefits Handbook* or McGurk & Raynsford 1982). After the introduction of the scheme further adjustments were made to the tapers, in order to cut benefits by reducing the entitlement of those nearest the top of the entitlement scale. Although in spite of these the costs of the new scheme rapidly increased, because of the government's policy of increasing council rents.

The only really significant improvement in the 1982 reform was the introduction of *Housing Benefit Supplement* in order to remove the better-off problem for the non-working poor. It is in fact a payment of SB to top up the Standard HB of those who would otherwise be better off moving entirely on to SB. But the process of claiming and administering it is extremely tortuous, involving separate claims at both the local authority and the DHSS, and it is probable that many of those who might be entitled do not receive it in spite of at some time having made an application for SB (Kemp 1984, p. 41).

The unification of support for housing costs thus fell far short of Donnison's hopes, but to make matters worse the expanded role of local authorities in the administration of the new scheme proved to be little short of a disaster. Few authorities were prepared for the extra burden of work that the transfer of authority was to mean and most struggled to meet the statutory time periods for processing claims, let alone improve on the previous inadequacies of the DHSS.

Different local authorities administer HB through different

departments, either housing, education or finance, or a mixture of all three. For claimants already dealing with one or two government departments this is yet another bureaucratic hurdle that they may fail to clear. In the early years following the introduction of the scheme there was also little publicity encouraging claims as local authorities had not published leaflets about entitlement, and in spite of hopes to the contrary it is unlikely that take-up of Standard HB was any better than that of the old rebates.

Further complication resulted from the power which authorities were given under the scheme to introduce improvements (enhancements) to the Standard HB scheme, up to a maximum of 10 per cent of the cost of the scheme, if this cost was borne by the local rates. By the mid 1980s around a half of authorities were doing this by amending the levels for entitlement in various ways. Although this may have been to the benefit of some claimants, the price paid in confusion (especially for people moving from one area to another) was high, making a nonsense of the advantages of having a single national scheme.

The 1984 review of HB was the only part of the process not chaired by a government minister [doc. 8], and in their report the review team concluded that simplification and equalisation of treatment across the two parts of the scheme were necessary (Rowe Report 1985). The proposals for the reform of HB did not entirely follow the review team's recommendations, however. Some simplification is planned through a replacement of the current six tapers for calculating Standard HB with only two (one for rent and one for rates) and an alignment of income levels with those in FC and IS, thus hopefully removing the need for HB Supplement. The power of local authorities to make enhancements to Standard HB is also to be removed, except for war pensioners and individual cases of hardship.

As well as simplifying entitlement however, the changes to HB are also expected to reduce expenditure on it by cutting benefit entitlement further. 'Savings' are certainly expected to flow from what was probably the most controversial aspect of the proposed reform, the requirement on all claimants (including those on IS) to pay a proportion of their local rates, probably 20 per cent. This idea was rejected by the review team itself and opposed by the House of Lords; but the government pressed ahead with it in any case, with the claim that forcing poor people to pay rates would be 'an indispensable part of a healthy local democracy' (White Paper 1985, p. 30). It is certainly likely to be a major headache for local authorities, who will have to collect some rates from all of those claimants previously on 100 per cent rebates, all of whom, by definition, are going to be poor people who will find it hard to budget for this extra expense.

As we mentioned, support for claimants with mortgage debts was not covered by the HB scheme and remained as part of SB administered by the DHSS. It did not escape review, however, and after the proposed reforms of HB had been published the government announced their intention to cut this too by removing entitlement of claimants on SB or IS to the full repayment of the interest on the mortgage debt for the first six months of dependency on benefit, but after this period any debts built up would be paid off. For those on benefit for less than six months this will be a major cut, and may force many to sell their homes in order to survive. It will, ironically, penalise those who following government policy had bought their homes before becoming dependent upon benefit, adding further to the contradictions between direct subsidisation of housing for some and means-tested support towards its costs for others. Without an attempt to plan these two forms of state support together, the problems which HB and other forms of benefit for housing costs fail to solve are likely to remain.

EDUCATION BENEFITS

Housing Benefit is not the only social security benefit administered by local authorities. Throughout most of this century they have also been able to provide benefits in the form of milk, meals, clothing and income support for school children or their parents. The initial rationale behind the granting of power to do this was that it would assist authorities in their duty to provide compulsory education for children, since poor children would not be able to attend school if they had to pay for meals and uniforms, and could not be expected to go without. Thus in 1906 local education authorities (LEAs) were permitted to provide school meals, free of charge if they wished, and in 1934 they were permitted to provide milk also (Cooper 1985).

In the 1944 Education Act these powers were consolidated and extended; LEAs were required to provide school meals for all, with free meals for those who could not afford to pay, and to provide free milk for all children. They were also required to provide free transport to school for children living outside prescribed limits and had the discretion to provide transport within these too. They were further given the power to provide grants for school clothing and Education Maintenance Allowances to help support the children of poor families to stay on at school after compulsory leaving age. However, the 1944

Act did not go as far as providing free meals and allowances for all, and since then there has been further reduction in the scope of education benefit support, as a result of both local authority and government policy.

In general the changes in education benefits have been a consequence of moves to reduce public expenditure and restrict universal provision, and to provide selective, means-tested support for those unable to pay the increased costs involved. School meal charges have been increased and grants for clothing and maintenance restricted in most local authorities, although the effects of cuts have been different in different areas as a result of the differing policies of LEAs (Tunnard 1977; Burghes & Stagles 1983).

In 1972 the entitlement to free school milk was removed and the subsidy for LEAs to provide it withdrawn by the government. After 1980 moves to cafeteria-style school meals reduced the take-up and the quality of these, and LEAs were no longer required to provide free meals merely to make 'such provision as was requisite' for children of SB and FIS claimants. In many cases this increased the stigma already associated with entitlement to free school meals by the physical separation of children on free meals from those who were paying for theirs, and this reduced the take-up further (Bissett & Coussins 1982). Although authorities could continue to provide free meals for the children of those on low wages, about a third restricted their provision to the statutory minimum, and provision amongst the rest varied widely.

The 1988 reforms will remove this fluctuation in the case of school meals, though not clothing and maintenance allowances, by removing the LEAs' power to provide meals for those on low incomes, even those receiving the new FC. The argument in favour of this is that benefits 'in kind', such as meals, are undesirable and anyone who can afford to pay for their children's meals, including those on low pay, should be required to do so – leaving free school meal entitlement, and no doubt all the stigma associated with it, to those on IS.

As with other aspects of the 1988 reforms this is largely an extension of existing trends in benefit policy towards restricted means-tested provision for the very poor. Although it will simplify entitlement on a national basis, fluctuations in entitlement to clothing and maintenance allowances will remain. In the case of the latter increased pressure will be put on LEAs to provide for poor children who stay on at school by the plan to remove entitlement to IS from sixteen- to eighteen-year-olds and its replacement with compulsory youth training for those who leave school. However, there is no evidence of any moves towards national provision of maintenance allowances for sixteen- to eighteen-year-olds at school (Burghes & Stagles 1983).

NATIONAL HEALTH SERVICE BENEFITS

The extension of means-tested benefits in education since the early post-war period has been accompanied by a growth of selective provision within the health service also. The post-war NHS, free for all at the point of need, was heralded at the time as a major, if not *the* major, achievement of the new welfare state. However, as early as 1952 the Conservative Government began a retreat from the principle of a free service with the introduction of charges for prescriptions. As with charges for education provision such as school meals, it was recognised that some might be unable to pay and so means-tested exemptions for the poor were introduced.

As charges have been introduced subsequently for other aspects of health service provision, and the level of existing charges raised, means-tested exemptions have become more widespread. They now cover free prescriptions, free or reduced charge dental and optical treatment, free milk and vitamins for young children, and the provision of aids such as wigs and fabric supports. Each of these exemptions constitutes in effect a separate means-tested benefit from the state. They are administered nationally by the DHSS according to annually fixed entitlement levels. They are available automatically, however, to claimants on SB who are *passported* on to entitlement, although if they do not realise this they may still not claim the benefit. Most are also available to those on low pay, although amongst these take-up is, not surprisingly, lower. One study in 1972 estimated only 44 per cent take-up of free prescriptions (Deacon & Bradshaw 1983, p. 94).

In 1971 the Conservative Government substantially increased NHS charges and extended means-tested exemptions. This was followed by a major advertising campaign to increase take-up, which went up to around 49 per cent and then fell back after the campaign was ended. In 1971 the government also abolished cheap welfare milk and as a replacement increased the income levels for entitlement to free milk and vitamins. They claimed that, following advertising for this, take-up rose from 1,509 families to 65,907, though it later fell back to 26,269 (Deacon & Bradshaw 1983, p. 94). Impressive though this may appear, it is really a telling condemnation of the proliferation of such means-tested benefits and their failure to provide adequately even for those supposedly entitled to them. Such massive advertising campaigns are not sustained, and arguably over a long period of time would anyway begin to lose their impact. And even the apparent success of this one is tempered when it is realised that in all about 340,000 families were estimated to be entitled to the benefit.

It is arguable that this is not just a problem with minor, and comparatively obscure, means-tested benefits such as free milk and vitamins, however, but is a chronic feature of any means-tested provision of state support. It is also not the only problem to which such benefits give rise. We will turn to look at these problems, and what might be done about them, in the final section of this book.

Part four
ASSESSMENT

Chapter nine

PROBLEMS AND CONTRADICTIONS IN BENEFITS

COMPROMISES AND CONTRADICTIONS

Social security provision in Britain is a product of state policies developed to provide income support for the poor. However, different perceptions of the nature of poverty itself and the role of the state in providing for it lead to different judgements about what is being done and why. In this context we have suggested that British social security policy is a *compromise* between the prevention of absolute poverty alone and some measure of redistribution of income to maintain a standard of living for benefit claimants relative to that of those in paid work; and also that it contains a *contradiction* between progressive gains for claimants in terms of an increased standard of living and control and containment of them at the bottom of an unequal capitalist society. Social security is not one or other of these – but both at the same time. And the predominance of one aspect rather than another is a product of changing political, ideological and economic pressures on the state.

As we have seen, these changing pressures have over the past forty years produced changing (compromising and contradictory) social security policies within Britain which have resulted in the complex mass of benefit provision experienced in the mid 1980s. Within it are compromises between universal and selective provision and between the insurance and taxation bases for funding state support. And between these the pendulum has been swinging in recent years towards a greater emphasis on means-testing, with important consequences for the way the benefit system operates on a day-to-day basis.

However, to say that the benefit system operates at all is in reality something of a truism, for its operation is debilitated by serious problems. The problems are not new, and they are not (all) confined to social security in Britain and thus to some extent we have learned to live with them. But they are very real, and for those who suffer under the social security system, indirectly all of us, they can be very serious. In any analysis of poverty and state support they must play an important part – and in any proposals for change their resolution must have a high priority.

The problems within social security, however, are no unhappy accident or unexpected coincidence. They are a product of the policies for social security which have been adopted by the state – an inevitable and predictable consequence. That the impact of these problems is contradictory is a result of the fact that the policies themselves are the contradictory products of the political process. And thus depending upon which political perspective is adopted, the nature and causes of the problems themselves will be different. In spite of this there is a fair degree of agreement about the effects of them in practice.

One of the major roles played by critics of social security policy, notably those in the poverty lobby, has been to point out these problems within the benefits system, to catalogue their effects on claimants and on society generally, and to argue that they should be alleviated or removed (see MacGregor 1981, Ch. 7 and Whiteley & Winyard 1983). Of course, since the problems are an inevitable consequence of the policies pursued, they could only be alleviated if the policies were changed. In spite of comments such as Deacon & Bradshaw's (1983, p. 157) on the poverty trap, 'If it was widely realised it would surely cause an outrage', pointing out the consequences of policies without looking at the reasons for them is of limited value. For what are problems for some may be benefits for others, and in the case of the poverty trap, as we shall see, this is certainly true.

This is not to say that problems cannot be alleviated, only that in order to achieve that we must change first the aims of policies which have given rise to them. In the rest of this chapter, however, we will consider some of the worst problems (or contradictions) within the social security system, their causes and their consequences, before moving on later to discuss what is being, and what might be, done about them.

CONFUSION, COMPLEXITY AND IGNORANCE

As we have seen, one of the most obvious problems with the post-war social security system has been the failure of the insurance scheme. Because of its inadequate benefit rates, arbitrary contribution conditions and limited benefit provision most benefit claimants have to rely on SB and other means-tested benefits, whether they can claim NI benefits or not. The separation of insurance and means-testing in principle and yet their overlap in practice are a major source of confusion for claimants. Even for those who understand the distinctions between the two schemes, their separation means making different claims on different forms for benefits paid under different criteria for entitlement administered from different offices run by different government departments, all in order to receive a basic income. For the majority, who are probably not aware of the distinct principles and processes, however, confusion over the roles of different offices and officers is common, frequently leading to delays before claiming and receiving all benefits or failure to receive full benefit at all.

In practice this confusion could be mitigated by close co-operation over the administration of the different benefit schemes; but in fact almost the reverse has occurred. They are administered by separate officers with separate responsibilities and training and, in large towns and cities, usually in separate offices. Their management structures, records and filing systems are different. It was only after an appeal had been made in one case to the Social Security Commissioners that it was established that claimants who notified one department of changes in their circumstances could assume that another one would be told. It was policy before that to require claimants receiving more than one benefit to notify all offices separately. It was also only after 1982 that claimants of NI Unemployment Benefit were automatically issued with a claim form for SB, though most are likely to be entitled to both.

The transfer of HB administration to local authorities has compounded rather than alleviated the confusion of bureaucracy with which claimants have to wrestle. Now all householders must make a claim at the local authority as well as at the government departments, and in the case of HB Supplement can end up being shunted back and forth between the two. When we add to this claims for NHS and education benefits the confusion multiplies and the process of claiming benefit becomes like an examination in the responsibilities and processes of central and local government – an examination in which large numbers of claimants fail to get 100 per cent.

Confusion does not arise only from the overlap of different benefit schemes, however. It is also an inherent feature of many of the benefits themselves, notably the means-tested SB scheme. Because of the basic assumption underlying SB, that it should meet claimants' subsistence needs but no more, the regulations governing entitlement must contain detailed definition of needs and means. As we discussed in

Chapter 7, this leads to thousands of rules covering everything from hot water bottles to baths – although of course they cannot cover everything, and even after this much is left to the interpretation of phrases such as 'normal wear and tear' or 'suitable alternative accommodation'. As the 1982 survey of the new SB scheme found (Berthoud 1984), the effect of this was widespread confusion and ignorance about benefit entitlement amongst claimants *and* DHSS officers.

Complexity and confusion could to some extent be mitigated by sympathetic administration of benefits, but unfortunately this has never really been the case. Indeed it appears that as entitlement has got more complex, administration has got worse. Officers in the DHSS were inadequately prepared for the 1980 reforms, and as the 1982 survey showed many failed to understand the scheme fully when it was in operation (Berthoud 1984, Working Paper C). In spite of massive increases in the numbers of claimants the numbers of administrative staff were reduced in the 1980s. Between 1979 and 1983 the staff to claims ratio worsened from 1:100 to 1:132 (McKnight 1985, p. 30). Staff turnover is very high and levels of pay and training are low, and, not surprisingly, so is morale. In such a climate sympathetic administration is not likely to be a high priority, and this seems to be confirmed by the DHSS instruction that officers should not advise claimants on potential entitlement, but merely respond to claims made.

The result of the increased pressure is that even many of those who do claim do not always get the correct benefit. A survey in London in 1984 found that 40 per cent of claimants were not receiving correct entitlement due to errors by the DHSS (McKnight 1985, p. 35). And in the 1982 survey it was found that 70 per cent of those whose claims were taken up and pursued by welfare rights officers subsequently received more benefit (Berthoud 1984, Working Paper D).

Claimants themselves are generally unable to do much about inaccurate benefit assessment, however, because as a result of the complexity and confusion of the benefits system many are ignorant of their entitlement to benefit. Apart from some of the high profile advertising campaigns, such as those mentioned in Chapter 8, publicity about benefit entitlement is generally poor. In the mid 1980s the DHSS was spending around £3 million a year on advertising, out of a total budget of about £40 billion. Leaflets explaining benefits are the major form of publicity, but these are generally only found in DHSS offices and then frequently in short or incomplete supply. Furthermore only a few have been translated into other languages, creating particular problems for many black claimants (Gordon & Newnham 1985, Ch. 3). The maxim that ignorance of the law is no excuse seems to apply to benefit administration too. Claimants are generally assumed to be relied upon to know about their entitlement to benefit and ensure that they receive full entitlement. Yet as we shall discuss shortly it is more likely that the reverse is true.

SCROUNGERMANIA

The assumption that claimants can be expected to know and claim their rights is sometimes carried further into a fear that some will *know* and *claim* too much, thus abusing or even defrauding the system. In this sense the problem of abuse is an inevitable one for any means-tested system. For if benefit entitlement is closely tailored to means and needs there will always be the possibility that those who do not need benefit are inadvertently, or deliberately, receiving it. The problem has always dogged state support for poverty; Golding & Middleton (1982, p. 9) quote sixteenth-century legislation concerned about 'divers subtle crafty unlawful games and plays' engaged in by rogues, vagabonds and vagrants. And, from the Poor Law on, state support has been based upon the assumption of less eligibility – that without active discouragement those who do not need (or deserve) state benefits will naturally abuse them.

Golding & Middleton (1982) trace the concern with the vagrant into the scroungermania of the 1970s and 1980s, exemplified by the view of one of the respondents in their survey of attitudes to welfare: 'There are some genuine ones but the majority just bleed the country dry ... 80 per cent are scroungers' (p. 173). They argue powerfully that the fear of scroungers and spongers is an inevitable product of the structure of welfare provision.

They also discuss how more recent concern has been stirred up by politicians and fanned by the at times obsessive media. The respondent quoted above cited the television and newspapers as the source of her knowledge about scrounging. Based on isolated cases and unsubstantiated allegations, notably those of Conservative MP Iain Sproat in the 1970s, the media in the 1970s and early 1980s fuelled a moral panic about the extent and the seriousness of social security abuse (Golding & Middleton 1982, Ch. 5), which exaggerated the already deleterious effect of scroungermania on social security provision. It also included racist stereotyping of increased social security abuse by black claimants, based in many cases on completely spurious evidence of generous payments received (Gordon & Newnham 1985, p. 71).

Governments too have colluded in the concern over fraud. In 1971 Secretary of State Keith Joseph appointed the *Fisher Committee* (1973) to investigate abuse of social security benefits. The committee were in no doubt about their remit: 'Quite clearly we were appointed because there was judged to be public concern and disquiet about abuse of social security benefits' (p. 2). Keith Joseph said they 'would be after the layabouts and work shirkers' (p. 93). The committee's definition of abuse [doc. 14] did not include the most obvious forms of fraud such as Giro forgery, and they were clear that the 'ultimate aim' of measures against abuse was not the detection of abusers but the deterrence of others by engendering 'an attitude among the public of disapproval' (p. 12).

Their concern was thus with potential scroungers rather than with the identification and prosecution of fraud. Indeed they found no arguments in favour of control over abuse itself. They did nevertheless recommend the creation of more specialist posts within the DHSS to deal with abuse. And this is increasingly what has been happening over recent years. The numbers of UROs and LROs have been growing steadily since the 1960s, as has the number of special fraud investigators.

In the early 1980s the Conservative Government appointed Derek Raynor (of Marks and Spencer fame) to investigate problems within the administration of benefits. He alleged that fraud was a major problem, with up to 8 per cent of unemployed claimants illegally working (Raynor 1981). Even before this, however, the government had appointed an extra 1050 specialist staff to deal with abuse, including the establishment of *Specialist Claims Control* teams who would tour from office to office searching the files for evidence of abuse. These teams symbolised a new (even) higher profile for concern with abuse of benefits; with their unofficial local magazines chronicling their successful 'discoveries' (see Smith 1985, p. 118). Raynor's 8 per cent figure was used as a target for fraud detection work; if the rate in any particular office was below that then obviously some abuse must be going undetected.

Perhaps the most prominent measure taken to *crack down* on abuse of social security in the early 1980s was the so-called *Operation Major* in 1982. It was a substantial police and DHSS exercise in which 283 homeless claimants were induced to register at a fictitious benefit office in Oxford and were then arrested *en masse* ostensibly for giving false information about their lodgings. In fact over a third of those arrested were completely innocent, the exercise was a major invasion of claimants' civil rights and very little in the way of benefits was saved (Franey 1983). However, its symbolic impact was substantial in confirming fears that social security payments are inherently subject to abuse, and that *any* measures necessary should be taken to reduce such activity.

Of course there is abuse, and defrauding, of the social security system. Given the size of the undertaking such activity is bound to occur, just as shoplifting does in large department stores. But the amount of abuse must be placed in some perspective. The DHSS estimated in the 1980s that £1–2 million a year was lost through fraud. The 1980 *crack-down* was estimated to *save* around £50 million, though this was only arrived at by assuming that those pressured by officers to withdraw their claims for benefit did not claim again for at least a whole year – an optimistic assumption. This must be compared with an estimate of £5–6 *billion* lost through tax and VAT fraud, where considerably less is spent on detection work.

The more serious problem with the social security system is not the scroungers but the scroungermania. The constant and escalating concern with abuse now pervades the administration of all benefits. The working ideology of DHSS officers has become one of suspicion rather than empathy, creating a gradually widening gap and hostility between them and claimants. Concern with abuse also colours perceptions of social security within society more generally. In a European opinion questionnaire conducted in 1976 43 per cent of UK respondents cited laziness and lack of will-power as the major causes of poverty, a far higher proportion than other EEC countries where injustice and misfortune were more frequently cited (Walker *et al*. 1984, p. 57). And as Golding and Middleton conclude from their study of images of welfare, 'while blaming the victim remains the cornerstone of our conceptions of poverty, the grinding and enduring misery of the poor is unlikely to evoke other than contempt, malign distrust or a corrosive pity' (1982, p. 244).

STIGMA

Scroungermania is in fact only one aspect of a more generally negative perception of social security and social security claimants within society. The impact of the principle of less eligibility has been significant throughout the history of the benefit system and has contributed to the now dominant view that dependency on benefits is a devalued and ultimately undesirable status, bestowing considerable *stigma* upon those who are forced to sink to it. The problem of stigma, however, is a twofold one including, as Taylor Gooby argued in 1976, subjective feelings of humiliation as well as a more general process of being treated as inferior.

Whether or not individual claimants experience the stigma of dependency is to some extent an unanswerable question. However, ever since the 1950s the stigma associated with means-tested benefits has been given as a reason for, particularly elderly, NI claimants not claiming supplementary allowances to which they may have been entitled. In Taylor Gooby's 1976 survey, although claimants did not all admit to experiencing stigma themselves, over a quarter suggested that *others* might experience it.

The process of claiming, in particular, means-tested benefits is one which is certainly likely to give rise to feelings of inferior treatment. In DHSS offices queues start early, offices are bleak, dirty and poorly furnished – in few other public buildings can the boundaries between *us* and *them* be so clearly demarcated. Bissett and Coussins's (1982) study of free school meals found that benefit recipients were frequently served separately and that parents often paid for meals to avoid their children being identified and picked on through this process. Recent exaggerations of the problems of fraud and abuse have served to underline rather than undermine the degradation associated with the process of claiming benefit.

However, it is not just the degradation experienced by claimants themselves which makes stigma a problem for the benefit system. The notion of less eligibility has always been directed not so much at claimants themselves but at others for whom the undesirability of dropping on to state dependency will maintain commitment towards, and control within, unrewarding and poorly paid employment. Where the positive values of industry and honesty are not so clear to see, the negative values of dependency become all the more important, hanging like a spectre over those struggling in inadequately waged work. Golding and Middleton's survey of attitudes to welfare revealed the harshest and most hostile views to be most likely to be held by those in low-paid, unskilled jobs, 'who feel most resentful of the apparent failure of their labours to provide a noticeable advantage over those outside the labour market' (1982, p. 169), an attitude that underpins a view that 'there but for hard work and honesty go I' (p. 172).

This is exaggerated for many black claimants by the requirement within the immigration legislation that entry into Britain can be made conditional upon being *sponsored* by an existing resident, and thus not having 'recourse to public funds'. Not only does this enforce a dependency upon relatives already in Britain, which can be pursued by the DHSS through the magistrates' courts; it also leads to unjustified suspicion and questioning of black claimants, and frequently to suspension of benefit (Gordon & Newnham 1985, Ch. 2). This adds another level of degradation and insecurity to the problems already experienced by black claimants and contributes to further divisions within and between those in work and those dependent upon state support.

Of course this general stigmatisation of welfare is a quite deliberate product of the controlling role of welfare in capitalist society – the other side of the welfare coin. And the divisions it creates within the working class and the unemployed divert attention and action from the inadequacies of the wage system itself. However, the division between those in work and those *sponging* on the state is a false division, even within the social security system itself, for in recent years welfare benefits have been extended to those on low pay as well as the unemployed; and the overlap in income between poor people in and out of work has become increasingly blurred. This has led to many poor workers not taking up benefits to which they are entitled, and to the unemployment and poverty traps.

TAKE-UP

Perhaps the most obvious problem with the social security system, and clearly a contradiction within it, is the fact that large numbers of people do not receive the benefits to which they are entitled because they do not claim them. And if benefits are not claimed they cannot be paid. This problem of *take-up* has in fact always been a feature of social security provision, not the least of the reasons for which are the ignorance, confusion, stigma and suspicion surrounding state dependency which we have just discussed. Abel Smith and Townsend's seminal study of poverty in the 1950s and 1960s stressed that in many cases a major 'cause' of poverty was the non-receipt of benefits to which people were apparently entitled (1965, p. 64).

Some have argued, however, that take-up should not be seen as a *problem* for social security since it saves expenditure on the scheme and is probably due to an element of self-selection amongst the poor based on subjective need. Such a view was expressed by the Institute of Directors to the 1984 review teams (see Bradshaw 1985, p. 109). To a large extent the policy of paying benefits only against claims made means that it is also an official view that those who need benefits will (eventually) seek them themselves. However, concern about levels of take-up of benefits does now appear to be more widely shared, if only because in many areas these levels are so distressingly low.

Measuring take-up is, of course, in itself a problematic exercise since by definition one can only guess at what people who have not made claims might be entitled to. The government have in recent years produced estimates of the take-up of major means-tested benefits based on national family expenditure and finance surveys, though the figures are always several years out of date. In a review of take-up levels in 1985 Bradshaw (1985) concluded that levels varied from around 70 per cent for SB and free school meals to 65 per cent for rate rebates and 50 per cent for FIS, giving an approximate total of unclaimed benefit of almost £2 billion, ten times the amount estimated to be lost through fraud and abuse.

More detailed calculations of take-up based on surveys of potential claimants are harder to come by, in part because they are very expensive to carry out. However, the DHSS-sponsored 1982 survey of the SB scheme did include a limited exercise to assess the extent of unclaimed benefit, by using welfare rights officers to follow up a sample of cases and attempt to secure full entitlement (Berthoud 1985, Working Paper D). In 70 per cent of these cases benefits were eventually increased for the claimants involved, suggesting that if such detailed investigation were done on a wide scale much more serious levels of non-take-up might be discovered than official estimates have so far accepted. And the increasing role of welfare rights work, discussed in the next chapter, would seem to support such a view.

The variation of rates of take-up between different social security benefits is significant and important. Universal Child Benefit is virtually universally claimed, and take-up of NI pensions and benefits is also very high. Whereas means-tested benefits generally have low rates of take-up, and those paid to claimants in full-time work (FIS and HB) the lowest of all. Clearly this must be a product of the nature of entitlement to and administration of benefits, as well as information and advice about their availability. Child Benefit can be claimed by anyone caring for a child, entitlement is determined by status only. Means-tested benefits, however, depend upon one's means and needs, these must be assessed before entitlement can be established. And in the first instance, of course, they must be assessed by claimants themselves. Those who already have an income from a wage or some other source may not make such an assessment of their needs and thus may never come to the point of considering entitlement at all.

In a society where in general income is determined by status this should hardly be surprising. It may perhaps partly explain the resignation with which the DHSS and successive governments have tolerated low levels of take-up of so many benefits. Apart from the limited advertising and leaflet provision discussed above, little is done nationally to improve take-up. As the NCC review of means-tested benefits concluded in 1976, 'Improved publicity, however excellent, cannot over any length of time sell a poor product; and so it is with means-tested benefits' (p. 7).

The proposals for benefit reform in 1988 are in part a response to the problems of confusion and complexity in social security and the low levels of take-up to which it is argued this can give rise, particularly in the case of FIS (White Paper 1985, p. 1). The simplifications and streamlining are expected to ameliorate the problem, and the removal of entitlement to some benefits such as free school meals and additions to weekly SB will certainly solve any problems of low take-up here(!). However, the new benefits will continue to be means-tested and administered by the existing central and local government departments. It is unlikely, therefore, that fundamental improvements will be made, especially as the serious problems caused by overlap with non-means-tested benefits and low wages will remain.

THE POVERTY TRAP

Almost certainly the most startling contradiction to emerge from the development of the post-war social security system is what is now called the *poverty trap*. It is a bizarre consequence of the growth of means-tested benefits which can lead to claimants who try and improve their income through paid work in fact being worse off in financial terms. The poverty trap thus appears as the nightmare product of irrational and unplanned policy development. But in fact it is the result of quite deliberate decisions with clearly anticipated aims and consequences. And at the end of the day whether the poverty trap is a *problem* for social security depends, as with all else, on the point of view adopted towards it.

In order to understand the poverty trap it is perhaps best to deal first with another contradictory product of benefit policy, the *unemployment trap*. As the Special Report of the House of Commons Treasury and Civil Service Committee (Meacher Committee 1983) explained, this is a consequence of the relationship between the growing impact of means-tested benefits and the receipt of low wages. Especially in the case of large families with only one (low) wage-earner, this can lead to a situation where the family as a whole would be better off with the wage-earner unemployed and receiving full means-tested benefit entitlement. Apart from the unlikely circumstances in which significantly higher wages could be expected, the claimant is then *trapped* in unemployment. Moving into part-time work is not an option, or at least not worth while, for people in these circumstances, for only the first £4 of any part-time earnings are of benefit to them (for single parents, as we shall discuss shortly, the situation is slightly more complex).

Whether many workers do leave employment in order to claim benefit is, of course, an unanswerable question, although as we already discussed, benefit dependency is not generally seen as a desirable option ideologically speaking, and the Meacher Committee themselves said they could find no evidence of claimants remaining unemployed because of higher benefits (1983, p. xxv). However, the *potential* problem is a large one. And it is represented by the appearance of high *replacement ratios* for low-wage earners. This is the ratio between net wages and potential benefit entitlement. The Meacher Committee calculated that in 1982 the replacement ratio for a couple with two children earning £100 a week was 89.4 per cent. In other words the £100 being earned was only increasing their income above benefit level by £10.60.

It is of course exactly this concern which has kept benefit rates, especially for the unemployed, so low throughout the history of state support and led to the introduction of measures like the wage stop. But with the extension of means-tested benefits in the 1970s, at a time when wage levels were being held down, it was presumed to be becoming more acute, and thus different measures were adopted.

As we have seen, the policy of the Conservative Government of the early 1970s was to introduce and expand means-tested benefits for the low waged, especially those with children. So FIS was introduced along with rent and rate rebates and expanded NHS and education benefits. Though as we have seen there were problems with the take-up of these benefits, their aim was to raise the take-home income of low-wage earners, thus reducing the replacement ratio and consequently the unemployment trap. What they also did of course was to provide an indiscriminate subsidy to low wages, effectively legitimising these and encouraging employers to continue paying them by mitigating their worst effects for employees.

There was, however, an unavoidable problem with means-tested subsidies to low wages. They had to be withdrawn as wages rose, otherwise the subsidy effect would not work. They could be withdrawn pound for pound if wages went up, but this would mean that any increase in wages would be of no effect in raising income.

Thus most are withdrawn on a gradual basis under a *taper* system: FIS provides 50 per cent of the difference between wages and the prescribed income level, thus it is withdrawn in effect on a 50 per cent taper (though of course this only takes effect after twelve months); HB tapers vary from 8 to 29 per cent and also depend upon rent paid; NHS and education benefits operate under a wide variety of different tapers. The effect of all withdrawals of benefit, however, is to act as a sort of tax on any increase in wages low-wage earners may get. In effect, FIS is a 50 per cent tax and the other benefits add to that.

Low-wage earners are not just paying tax by way of benefit withdrawal, however. Most are also paying NI contributions and income tax as well. The former are now earnings-related, but in order to include most workers they start at very low wage levels (£35.50 a week in 1986). Income tax was only paid by reasonably well-paid workers in the 1950s, but under a process known as *fiscal drag* tax thresholds have fallen (in practice they have not been raised to keep up with wage inflation) bringing the vast majority of wage-earners into the income tax system [doc. 15]. This has had the effect of shifting the burden of taxation increasingly on to the lower paid (Field *et al.* 1977, Ch. 2), a process which accelerated under the Conservative Government of the 1980s (Smail 1984). And most wage-earners are now paying tax at the standard rate.

If the effect of income tax, NI contributions and withdrawal of means-tested benefits is added together, then the *marginal* tax rates (the amount effectively paid out to the state from each extra pound earned) faced by the low paid are very high indeed – way above the 60 per cent rate which is the highest faced in the mid 1980s by a tiny majority of very high-wage earners. Indeed in many cases if the effect of the delayed 50 per cent loss of FIS is taken into account, for wage-earners with children it can amount to well over *100 per cent*. In other words, in spite of an increase in earnings, people end up worse off!

As the graph in document 16 shows, over quite a wide range of low earnings increases in wages either reduce or barely increase take-home incomes, and only once significantly higher wages are received does income begin to rise. The effect of this is that low-wage earners are *trapped* in poverty. Even if they could improve their wages they would be no better off. Deacon & Bradshaw (1983, Ch. 8) call it a *poverty plateau*, because over quite a wide range of earnings, between about £70 and £120 a week, take-home income for a family is more or less the same.

This has led to concern about the effect on incentives for the lower paid, who can hardly be encouraged to work harder or take on more (or any) overtime if this will not make them any better off. It has also led to problems in wage bargaining for the low paid, for whom the small wage increases which can sometimes be achieved through the bargaining process are of little or no value. The incentive argument, however, ignores the fact that in practice low-wage earners have very little control over their hours and patterns of work and wage levels – otherwise they would not be on low wages in the first place. The real incentive behind the subsidisation of low wages, is the incentive it gives *employers* to pay them, in a situation when trade unions can do little to prevent this.

As we saw, the development of the poverty trap was a product of policies to subsidise low wage levels in the 1970s. The phrase itself dates from analysis by Piachaud of the effects of government policy in 1971 (Field & Piachaud 1971). The aims behind the policy are clear, even if the effects on claimants appear quite contradictory. The planned reforms in 1988 will retain these policies and their effects, even though the poverty trap is recognised as a problem in the White Paper (1985, p. 1).

The introduction of the HB scheme in 1982 actually steepened the poverty trap in order to avoid increasing public expenditure (Lansley 1982). The 1988 changes to FIS and HB will modify it, by moving the basis of calculating withdrawal of benefit from a gross to a net income basis, reducing the highest marginal tax rates at the expense of spreading high rates over a larger proportion of the low paid. Without the provision of extra resources to increase benefits this will in effect redistribute existing resources from the very poorest to the not so poor – a rather niggardly case of robbing Peter to pay Paul. However, minor reforms which concentrate on the means of calculating withdrawal rather than the principles of payment themselves can only ever have such a restricted redistributive effect.

The other major change to FIS when it becomes FC is the reduction of the minimum qualifying hours of work a week from thirty to twenty-four. This will have the effect of giving all claimants working between those hours the choice that single parents have 'enjoyed' since 1971 between claiming a wage subsidy or claiming SB and having wages deducted from entitlement. Because of this more 'generous' treatment, and the generally low wages earned by single parents, over half of FIS claimants have tended to be single parents. For them the choice has frequently been a complex one because of the slightly more generous treatment given to their part-time wages under the SB scheme (they are able to keep, in addition to £4 a week, half of any more earned up to £20), and many may have consciously (or unconsciously) made the 'wrong' one.

For claimants of FC the choice will be simplified by the proposed alignment of the IS and FC entitlement rates, and the replacement of the tapered earnings rule for single parents (and for couples who have been unemployed over two years) with a flat-rate disregard of the first £15 of weekly earnings.

The problem of the poverty trap is caused by the interaction of policies on benefits, taxes and wages affecting the low paid. It is a direct, if contradictory, product of the decision to seek to alleviate the poverty caused by low wages via an indiscriminate subsidy to those receiving them, and could therefore only be resolved if policies on both benefits and wages were changed.

However, in the mean time the problems caused are real enough; and for claimants how they are dealt with can usually mean the difference between surviving on the welfare – or not. Whether and how claimants cope with our contradictory benefits structure are thus important issues. They turn upon the question of how far claimants, or those who can help them, are able to work within the system.

WHOSE PROBLEM?

The problems with social security provision which we discussed in Chapter 9 are first and foremost problems for those who depend upon social security for their daily livelihood. And for many their consequences are debilitating. Confusion, ignorance and stigma can readily lead to a resignation that living *on the social* is an existence to be endured without sympathy or comprehension until escape in the form of employment or some other source of independent income materialises. That this confirms, even amongst the poor themselves, the pathological perception of their own inadequacy within the social order, of course, is no coincidence. As with the problems which create it, it is an inevitable consequence of the structure of benefit provision. It reinforces also divisions between those dependent upon welfare and those 'providing' it, and contributes to the widely held, defeatist view that no benefits system could ever solve the problems *of the poor*.

However, the transfer of the problems of social security from the state, which has developed those policies, to the people who suffer under them has not gone entirely without challenge, and in the 1970s and 1980s has increasingly become a focus for direct practical and political action on benefits. It was the growing dominance of means-tested benefits in the early 1970s which provided the background to this challenge. With increasing numbers of benefits and claimants, the experience of the problems associated with them became more and more widespread. In such a climate the passive receipt of state benefits became increasingly less viable as a means of coping with life on benefits, if only because so many benefits required knowledge and activity to obtain them. As the problems of take-up testified, many failed to cope with this. But recognition of the problem itself was also a recognition that things would be different if claimants had the knowledge and ability to pursue their rights to welfare.

Poverty and state support

Providing claimants with such knowledge and ability could thus be a way of helping them cope with the system. However, it would also be a challenge to the passive and pathological position of welfare claimants – a transfer, to some extent, of the problem of claiming back from them to the state. This challenge has become an important, and dynamic, feature of the British social security system, providing a constant pressure upon the most problematic features of the benefits structure and forcing changes to be made within it or preventing less desirable changes which might have been made to it.

In one form or another this challenge has come from the pressing need to work *within* the system, though whether its ultimate effect is to sustain or transform that system is a question to which we will return later. It is perhaps best understood as the development of a *welfare rights* approach to welfare services, although as we shall discuss first, its roots perhaps lie mainly in the Fabian traditions of welfare reform which gave birth to the poverty lobby.

THE POVERTY LOBBY

The role of experts advising and seeking to influence the government on benefit policy goes back at least as far as the work of the Webbs and the welfare policies of the early twentieth century. Their belief, and that of subsequent Fabian supporters, that social security could gradually be improved through the reform of its most ineffective and problematic features has been of significant importance in the development of social security policy, particularly in the post-war period. It has produced within Britain a tradition of academic research and policy advice in the poverty and welfare field which is more well developed than that of many other Western countries, perhaps best exemplified by the work of Peter Townsend (1979, 1984; Abel Smith & Townsend 1965).

It was the work of academic researchers and policy advisers in the late 1950s and early 1960s which provided much of the impetus for the so-called *rediscovery* of poverty in the mid 1960s. And in 1965 Abel Smith and Townsend were themselves instrumental in the establishment of what has since become one of the most influential pressure groups on government in the social security area, the *Child Poverty Action Group* (McCarthy 1986).

The CPAG were initially formed to campaign against the problem of child poverty caused by inadequate incomes for poor parents, by pressuring the government to replace the existing child tax allowances with cash benefits for all children. However, increasing recognition of the broader problems of family poverty and the failure of government to respond to these, led the CPAG to take up a broader assault on policies for state support and to continue campaigning in this arena after Child Benefits had been introduced in 1977.

They were also joined in the late 1960s and early 1970s by other organisations campaigning on behalf of sections of the poor and deprived, such as *Shelter* (for the homeless), the *National Council of One-Parent Families* and *Gingerbread* (for single parents), *Help the Aged* (for pensioners) and the *Disability Alliance* (for people with disabilities). Together they came to be referred to as the *poverty lobby*. Whiteley and Winyard (1983) discuss their development and their influence upon social policy in the 1960s and 1970s. They distinguish between representational groups (those comprised of the poor themselves) and promotional groups (those like CPAG seeking to speak for them), and they quote one civil servant who was very scathing of the political base of the latter in particular: 'CPAG doesn't really talk for anyone' (p. 19). Though in general they conclude that *these* groups had a higher reputation in the corridors of power in Whitehall and Westminster.

Given their organisational bases the focus of most groups in the poverty lobby was upon the problems caused for particular claimants by existing benefit policies. And thus their aim was generally to encourage changes which would alleviate or remove these. Their concern was thus with the operation of the existing welfare system rather than any radical reform or transformation of it. As Field discusses in his analysis of the CPAG (1982, p. 62), this led to an increased concern with the operation of the existing system and the need to work within it to secure the best deal for claimants now.

Working to ensure receipt of maximum benefits for the poor now has thus become as important a part of the work of many groups within the poverty lobby as putting pressure on government for legal change. And the two have come together in the *test case* strategy developed by the CPAG in the 1970s to challenge the DHSS in the courts over the interpretation (and thus the extent) of benefit entitlement – in effect seeking to change the law through work based on assisting individual claimants (Prosser 1983).

The role of the CPAG in promoting and supporting advice and advocacy work with claimants became increasingly important in the 1970s. Their *Citizens Rights Office* became a major source of specialist knowledge and assistance on benefit entitlement, and their annually updated handbooks on benefits became invaluable guides to the complexities of the social security system for the growing numbers of people involved in helping claimants to secure their rights. In the 1980s after the reform of the SB scheme the handbooks became an influential interpretation of the new regulations, and CPAG-backed test cases began to be a growing embarrassment to a government endeavouring to restrict entitlement to means-tested benefits. Most notable was their campaign against regulations restricting entitlement to board and lodgings payments for young persons which, following a CPAG test case in 1985 the government had to withdraw (though they were later successfully reintroduced).

Their knowledge and experience of the benefit system made the CPAG natural leaders of the growing welfare rights movement of the 1970s and 1980s. But the rapid growth of a commitment to working within the benefits system also had its roots in developments in government strategy towards the problem of poverty in the late 1960s.

WELFARE RIGHTS

As we discussed in Chapter 1, part of the government's response to the rediscovery of poverty in the 1960s was to establish national anti-poverty programmes, targeting resources for the employment of specialist workers in urban areas where large numbers of the relatively poor were presumed to live. The assumption behind the urban programmes was rooted in pathological notions of the problem of poverty as being largely a product of the inability of the poor to take advantage of the opportunities of the new affluent Britain, and the expectation was that specialist workers would be able to help and encourage them to do this.

Of course, as the specialist workers themselves quickly found out, the problem of poverty was the result not of individual inadequacy but of national economic and social policy, experienced most acutely in run-down inner-city areas (Loney 1983). And the only opportunity existing for most poor people here was the opportunity to depend on state benefits. However, because of the growing complexity of the benefit system many were not even taking full advantage of these. Thus what most anti-poverty workers found themselves doing was advising local claimants about benefit entitlement and helping them to get all the benefits that they could.

It was somewhat ironic that those paid by the government to work to alleviate poverty should in effect be working primarily to alleviate the problems caused by the government's benefit policy itself. And in the case of the CDPs the contradictory role of the anti-poverty workers led to the closure of the programme in the 1970s. Other urban programmes continued, however, and began increasingly to take on this *welfare rights* work with claimants. And in the 1970s other state employees too began to question whether they should not also be working to ensure that poor clients with whom they dealt were getting all the support to which they were entitled from the state.

In social work in particular money advice was increasingly going hand in hand with psychological support for the poor (Hill & Laing 1979). Whether all individual social workers, trained largely in psychological approaches to client problems, recognised and acted on this is doubtful. But some did, and so did their employers. In 1972 Manchester Social Services Department appointed a specialist *Welfare Rights Officer* to do benefits advice and advocacy work on cases referred to him by other social workers. In the first year he dealt with 600 enquiries and claimed that his advice should have led to £10,000 in extra benefits (Simpson 1978, p. 22). Following this Manchester expanded their welfare rights service and other local authorities have since established provision by appointing Welfare Rights Officers to work alongside, or as support for, ordinary field social workers (Fimister 1986).

The influence of the new Welfare Rights Officers also raised the profile of such work generally within social services. In 1975 Cannan argued that it should be seen as a part of the new radical social work approach. In 1979 Hill and Laing put forward the case for welfare rights work as a social work specialism in its own right. And in 1982 Cohen and Rushton's practice handbook discussed it as a social work skill and a 'core activity' for all workers.

Cannan (1975), however, had also criticised welfare rights work for a tendency to reproduce the paternalistic, professional/client relationship typical of social work, in which the expert professional solved the problems of the individual client from a position of power and control over them. This was also criticised most strongly by claimants themselves. And in different areas throughout the country they began to organise for themselves *Claimants' Unions* to provide advice and support without the need for professionals, and to press for reform of the benefits system itself.

Claimants' Unions were potentially a powerful representational body, with a possible membership of millions. But in practice they were loose and often short-lived organisations involving relatively few claimants – a testimony perhaps to the continued isolation and debilitation of dependency on benefits. They achieved some success in supporting claimants challenging the exercise of discretion by DHSS officers, exposing the inconsistency and hypocrisy of this. But when

SB was reformed in 1980 their impact diminished as advice and advocacy became an increasingly complex and technical legal task, though their political demands for fundamental reform of benefits remained.

It was the changes made to SB in 1980 which greatly accelerated the growing prominence and importance of welfare rights work in social security. With discretion replaced by rights, the need for advice and advocacy became of crucial importance, especially when it became clear that the DHSS was instructing officers not to advise claimants about potential entitlement. And with the numbers dependent upon SB rapidly growing, demand for it soon outstripped the limited resources available in some social service departments.

Measuring the full extent of demand for welfare rights assistance is of course practically impossible, but by the 1980s the evidence was that it was likely to be of iceberg proportions. Wherever some provision was established, demand for help was found. And as a result of this there was a dramatic growth in the late 1970s and early 1980s of welfare rights support in a number of different agencies. The *Citizens' Advice Bureaux* which had since the war been providing a general community information and support role, began to experience heavy demands for advice on benefit entitlement, and many quickly moved over to a largely welfare rights service. They were also augmented in most urban areas by growing numbers of *independent* advice centres, set up with government urban aid and inner-city partnership money, and able to employ part-time and temporary workers on Manpower Service Commission job creation schemes. In Sheffield the number of advice centres increased from five to thirty-four in the decade from 1975 to 1985 (Sheffield Advice Centres Group 1985).

Most of the new advice centres were community based and responsible to management committees composed of local community representatives. They could, when successful, provide advice and assistance tailored to the particular needs of local communities, for example advising on the implications of immigration controls for benefit entitlement where there was a substantial local ethnic minority population. Their flexibility and community base could therefore make them a less paternalistic and controlling source of help than social services departments. However, there was a drawback to their informal, independent status, for the urban aid and job creation money on which many centres were based were extremely unreliable sources of support. This meant that provision was largely *ad hoc* and isolated, and even where centres were able to attract more stable funding from sympathetic local authorities there was little strategic planning of resources to meet estimates of local need. In the mid 1980s the pressures on local authorities themselves undermined the limited stability of this form of support too, as many of the centres funded by the ill-fated Greater London Council found when the council was abolished in 1986.

TAKE-UP CAMPAIGNS

The increased pressure on welfare rights provision in the 1980s forced some workers to question whether direct advice to individual claimants was the best way to secure benefit take-up. Means-tested benefits can only be received if they are claimed, but once a claim has been made the onus of determining entitlement is on the DHSS (or the local authority). Thus if all those who might be entitled could somehow be encouraged to claim then the DHSS would be forced to assess the entitlement of all and pay the necessary benefits.

In 1981, encouraged by their Welfare Rights Officers, Strathclyde Regional Council decided to try and ensure that all its residents received their full entitlement to benefit by encouraging them all to make a claim. Some 100,000 postcards were distributed stating the range of benefits available and including a self-complete claim form to be presented to the DHSS. This led to an estimated 35,000 claims and awards of benefit said to be worth £1.3 million a year in weekly payments and £2.75 million in single payments (Strathclyde RC 1981). But of course many of those who claimed received nothing because they were not entitled to any of the benefits listed.

The Strathclyde *take-up campaign*, as it came to be called, received much publicity, and the initiative was soon followed by other local authorities including Bradford, Coventry, Lothian, Manchester and Nottingham. However, doubts began to be expressed about the tactic of *blanket* leafleting of all residents, which was bound to lead to disappointment for many who would be encouraged to make 'hopeless' claims. More sophisticated approaches to take-up campaigns have thus been advocated, concentrating mainly on the issues of *targeting* and *back-up*.

Targeted campaigns seek to limit the disappointment of hopeless claims by concentrating take-up information in particular deprived areas, where large numbers of potential claimants might be expected to live. A take-up campaign in South Tyneside in 1985 used a local survey of poverty and unemployment in the area to target advertising and leafleting on particular districts with high levels of deprivation (South Tyneside Welfare Rights Service 1985).

The South Tyneside campaign also included back-up advice and assistance to individual claimants from temporary Welfare Rights Officers placed in local centres. Given the extra pressure which would be placed on an already overworked and unreliable DHSS, the expectation was that the campaign would itself generate demand for advice and help from claimants, leading to frustration and anger towards the council if this were not provided. Other campaigns such as Cleveland and Birmingham have also used temporary welfare rights back-up.

Geographical concentration is one way of targeting take-up campaigns. However, information may already be possessed about claimants which could permit even more sophisticated targeting of information to those most likely to be entitled to benefits. This could be done, for example, by screening users of centres for the elderly or disabled. The transfer of the administration of HB to local authorities in 1982, however, gave them automatic access to information about all SB claimants in their area. This could be used to direct benefit information to those people already known to be entitled to SB. The information could also be included in general mailings to council tenants. This *piggy-back* mailing, as it is called, could expect to encourage a much higher rate of successful claims, and a much lower rate of disappointment. Sheffield used this method to mail out specialised leaflets and claim forms for specific SB payments to claimants, leading to successful claim rates of between 8 and 48 per cent (Fitch & Reid 1983).

With the growing impact of new technology in the mid 1980s, the potential for using microcomputers to advise on benefits and encourage claims began to be widely discussed. Software packages had been developed to allow claimants to use computers to calculate their own benefit entitlement, and to provide instant access to benefit information for welfare rights workers. In 1984 the Community Information Service in Belfast ran a twelve-month project using computerised welfare rights advice (Belfast Community Information Service 1985), and many local authorities and advice centres have bought microcomputers and software packages. Once DHSS and local authority benefit administrations become fully computerised in the late 1980s and early 1990s the potential for computer-based welfare rights work will take on a new dimension, of which by the mid 1980s existing welfare rights workers and campaigners were only just beginning to become aware.

THE LIMITATIONS OF ADVICE AND TAKE-UP WORK

In an issue of their journal *Poverty* (CPAG 1984, No. 57) the CPAG summarise a number of the different initiatives taken by local authorities to alleviate poverty in their area through support for welfare rights and benefit take-up work. As well as securing additional benefits for claimants such work also brings extra resources into the local area, a not unsubstantial political and economic advantage. Few would claim to have attracted the millions quoted by Strathclyde, but Milton Keynes claimed around £200,000 in extra benefits (Milton Keynes Welfare Rights Group 1985) and South Tyneside £500,000 (1985).

However, the gains are short-lived, unless the campaign can be sustained over a long period – and few have been. Advice and advocacy work are a more permanent resource, though as we have discussed, much of this too is uncertain and limited. *And*, however successful welfare rights workers are in getting claimants full benefits, at the end of the day that is *all* they are doing. If those benefits are not adequate to meet the needs which have generally motivated people to seek assistance in the first place – as they usually will not be – then, in spite of all the effort, poverty remains. Indeed one of the most painful, and yet most common, tasks facing welfare rights workers is that of explaining to people that they are not entitled to the benefits that they need or want – and in practice, of course, to some extent doing the job of the DHSS for them.

Welfare rights workers are not by and large under any illusion that this is a satisfactory role. By the very nature of their task they are made more aware than most of the problems and limitations of the existing benefit system, and many have become prominent in campaigns for changes in benefit policy. This of course has always been a feature of CPAG's work and in the 1980s other campaigning groups drawing on the work of welfare rights activists began to spring up, notably the *Action for Benefits* campaign to counter the benefit policies of the Conservative Government, and the *National Campaign Against Social Security Cuts* formed to campaign specifically against the proposals for reform following from the 1984 reviews. In 1985 three welfare rights workers in London turned their experience of the problems encountered in working within the benefit system into a manifesto for a fundamental review and reform of the social security system (Esam *et al.* 1985).

The local authorities who supported advice and take-up work also became increasingly aware in the 1980s of the limitations of working to secure entitlement to benefits which were inadequate for people's needs. Their administration of the HB scheme after 1982 also made them aware of the inherent problems and limitations of means-tested benefits, and with the best will in the world (which few in fact have had) they have not been able to improve HB provision or deliver a better service than the DHSS. And so by the mid 1980s, after the publication of the government's proposals for reform of social security, many Labour-controlled authorities began to campaign openly against Conservative social security policy, and to call for alternative policies for state support for the poor [doc. 17].

It is of course no surprise that the problems and inadequacies of benefit provision could not be overcome by welfare rights work, for as we have discussed, these problems are a direct consequence of the policy decisions on which provision is based. Because of this any attempts to work pragmatically within the benefit system in order to provide bread today rather than jam tomorrow, will inevitably bring claimants, workers and local authorities into conflict with existing social security provision and the principles on which it is based, leading to demands for reform. It is to the scope of these demands, and their potential, that we turn in the final chapter.

Chapter eleven
THE REFORM OF SOCIAL SECURITY

THE POLITICS OF REFORM

Any discussion of proposals for reforming social security must take into account the political context in which the current social security system has been constructed and reconstructed, for it is through the political process that reform must be argued for and won. Furthermore that political context is itself constrained by the economic and ideological structures of British society. These structures are not immovable, they contain contradictory and conflicting tendencies and they are changing and changeable; but they cannot be restructured overnight, and if not changed themselves they will continue to constrain the process of political change.

This does not mean that political, economic and ideological pressures will prevent any fundamental reform of current social security provision – as we have argued, if existing problems and contradictions are ever to be resolved then change must be fundamental. But it does mean that proposing alternative principles for social security policy will be an academic exercise if those principles cannot be achieved by reforms from within current political, economic and ideological frameworks as part of a more general process of social change.

In the early years after the war it was assumed that the goals of social security reform had been achieved in Britain with the implementation of Beveridge's social insurance plan. As we discussed in Chapter 4, Beveridge intended his proposals to remove want forever from the country through the introduction of national provision for welfare benefits; and this aim seemed to have popular approval and government support. However, the insurance plan failed to realise Beveridge's hopes. At the time of its introduction compromises were made with Beveridge's original ideals, and since then policies have drifted further and further from his intended comprehensive insurance scheme.

In fact, of course, although there was much political support for Beveridge's proposals, there was never a complete consensus over their desirability. As we shall see, other radically different approaches to social security policy were being proposed at the time, and many, including Conservative MPs, had their doubts about the feasibility and desirability of the insurance plan [doc. 4]. However, once the post-war benefits system had been established, ostensibly at least on the lines laid down by Beveridge, discussion of alternative principles for benefit provision was effectively quashed. And after this experts in social security policy, most notably the Fabian academics and the poverty lobby, concerned themselves largely with seeking changes within current parameters, to iron out problems or anomalies in the scheme or to make gradual, incremental improvements to it.

The assumption behind the concern with incremental reform was the widely held belief that restructuring of welfare policy was only sustainable if it could be financed out of economic growth. And by the 1960s this was a view shared by both major political parties. Thus when economic growth became stagnation and then slump in the 1970s, incremental changes became more and more difficult to achieve. The introduction of SERPS was delayed twenty years, and Child Benefit was almost abandoned. Many reforms made were designed to support, rather than challenge, existing economic policies, for instance the earnings-related addition to Unemployment Benefit which was intended to cushion the blow of redundancy during the labour 'shake-outs' of the technological revolution.

In such a context social security policy no longer attracted the high political profile in had had in the early post-war years, and discussion of benefit policy increasingly became restricted to the experts in the poverty lobby and the DHSS. Though alternative proposals for benefit reform were made in the 1960s and 1970s, they were debated largely in academic and informed circles, and had little effect on the policy process. Indeed the increasingly technical and specialist aura of social security policy had to some extent strengthened the hands of those arguing for incremental reforms by obscuring from debate more fundamental questions about the principles behind policies for state support.

However, the failure to achieve much by way of incremental reform and the increasing prominence of the problems and contradictions of current policies were a constant threat to the restrictions which appeared to be placed on discussion of benefit reform, and in 1984 the relatively closed world of social security politics was blown open with the establishment of the Conservative Government's reviews of social security policy. The reviews invited evidence from anyone wishing to propose alternative policies, and attracted a wide range of responses. When published they pointed directly to the obvious failings of the existing benefits system in making the case for major reform. And the case for reform was presented as *unchallengeable*. In 1986 Secretary of State, Norman Fowler, could say, 'we have changed the whole nature of the debate on social security. The debate is not about *whether* social security should be reformed but *how* it should be carried through.'

The process of review itself and the subsequent publication of the Green and White Papers and the legislation stimulated the most wide-ranging public debate on social security since the time of Beveridge, with meetings and even demonstrations held throughout the country. Of course this revived public interest should not be misinterpreted. It must be judged relative to the generally ignorant and divisive perception of social security predominant prior to the reviews, and it was largely in the form of negative protest against the reforms proposed by the government rather than any campaign for alternative strategies for reform. And it was not successful in preventing the government carrying through the legislative reform. What it did do, however, was to raise the profile of debates about alternative policies to fill the gap between the now abandoned principles of Beveridge and the new means-testing of the Fowler plan.

THE PRINCIPLES OF REFORM

As we have discussed, social security policy in Britain has often been presented as based on a choice (or perhaps a contradiction) between two different principles for the provision of benefits: universalism or selectivity. Universal benefits, like Child Benefit, make state support available to all in accordance with their membership of society and social situation. Selective benefits target state support on those who are presumed and defined to be in need of help, and is paid only if need cannot be met from private resources.

The aim of selective benefits is the *relief* of poverty. Thus poverty must be established under a means test before benefit can be received, and benefit is paid only at a subsistence level to meet presumed absolute needs. To pay benefits beyond this level, or to those who are not poor, would be 'wasting' state support on those who do not 'need' it.

Beveridge's social insurance plan was based upon a rejection of selectivity and means-testing. However, apart from the Family Allowances which he hoped would accompany his insurance plan, Beveridge did not advocate universal benefits but rather insurance-based (or contributory) ones. And as we discussed in Chapter 6, these excluded many people who might be in need of state support. The aim of insurance was the *prevention* of poverty, via collective insurance against the contingencies which it was assumed gave rise to it. Prevention of poverty, however, meant only that; it was not intended that insurance would interfere with the distribution of resources through the wage system or with private individual support. Thus benefits were restricted to a subsistence level. As with means-tested benefits this implied an absolute notion of the nature of poverty, which it was expected could be removed forever once adequate cover for its presumed causes had been made.

Thus both insurance and means-tested benefits have been based upon attempts to deal with absolute poverty. However, as we discussed in Chapter 1, the notion of absolute poverty is an extremely dubious one on which to base policy. Once we begin to conceive of poverty as a relative phenomenon resulting from inequalities in the distribution of resources and power in society, then the question of relieving or preventing it becomes a very different one. And this requires a different role for state support. For, rather than responding *ex post facto* to the problems caused by the existing distribution of wealth and resources, the state would have to intervene directly in that distribution in order to redistribute from those with more to those with less. And to do this social security policy would have to encompass not only the benefits paid to those without other resources, but also the wages and taxes paid by everybody else. For without changes in wage and taxation policy there will be no resources to redistribute to those receiving benefits.

The issue is therefore not just one of *how* benefits are paid (to relieve or prevent poverty) but also what levels they are paid *at*, and how they are paid *for*. Consequently it crosses the traditional divide between economic and social policy, which has dominated incremental approaches to reform throughout the post-war period, and in a situation of economic decline has seen improvements recede over the horizon to be replaced by cuts.

Of course the cuts in benefit provision made and planned by the Conservative Government of the 1980s *were* a direct product of the link between economic and social policy. They were an attempt to reduce expenditure and further control the labour force in order to encourage privatisation and private investment. And they did involve intervention into the wage market and taxation policy in order to redistribute resources. Though in this case, however, the redistribution was *from* the poor *to* the rich rather than vice versa – 44 per cent of the £4.5 billion made in tax cuts between 1979 and 1984 going to the richest 5 per cent of the population, at a time of minimal growth in the economy.

In fact, as we saw in Chapter 9, benefit policies do already overlap and interfere with wages and taxation; the poverty trap is a direct product of the interrelationship of all three. And although this causes serious problems for low-paid workers in particular, it also helps employers to keep wages down and helps to spread the burden of taxation on to the low paid. A social security policy seeking to improve the situation of the poor would have to tackle these low wages and the taxes paid on them as well as the benefits which currently support them.

Existing benefit policies are also based, almost entirely, on family units. As we discussed in Chapter 3, this has had the effect of forcing women into relationships of dependency upon men. It is also responsible for many of the problems and complexities of benefit provision, for it requires tests of household and marital (or quasi-marital) status, rules about earnings and dependency additions, arguments about whether benefits should be paid to 'breadwinners' or 'carers', problems of access to spouses' contribution records, and many more. The main argument mounted in favour of the family base is that most people do live in family relationships (though in fact only about a third of households are married couples with dependent children (Study Commission on the Family 1983, p. 10) and that to abandon that basis would involve paying benefits to many women (the wives of wealthy men) who do not 'need' them.

Of course the effect (and intention) of the family base *is* to reinforce female dependency and male breadwinning within the 'traditional' family through the form of provision of state support, even though in practice this is not a viable life-style for most poor men and women. A redistribution of resources through social security policy would therefore have to encompass redistribution on a gender basis as well as on the basis of overall household income. And with changed taxation policies there would in any case be every possibility for ensuring that a married woman's individual entitlement to benefit was financed, indirectly, by her (now less) wealthy husband.

Changes to the principles governing entitlement to state support must also encompass measures to combat racism within the social security system. Much of the oppressive treatment experienced by black claimants, notably passport checking, flows from the use of the administration of state support as an internal control on illegal immigrants. Such controls must be removed, and immigration checks reserved for the appropriate authorities. Unequal treatment also arises as a result of the *sponsorship* regulations, which can permanently deprive black claimants of access to benefits (Gordon & Newnham, 1985, Ch. 2), and reinforce racist attitudes that members of black communities will receive local support and do not need state benefits. If such attitudes are to be removed, then the principle of equal access to state support for all persons resident in Britain must become a central feature of benefit provision.

Alternative policies for state support thus raise the question of alternative principles for benefit provision. And unless the principles, as well as the practice, of benefit policy are opened to question, then the existing practical problems and contradictions will not be resolved. At the same time, however, alternative principles must be part of a strategy for reform within existing political, economic and ideological frameworks. Over recent years a number of different strategies for social security reform have emerged, spurred on in the mid 1980s by the debate engendered by the 1984 reviews. Some do tackle the issues of politics and principle, as well as the practical problems with current provisions, although not surprisingly some are more far-reaching than others. It is against the issues of politics and principle, as well as practical change, however, that alternative proposals will be examined and their prospects for reforming our policies on poverty and state support assessed.

INCOME-RELATED BENEFITS

Income-related benefits is the phrase used by the Conservative Government for their plans for social security reform in 1988. They are based upon a commitment to maintaining means-testing as the central feature of state support for the poor in Britain, but with some simplifications to reduce overall costs within broader economic and social policies designed to reduce state welfare.

The objectives of reform outlined in the Green Paper seem to confirm this [doc. 18], and, as has been argued elsewhere, the changes to be made in 1988 are an accentuation of existing trends towards greater selectivity in social security rather than any radical departure to a new basis for benefit entitlement (Alcock 1985b). Indeed, as we discussed earlier, it seems that many of the new benefit provisions are designed to reproduce more or less existing patterns of entitlement and existing divisions between claimants.

As many critics have pointed out, the effect of the changes is likely to be limited, penny-pinching redistribution amongst those dependent upon state support, as some lose and some gain in the general simplification within existing budgetary constraints (Berthoud 1985; Lister *et al.* 1985). This is likely to be a painful process for many, and it will do nothing to solve the existing problems and contradictions in benefit provision. The problems of stigma, of take-up and of the poverty trap will remain, because the basic structure of benefits will remain. They could only be removed if these structures were challenged; such a challenge could come, some have argued, from proposals to merge *benefit* provision with *taxation*.

COMBINED TAX AND BENEFIT SCHEMES

Although the arguments for merging taxation and benefit provision have received increasing prominence and support since the 1970s as the problems of the existing overlap between taxes and benefits became more and more obvious in the unemployment and poverty traps, they are not new. Proposals for a joint tax and benefit scheme were being proposed at the time of the Beveridge Report itself (Rhys Williams 1943). They are also not confined to one particular political position. They have received the endorsement of the Adam Smith Institute (1984) on the right and the Federation of Claimants' Unions (1984) on the left.

Not surprisingly, therefore, tax and benefit schemes differ considerably in their aims and their scope. However, they all have in common the idea of paying state credits or dividends to those in and out of paid work in order to guarantee a certain minimum income level and recovering back the cost of this from the direct taxation of incomes above that level. And, as we shall see, they all therefore contain similar, and unresolved, problems of implementation.

1. Negative income tax

Negative income tax (NIT) is misleadingly used to refer to a wide range of proposals for combining taxes and benefits, including the recommendations of Lees (1967) which formed the basis of social security policy discussion within the Conservative Government of the early 1970s, and which are really more accurately described as a plan for *tax credits*. For the sake of simplicity we will use the term to refer only to schemes designed to replace completely existing taxation and benefit provision with a system under which a negative tax payment is used to guarantee a fixed minimum income for *all* households, and positive tax is levied on all extra income earned.

Such schemes have been advocated by Milton Friedman (1962), by Patrick Minford of the Institute of Economic Affairs (1984) and by the Adam Smith Institute [doc. 19]. In all these cases they are part of plans to reduce significantly the welfare role of the state within capitalism – Minford also proposed compulsory private health and education insurance. For the most part, therefore, the income levels which would be guaranteed by the payment of negative tax proposed are very low in order to create an incentive to work and take out private insurance. They need not necessarily be low, of course. In theory any level could be fixed. But the higher the level, the greater the proportion of income above that level which would have to be paid in tax (tax rates of 40 and 50 per cent are commonly referred to), and the more the fixed minimum income would interfere with the incentive to take paid work.

In fact the problem over work incentives in NIT proposals runs deeper than the issue of minimum levels alone, however, because of the wage subsidy effect which the NIT payment has. If all of those with incomes below the fixed level receive NIT payments to bring them up to it, then if their income rises the payment must be withdrawn. If it is withdrawn completely to maintain only the fixed income level, then it acts as a marginal tax rate of 100 per cent, destroying entirely any incentive for private improvement and reproducing the worst effects of the poverty trap. Few proponents of NIT wish to destroy incentives in this way, however, and most thus propose slightly reduced rates of withdrawl. The Adam Smith Institute suggestion is the 'modest incentive' of a 90 per cent marginal rate for those just above zero earnings level (1984, p. 15).

For many low-wage earners this would be worse than the current poverty trap. But within NIT schemes there is no way of escaping from such high marginal tax rates, coupled usually with low rates of benefit, if they are to operate within the private wage economy. In such an economy what NIT payments do is subsidise low wages, much as current benefits do, but more openly and honestly. This is no doubt what most proponents intend, though it is not generally presented as a major aim, and it is not a policy which would be likely to attract much support on the left. Many proponents of combined tax and benefit schemes have thus looked for more sophisticated ways of using taxation to supplement existing income, or of circumventing the problem of low wages altogether.

2. Social dividends

In principle the idea of a social dividend is quite different from proposals for NIT. But as many commentators have pointed out their operation and their practical effects are usually very similar (Collard 1980; Creedy & Disney 1985, Ch. 9). They were proposed as an alternative to Beveridge's social insurance plan by Lady Rhys Williams in 1943, and they have more recently received the support of Conservatives (Sir Brandon Rhys Williams MP, see Parker 1984), Liberals (Vince 1983), claimants (Federation of Claimants' Unions 1984) and some on the left (Jordan 1984). In 1984 they also received the endorsement of the National Council for Voluntary Organisations (NCVO) who established a Basic Income Guarantee Research Group to discuss and promulgate proposals for dividends (Ashby 1984).

The basic idea is a simple one, to replace all existing benefits and taxes with a social dividend (or *Guaranteed Minimum Income*) paid to all whether in or out of work. Wages, whether full time or part time, would then act as a supplement to this and would be taxed in order to finance the cost of the dividend [doc. 20]. It is claimed that such schemes would break down existing divisions between workers and claimants, since all would receive the same dividend; and would remove the problem of the poverty trap, since all wages would be taxed at the same rate. Problems of take-up would also be wiped out as everyone would be sure to get their dividend. The attractions are obvious; but so are the pitfalls.

If the dividend is to be high enough to prevent poverty and improve the incomes of benefit claimants, as the Federation of Claimants' Unions and others on the left imply it must, then the tax rates levied on the wages of those who were in work would have to be very high indeed – well above the average 50 per cent tax rate which Vince (1983) and Parker (1984) anticipate for much lower social dividends. In these circumstances wages would no longer be a major means for distributing resources, and would in practice become something of an individual luxury. With high rates of unemployment flowing from deindustrialisation and the growth of new technology, Jordan (1984) and others argue that this is only a recognition of the inevitable. However, it would involve a fundamental break with current political and economic expectations in social and economic policy, especially within the labour movement, whose support for such reforms would have to be enlisted by the left. There is virtually no basis of support for such proposals within the labour movement of the mid 1980s, and the prospects for securing it look extremely remote.

If dividends are not set at a high level, then they become a much more feasible proposal for reform; and it is in this form that they have attracted the support of Parker (1984), Vince (1983) and the NCVO (Ashby 1984). Their proposals are for a dividend (or *Basic Income Guarantee*) fixed roughly at or below current benefit level, to be paid to all, with wages as an additional, taxed income. Parker describes it as a minimum, upon which people could build, without necessarily interfering with existing living standards (1984, p. 41). Ashby argues that it should not pose unreasonable demands on public expenditure and thus threaten cross-party support for the scheme (1984, p. 9).

For those in paid work the dividend could act as deduction against tax, to avoid a claim having to be made for it. For those with no other income it might be insufficient to meet basic needs, and thus additional payments could be made for children, pensioners, single parents and others. Additional payments would also have to be made to cover the housing costs of those with no other income, but these could be withdrawn if income were received, creating in effect a form of increased marginal taxation.

The proposals to deal with housing costs obviously weaken the apparent attractions of dividend schemes of this nature, reproducing as they do means-tested support and the problem of the poverty trap. However, if low social dividends are paid these problems cannot be removed, because in such circumstances the effect of the dividend would be to act as a subsidy to wages for everyone in paid work and an inadequate, subsistence income for everyone else. This would retain an incentive to take paid work, as Parker (1984) and other proponents are keen to do; but in practice it would mean that the major beneficiaries from the dividend scheme would not be the poor, but the employers, who would find part of their wage bill automatically guaranteed by the state.

It is in this sense that the aims and the effects of social dividends are very similar to those of NIT proposals. And if they do not challenge existing relativities between those on benefits and those paying taxes this is inevitable, as Collard commented in 1980, 'There is no painless way of redistributing income in favour of the poor. Given the need to keep the typical taxpayer's average and marginal rates as low as possible, the original schemes for a social dividend have been diluted ... to the point where the practical recommendations of several of them are remarkably similar' (p. 201).

3. Tax credits

The third group of proposals for combined tax and benefit schemes are not generally based upon attempts to change or challenge existing priorities for income distribution. Indeed the most recent proponents of tax credits, the *Institute for Fiscal Studies* (IFS) (Dilnot *et al.* 1984), argue that one of the merits of their scheme is that it can reproduce, on a more rational basis, more or less exactly the existing distribution of income in Britain. Rather they are attempts to replace the existing complex and contradictory pattern of taxes and benefits with a simple and rational means for allocating state support within existing economic constraints. In 1974 Pinker called them a 'pragmatist's solution to poverty'; and certainly it is to their technical merit rather than their reforming potential that most of their proponents appeal.

In 1967 Lees proposed a tax credit system to rationalise and replace Family Allowances and tax allowances, and in 1972 similar proposals formed the basis of a Green Paper and Select Committee report supported by the Conservative Chancellor, Anthony Barber. The Conservatives' proposals were for a truncated merger of taxes and benefits, and they did not involve the replacement of existing benefit provision. The plan was to replace tax allowances, Family Allowances and FIS with a weekly tax credit for all which would then be added to income for tax purposes, and set against tax liability or paid as cash if no tax was due. The credit was not a guaranteed income (it was provisionally fixed at £4 a week for a single person) and if no other income was received then SB would have had to be claimed. However, even this limited scheme was felt to be too costly to introduce and was shelved in 1973.

The Conservative Government of the 1980s did not resurrect the tax credit proposals of the early 1970s, but during the 1984 reviews of social security they did reappear, in a much more sophisticated and further-reaching form, in the proposals for the reform of social security published by the IFS (Dilnot *et al.* 1984). The IFS proposals spring from a desire to replace entirely existing tax allowances and benefit payments in order to simplify drastically the administration of state support. They discuss NIT and dividend proposals and argue that both would be either too expensive or ineffective in removing poverty, and conclude that what is required is a modification of these ideas in order to avoid high tax rates and to target resources on those most in need. This would be done by means of a joint tax credit and benefit system [doc. 21].

A low tax credit would be paid to all, or set off against tax liability for those with sufficient income, and a benefit credit would be paid to those without other resources in accordance with their needs, such as numbers of children and housing costs. Entitlement to both would be calculated annually from the tax returns completed by all, thus removing the stigma associated with having to make separate claims for benefit, and massively reducing the problem of take-up. If wages were earned, or increased, then the benefit credits and tax credits would be withdrawn until a net tax liability situation was reached and income would then merely be subject to tax at the standard rate of 39 per cent (the then 30 per cent basic rate plus 9 per cent for NI contributions, which would be abolished).

Credits must be withdrawn as income rises, just as current wage-related benefits are, because otherwise those above the thresholds would be receiving them, thus destroying the targeting effect of the scheme. If they are withdrawn, however, they will lead to high marginal tax rates on the low paid. The IFS propose a withdrawal rate of 50 per cent, leading to marginal tax rates of up to 89 per cent (when added to standard income tax). That this would be better than the current rates of over 100 per cent, which the IFS castigate as 'absurd and immoral', is true; but it is still a retention, and a clear legitimation, of the poverty trap and an indictment of the ability of the proposals to overcome one of the major problems with existing provision.

The claims to remove some of the other problems associated with the current benefit system also seem a little far-fetched on closer examination. Although the problems of stigma may be reduced by the merger of benefits with taxes, differences will still remain. Claimants will still have to get their credits in cash from DHSS offices or post offices (although the IFS talk of a future in which new technology could replace these with plastic cards and cash dispensers), whereas taxpayers will have their credit automatically deducted from tax liability. Confusion and complexity are also likely to remain for many. Although the annual tax return may serve as an adequate basis for determining the entitlement and liabilities of those in secure employment, for part-time and temporary workers with changing home and family circumstances, who form a large number of current benefit claimants, this will be hopelessly inadequate, and many may miss out on entitlement altogether or receive credits too late. Some may even end up owing money to the state at the end of the year, in which case the IFS propose that this be repaid by reducing the following year's credits.

It is also proposed that the family basis of entitlement be retained for benefit purposes (though not for tax liability) on the grounds that families want and expect their needs (though not their liabilities) to be assessed jointly – although apart from personal prejudice (Dilnot *et al.* 1984, p. 112) it is not clear what evidence such judgements are based on. In such circumstances it would obviously be unfair to treat cohabiting couples any differently from those legally married, thus the existing cohabitation rule is proposed for retention. However, somewhat naïvely, the IFS suggest that it should be enforced merely by asking couples in the tax return whether their living expenses were shared and accepting them as single persons if they said no.

Thus although technical simplicity is one of the major claims made for their tax credit proposals by the IFS, many of the problems of the current benefit system would be likely to be repeated in them. The main reason for this is that, in spite of their organisational innovation, tax credits are largely based on similar assumptions to existing benefits about the role of state support in providing for the poor. They seek to relieve absolute poverty by targeting benefits (or benefit credits) on to those who can establish, via a new means test, that they have an inadequate or non-existent income; and, to avoid providing for those who do not 'need' them, these are withdrawn rapidly in income rises. Their effect, and again no doubt their aim, is to subsidise and encourage low wages and exact the cost of state support most heavily from those trying hardest to escape from it. Although they involve a merger of tax and benefit policy, they cannot alter the priorities of existing policies without also tackling wage policy, and this would involve a much more extensive role for the state than most proponents of tax and benefit schemes would be prepared to support.

SOCIAL INSURANCE

As benefit provision in Britain has departed further and further from Beveridge's insurance plan, many critics and commentators have begun to argue that the most feasible and desirable strategy for benefit reform would be a return to, or a revitalisation of, the Beveridge ideal of comprehensive insurance. Like Beveridge himself, most commentators compare the advantages of benefits paid as of right through insurance with the growing dominance of means-testing within benefit provision; but some also argue that insurance is generally a more desirable basis for benefit provision than other alternative proposals. In 1969 Atkinson contrasted a 'back to Beveridge' approach with social dividends and tax credits, and in 1984 he reiterated his support for reform based on an 'improved' social insurance scheme.

In the intervening period other influential voices within the poverty lobby have lent their support to proposals based on the ideals of Beveridge. In 1975 the CPAG called for a move *Back to Beveridge* (Lister 1975). In 1978 the Meade Committee (including the IFS) proposed a *New Beveridge* scheme (Meade 1978). And in the same year a group called the Outer Circle Policy Unit (1978) proposed a *Beyond Beveridge* package of reforms. More recently the NCC (1984) have supported a social insurance basis for social security reform. And such an approach has also attracted the support of the major civil service trade unions (Society of Civil and Public Servants 1985).

Although proposals within this area differ significantly, their basic aims are generally the same. They wish to reduce the scope of means-testing to the minimal safety-net role envisaged by Beveridge by *floating* claimants off the SB and FIS schemes. This would be done by raising and extending NI benefits (SERPS was seen as a major step towards an extended Beveridge scheme, though Beveridge himself did not support earnings-related provision) and by increasing Child Benefit significantly. Most also favour an improved, non-contributory benefit for the disabled, as demanded by the Disability Alliance. Housing Benefit and other minor means-tested benefits would generally be retained, as would SB for those who still managed to fall through the expanded insurance scheme.

Such proposals would improve the incomes of significant numbers of existing claimants and would thus increase expenditure on social security. This would have to be paid for. The NCC (1984) suggest that this could be done by the abolition of the married man's tax allowance, reductions in mortgage interest tax relief, and a 3 per cent rise in the basic income tax rate. Atkinson (1984) proposes the introduction of more progressive tax rates on higher incomes. What is not generally proposed is an increase in NI contributions, though this would be the logic of a return to the Beveridge Plan. Most social insurance proponents are well aware that NI contributions are a relatively regressive way of raising income to finance social security, because of the lower and upper earnings limits, and they would not wish to exacerbate this. The NCC propose aligning NI contributions with income tax, and Atkinson proposes abolishing employees' contributions altogether.

Proponents of social insurance are also lukewarm in their support for contribution conditions for receipt of benefit. Once again they are aware that the arbitrary nature of these exclude many from the NI scheme. The CPAG have more recently proposed removing them altogether (Lister & Fimister 1980). If such adjustments are made, however, it is difficult to see in what sense the proposals are a return to the ideals of Beveridge, or indeed are an insurance scheme at all. As we discussed in Chapter 6, of course, the current NI scheme is not really an insurance scheme anyway; and it has never operated in the way Beveridge originally envisaged. Making a case for insurance in principle, therefore, is something of an unreal exercise, as the Society of Civil and Public Servants (SCPS) found in presenting their proposals for it [doc. 22].

Of course the civil service trade unions might be expected to support the NI scheme, as many of their members' jobs are currently based upon it. But apart from this, the major arguments mounted in favour of the insurance ideal is that it is better than means-testing and that it has widespread popular support. It is these attractions which proponents hope will make reforms based on social insurance politically feasible. Indeed it is the political feasibility of reform which is the most crucial issue for supporters of insurance proposals, many of whom are hardened campaigners only too well aware of the difficulties of tackling the established wisdom (or established ignorance) on the desirability of social security reform.

Thus the retention of the reference to Beveridge is symbolic of an intention to build on the *good bits* of existing provisions (NI, SERPS and Child Benefit) and maginalise the *bad bits* (means-testing). The fact that many are proposing insurance in no more than name does not matter very much, providing people *think* it is a good idea. Building on the existing system is the important feature of proposals, for it will permit reform to be gradual, and thus more likely to attract political support.

However, enlisting support for something you do not actually intend to pursue is a dangerous business, which could backfire when real intentions are revealed. In any event securing political support for insurance has a number of obvious problematic consequences. As we have already discussed, the principles of insurance which Beveridge championed are those of self-financing, family-based, subsistence benefits paid in return for contributions made. They exclude many who need state support and do not contribute to a redistribution of resources to reduce inequality. The earnings-related benefits which many proponents of social insurance support would remove the subsistence basis, but at the cost of importing existing inequalities into the system of state support. In supporting SERPS Ward (1985) argued that where inequalities already exist it would be harsh for the social security system not to recognise and cater for them, until they can be removed at source. Once again, however, this is making social security policy conditional upon economic change, and as Esam *et al.* (1985,

Ch. 5) point out, it would continue to leave those currently experiencing the harshest poverty with lower incomes than others within the same benefit scheme.

Given the expectation that means-tested provision outside of the new insurance scheme would also remain, further divisions within state support would also be continued. To say only a few would be affected is no real justification for maintaining the distinction – and small comfort for the few. And until the 1980s it was generally the intention of social security policy to restrict means-testing to only a few, with remarkably little success.

Most social insurance supporters also propose retaining the family unit as the base for state support, with all its problems. The requirement for benefits to be based on contributions will always exclude women with inadequate contribution records. Those who propose removing contribution conditions, however, do not usually propose paying separate and equal benefits to married women and men, the expectation is generally that there would be a couple rate which either could claim. If one partner was in paid work, however, there would be no entitlement, although some proponents do suggest the payment of a *carer's allowance* to women who are not in paid work because of child care or disabled adult care responsibilities.

The other problem which would still remain in an expanded insurance scheme is the poverty trap. Most proponents would not want to abolish FIS, HB and other means-tested benefits for the low paid, but would hope to see their scope drastically reduced as a result of a substantial rise in Child Benefit. Such a rise would have to be substantial indeed to remove the need for these, and would threaten the political support for gradual reform on which the success of such proposals is based. Yet without it the spectre of the means test still looms large.

As we pointed out before, the poverty trap is a product of the use of state benefits to subsidise low wages, and the relegation of social security policy to the support of capitalist economic demands. Such priorities would have to be reversed for social security reform to tackle the issue of the redistribution of resources rather than the relief of poverty; and this requires policies on benefits, taxes and *wages* to be subsumed within the planning of state support.

A WAGE AND BENEFIT POLICY

If social security reform is to move beyond the prevention or relief of poverty and begin to tackle inequality within British society, then it must be linked to wage and taxation policies designed to interfere in the existing mechanisms for distributing resources in order to *re*distribute these to the poor and the less well off. Such a policy would involve economic as well as social change, and would have to be linked to policies to control and direct capital investment and to create and subsidise employment. This would mean a commitment to an enhanced role for the state in transforming current economic priorities and economic power. And this inevitably means embarking upon plans for social change for which political support would have to be mobilised and won. However, without such support and such change, redistribution and improved social security will not in any event be possible – for improving the relative lot of the poor involves intervening simultaneously to reduce the wealth and power of the rich.

Benefit reform must therefore be related to policies for tax and wage reform. However, this does not necessarily mean a tax/wage/benefit merger. The technical merging of administration is not in itself a guarantee that redistributive policies will be pursued; and such policies do not require technical merger to achieve the objective of a co-ordinated role for state support. Proposals for benefit reform linked to policies for a guaranteed minimum wage and a more steeply progressive taxation system have been discussed by Esam *et al.* (1985) and by this author (Alcock 1985a). They involve the abolition of all means-tested and insurance benefits, the introduction of a statutory minimum wage, the replacement of the current standard rate of income tax with banded tax rates increasing as income rises, and the establishment of effective wealth and corporate taxation.

1. Benefits

The abolition of means-testing and insurance as a basis for the payment of benefits involves the establishment of a different basis for determining entitlement to state support. Esam *et al.* (1985) propose instead *positional benefits*, relating entitlement to the social causes of need which lead to the lack of an adequate income. Thus benefits would be paid automatically to all those not in full-time paid work, either through unemployment, disability, caring responsibilities or retirement. These would be supplemented with *cost-related benefits* for those who, because of their circumstances can be presumed to incur extra expenditure, for example a housing allowance for householders and a disability allowance for the disabled [doc. 23]. These would be payable to people whether in or out of work.

Both benefits would be paid at a flat rate, without test of means.

They would, however, be taxable income, and thus if claimants had other resources then tax liability might be reached. It is also proposed that benefits be paid to individuals and not to presumed family units. Only via individual entitlement, it is argued, can financial dependency be avoided. This would have to be applied irrespective of marital status, in order to avoid a situation in which married women were treated unfairly in comparison with those in other relationships. It would thus involve a significant redistribution of resources towards married women not in paid employment. This might well be resented by their husbands, especially if in effect they will be required to some extent to finance such a transfer through increased direct taxation. As we saw, the IFS see this as a major obstacle to moving from family to individually based benefit entitlement, and it has in the past received a somewhat hostile response from sections of the trade union and labour movement, because of its likely effect in depressing men's *family* wages.

Certainly political support for *disaggregation*, as individual benefit entitlement is frequently called, would have to be won in order to achieve a redistribution between genders. But the political support that was mobilised in opposition to the 1986 plan to pay the new FC to male wage-earners rather than women caring for children suggested that the issue of dependency and inequality within marriage could be an arena for political mobilisation in the future.

The proposed flat rate for benefit would mean the abandonment of SERPS, which, when proposed for abolition in the 1985 Green Paper, appeared to attract much political support, and over which the government eventually backed down. Esam *et al*. (1985, Ch. 5) argue that in principle earnings-related additions contradict the aims of an egalitarian policy of state support, and would not in any case provide the protection for many low-paid and part-time workers which supporters sometimes imply that they will. They propose a change in direction by replacing gradually the earnings-related additions to pensions with an increase in the basic rate for all, irrespective of past contributions. They also propose a withdrawal of the state support for private pension schemes and argue that this would make these considerably more expensive and financially less viable, restricting further movements towards private welfare for old age.

In spite of this it has been argued that SERPS is seen by many in the labour movement and the poverty lobby as a major progressive move for welfare provision, and that the feasibility of removing it, even in gradual moves towards more egalitarian provision, may therefore be doubted (Ward 1985). At present the earnings-related element is calculated in accordance with NI contributions made whilst in employment and will not be fully operational until 1998. If contributions were to be abolished then this would open up the question of whether the earnings-related element should not merely be based on average earnings and extended to all pensioners now. Such a policy would at least increase the incomes of existing pensioners and would give a clearer idea of the overall cost of the scheme, and the priority therefore to be accorded to the earnings-related principle.

Child Benefit is already a universal, positional benefit. Naturally it is proposed to retain it as a benefit for those with dependent children, and to increase it significantly to cover a more realistic assessment of the costs of child care.

Esam *et al.* (1985) also argue for a substantial general increase in rates of benefit. The priority is to redistribute resources to the poor as well as to change the principles of entitlement. And, once established, it is proposed that these rates be linked to the rise (or fall!) in the level of average earnings. Commitment to a relative concept of need requires commitment to a relative basis for state support, though of course the nature of the relativity (the proportion of wages at which benefit levels were fixed) could always be changed.

2. Minimum wages

A statutory minimum wage is an essential feature of proposals for reform which seek to replace current means-tested benefits for those in low-paid employment. If removing these is not to leave low-paid workers much worse off then their income from wages must be raised, though of course positional Child Benefit and cost-related housing allowances will assist in this for many.

This will obviously involve a rise in the wage levels of the low paid, especially women workers. Though since wages, like benefits, would only be expected to meet individual needs, the family wage argument which has been used to support higher wage levels in the past would no longer apply. In such a context the minimum wage need be no higher than a proportion of average earnings slightly above that fixed for benefit levels, although this would mean a significant increase for many women workers.

It is argued that wage levels must be fixed above benefit levels in order to preserve some incentive to undertake socially desirable employment. Especially as proponents also recommend removing the current negative incentives to take paid work contained in the requirement on benefit claimants to demonstrate that they are actively seeking employment. This would apply at an hourly as well as a weekly level. So that a part-time worker could be entitled to positional benefits on a proportional basis (for the hours of an average working week when they were not in paid employment) and be guaranteed a minimum wage (at least) above benefit level for every hour worked. It is likely that this could significantly reduce the black economy of part-time work which is undisclosed for benefit purposes; and this could also be more strictly controlled by effective enforcement of minimum wage levels paid by employers.

It is perhaps no coincidence that the statutory minimum wage has for some time been supported by the *Low Pay Unit* as the only effective way of removing the problem of low pay (Pond & Winyard 1983). It also received the support of the Labour Party and TUC conferences in the mid 1980s, in spite of the reservations by some unions over its effect on overall wage differentials. However, opposition has always been strong from employers, who argue that many could not afford to pay minimum wage levels and thus would have to sack large numbers of workers, leading to higher levels of unemployment. Of course many are at present supported in their payment of low wages by means-tested subsidies to low-paid employees. If these were removed it would be possible to subsidise employers direct to employ workers whom they could not otherwise afford. This would require a change in the nature of, and no doubt the criteria for, intervention by way of state support; but the principle of subsidy is already well established.

Supporters of statutory minimum wages have also expressed support for statutory *maximum* wages (Meacher 1985) and even general state policies on all wage levels. These are a logical extension of a concern to use social policy to transform the existing distribution of economic resources. However, this is a goal which can also, and perhaps more swiftly, be achieved by taxation reform.

3. Taxation

Taxation is a means of raising revenue for government expenditure. However, it is also, or could be, a major vehicle for redistribution of resources within society, especially through the use of direct taxation to finance benefit payments. Proponents of tax and benefit reform of social security of course all support this to some extent; but its effect can also be achieved without the merging of the benefit and taxation systems, by the joint planning of taxation and benefit policy so that receipt of benefit and liability to taxation do not overlap for those with no other resources, and so that benefits are financed out of taxation on the relatively better off.

In fact the direct tax system in Britain has become considerably *less* redistributive over the forty years since the welfare policies of the immediate post-war period. Tax thresholds are very low so that most earners now pay direct taxation, yet higher tax rates on the higher paid have been significantly reduced, and the vast majority of taxpayers now pay at only the standard rate. That this has led to the increasing unpopularity of taxation generally is only to be expected. However, it has also led governments to seek concessions, for the sake of popularity, by reducing the standard rate and/or raising tax thresholds, both of which, given the current system, always benefit the higher paid proportionately more. Coupled with this has been a significant decline in the size and scope of corporate and wealth taxation.

The general effect of all this is a taxation system in Britain with higher rates starting at lower levels of income than most other comparable countries, yet lower rates of tax for the wealthy and significant non-personal tax reliefs (such as mortgage interest relief) which disproportionately benefit higher earners (Smail 1984). The details of current, or alternative, taxation policies are really beyond the scope of this book, but suffice it to say that these policies could be reversed (see Esam *et al*. 1985, Ch. 8). Tax relief on non-personal expenditure, worth around £15 billion a year in the mid 1980s, could be withdrawn. Tax rates could be lowered for the low paid (via a reduced starting rate) and raised steeply for the higher paid – progressive rates of 25, 40, 60 and 75 per cent for instance could be used. Taxation on wealth and corporate holdings could also be introduced.

For the purpose of social security reform perhaps the most important question in tax reform is the retention, or otherwise, of NI contributions. If contribution tests as an entitlement to benefit are to be abolished, then the logic of retaining separate contributions seems faulty. They are also a relatively regressive form of taxation, and therefore the case for merging them into ordinary direct taxation appears to be strong. It is argued by some, however, that NI contributions are more willingly paid than other forms of taxation because they are earmarked for social security expenditure; although this is only partly true, and in any event payment of both is compulsory. The attitude survey commissioned as part of the 1984 reviews revealed widespread ignorance about the scope and purpose of NI contributions (Green Paper 1985, Vol. 3, p. 78), suggesting that public support may be more complex, or confused, than is frequently assumed. Perhaps few would notice the difference if a part of taxation retained the name of National Insurance albeit merged with direct tax – a proposal not dissimilar to that suggested by Atkinson (1984) as part of a supposedly social insurance basis for social security reform.

Of course NI contributions are not only paid by employees, employers also pay them for each employee. If these were abolished they would be a substantial redistribution of resources to employers. If they were then transferred to employees' direct taxation they would *appear* (even if employers could be trusted to pass them over) as a major addition to direct taxation. Thus a common compromise is the retention of employers' NI contributions as a payroll tax, although the future of this might more logically be discussed in the context of policies for corporate taxation generally.

As we suggested earlier, it may be that the retention of NI contributions in the 1980s is a pragmatic response to the perceived unpopularity of appearing to raise tax levels, rather than any continuing support in principle for the insurance base of funding for state support. If taxation (and benefit) policies are to be reformed, this perceived unpopularity must be challenged and changed. This is perhaps the most difficult of the political hurdles facing the radical reform of social security; although, if any commitment to re-distribution is to become reality, it is also the most important principle.

Part five
DOCUMENTS

Indeed, the poor often 'manage' their money very carefully – and still fail to get by. Tricia is a single parent bringing up two school-aged children on supplementary benefit. She finds herself forced to cut back on heating and food even though she accounts for every penny she spends:

> What I do is draw my money on a Monday, and I come home and I sort all my bills out, what I've got to pay there and then paid. Whatever I've got left, then I work from day-to-day. I do my shopping day-to-day. I've tried doing it in bulk but by the time you picked up what you think you need, the time you've paid for it you've got nothing left. So you can't shop like that, you've got to shop from day-to-day. You've got to be careful with what you buy. You can't just buy anything, you go for the cheapest. No matter what it is, you've got to go for the cheapest.
>
> I mean, when I go into Stockport I always walk because it's 30p down and it's 30p back, and if you walk there and back you are saving yourself 60 pence and that's just for one person. You can get a lot with 60p, you can get a loaf and you can get margarine.
>
> Usually by the time you get to Saturday, when most people are doing the shopping, you are down to your last pound. It's very hard for other people to realise what it's like to manage off that type of money.

From: J. Mack & S. Lansley, *Poor Britain*, George Allen & Unwin (1985), p. 127.

Document two
THE RELATIONSHIP BETWEEN WAGES AND PROFITS

Real wages may remain the same, they may even rise, and yet relative wages may fall. Let us suppose, for example, that all means of subsistence have gone down in price by two-thirds while wages per day have only fallen by one-third, that is to say, for example, from three marks to two marks. Although the worker can command a greater amount of commodities with these two marks than he previously could with three marks, yet his wages have gone down in relation to the profit of the capitalist. The profit of the capitalist (for example, the manufacturer) has increased by one mark; that is, for a smaller sum of exchange values which he pays to the worker, the latter must produce a greater amount of exchange values than before. The share of capital relative to the share of labour has risen. The division of social wealth between capital and labour has become still more unequal. With the same capital, the capitalist commands a greater quantity of labour. The power of the capitalist class over the working class has grown, the social position of the worker has deteriorated, has been depressed one step further below that of the capitalist.

What, then, is the general law which determines the rise and fall of wages and profit in their reciprocal relation?

They stand in inverse ratio to each other. Capital's share, profit, rises in the same proportion as labour's share, wages, falls, and vice versa. Profit rises to the extent that wages fall; it falls to the extent that wages rise.

From K. Marx, *Wage Labour and Capital*, Progress Press (1952), p. 35.

LIVING TOGETHER AS HUSBAND AND WIFE

GUIDELINES TO A DECISION

The adjudication officer is given the following guidelines to help decide whether a couple are living together as husband and wife:

Membership of the same household

Both partners must be living in the same household and neither will usually have any other home where they normally live. This implies that the couple live together the whole time, apart from absence necessary for employment, visits to relatives, etc. and that, for example, they usually share meals and do jobs around the home for each other.

Established relationship

Living together as husband and wife clearly implies more than an occasional or very brief association. When a couple first live together, it may be clear from the start that the relationship is similar to that of husband and wife. For example, the women takes the man's name and has borne his child. But in other cases it may take more time before such a close relationship develops.

Financial support

In most husband and wife relationships one would expect to find financial support of one party by the other, or sharing of household expenses, but the absence of any such arrangement does not prove that two people are not living together as husband and wife.

Sexual relationship

A sexual relationship is normally an important part of a marriage and therefore of living together as husband and wife. But its absence does not necessarily prove that a couple are not living as husband and wife, nor does its presence prove that they are. (You will not be asked about any sexual relationship, but you can give information about this if you think it will make things clearer.)

Children

When a couple are caring for a child or children of whom they are the parents there is a strong presumption that they are living as husband and wife.

How other people see the relationship

Whether the couple present themselves to other people as husband and wife is relevant. But many couples living together do not wish to pretend that they are actually married, and the fact that they retain their separate identities publicly as unmarried persons does not mean they cannot be regarded as living together as husband and wife.

From: DHSS, *Living Together as Husband and Wife, NI 247*, DHSS leaflets (1986).

Document four
QUESTIONING BEVERIDGE

Sir A. Gridley: I wish I would not be interrupted, because I think the hon. Member will find the ground covered in the very few minutes for which I propose to ask the attention of the House.

First, it is Parliament's duty to consider what are the total post-war obligations that the State must face, and decide on their order of priority, within the capacity of the State to meet them. In this connection – and this answers the point of my hon. Friend – we should consider whether children's allowances should not be the first of the major Beveridge proposals to be implemented, the whole cost of which must fall on the State. I am merely expressing my personal views, committing no body of friends and no party. The great value of this Debate should be that we are free to express our own views, irrespective of ties of any kind. I certainly am in favour of children's allowances being one of the first of the proposals to be implemented. Secondly, how are we effectively to control the cost of living? Thirdly, should the taxpayer's contributions be a percentage of the employer's and employee's contributions – in other words, is the liability of the State to be fixed, or is it to be unlimited? There is a great deal to be said for fixing it. Also, what should be the actual cash benefits? That is a matter to be hammered out.

Fourthly, who should be included for unemployment benefit? I sometimes wonder whether hon. Members realise how many hundreds of thousands of people there are in the country to whom unemployment is practically unknown. They include Civil Services, municipal services, public utility undertakings, the railways, the standing Fighting Forces, the police, many undertakings such as farming, tobacco manufacture, the co-operative societies, and the clerical staffs of many industrial undertakings. These must total up to many millions, and they get pensions on retiring. Should such people as these be compelled to contribute to Unemployment Insurance, which they may never require? Fifthly, should there be a national scheme of pooled benefits for workmen's compensation? That has to be hammered out.

Sixthly, should old age pensions be conditional on retirement, and should schemes of insurance by employers for their workpeople be encouraged, and the national Exchequer thus relieved? I have always been quietly proud of the fact that 98 per cent of the staff and the employees in the undertakings with which I am connected are already insured. They are insured for benefits on retirement, and a capital sum is payable for the benefit of their relatives in the event of their death. I should view with the greatest apprehension having to give up schemes of that kind, and I do not think it would be to the benefit of the State that they should be discouraged. Seventhly, should not funeral and death benefit be left as they are? There are 100,000,000 policies of this kind to-day. Why should that state of things be disturbed? Eighthly, is there any justification for setting up an Industrial Insurance Board? I doubt it very much, but we may be convinced later that it cannot be avoided. Ninthly, should all be eligible for health insurance benefits, or only those below a certain income limit? That is a big question about which views may differ. My own view is that a limit should be fixed at about £600 or £700 a year, and that below that figure people should be entitled to these benefits, but that above it they must go to their own doctors and pay for treatment. Finally, to what extent is it likely that international co-operation can be secured? All these are major problems for careful consideration. I ventured to tabulate them because I thought they might be of some use to Ministers who have to reply, and perhaps to some of my hon. Friends who have to make up their minds on these problems.

Finally, may I say this? I find myself in agreement with the main principles underlying the Beveridge proposals, subject to adequate – and they must be adequate – safeguards against abuse and over-organisation. The whole plan hangs upon our industrial prosperity and constant good employment. If prosperity is not achieved, the whole plan is bound to crash.

From: Hansard, *House of Commons Debates*, Vol. 386, HMSO (1943), Cols. 1635–37.

303. *Six Principles of Social Insurance*: The social insurance scheme set out below as the chief method of social security embodies six fundamental principles:

Flat rate of subsistence benefit

Flat rate of contribution

Unification of administrative responsibility

Adequacy of benefit

Comprehensiveness

Classification

304. *Flat Rate of Subsistence Benefit*: The first fundamental principle of the social insurance scheme is provision of a flat rate of insurance benefit, irrespective of the amount of the earnings which have been interrupted by unemployment or disability or ended by retirement; exception is made only where prolonged disability has resulted from an industrial accident or disease. This principle follows from the recognition of the place and importance of voluntary insurance in social security and distinguishes the scheme proposed for Britain from the security schemes of Germany, the Soviet Union, the United States and most other countries with the exception of New Zealand. The flat rate is the same for all the principal forms of cessation of earning – unemployment, disability, retirement; for maternity and for widowhood there is a temporary benefit at a higher rate.

305. *Flat Rate of Contribution*: The second fundamental principle of the scheme is that the compulsory contribution required of each insured person or his employer is at a flat rate, irrespective of his means. All insured persons, rich or poor, will pay the same contributions for the same security; those with larger means will pay more only to the extent that as tax-payers they pay more to the National Exchequer and so to the State share of the Social Insurance

Fund. This feature distinguishes the scheme proposed for Britain from the scheme recently established in New Zealand under which the contributions are graduated by income, and are in effect an income-tax assigned to a particular service. Subject moreover to one exception, the contribution will be the same irrespective of the assumed degree of risk affecting particular individuals or forms of employment. The exception is the raising of a proportion of the special cost of benefits and pensions for industrial disability in occupations of high risk by a levy on employers proportionate to risk and pay-roll (paras 86–90 and 360).

306. *Unification of Administrative Responsibility*: The third fundamental principal is unification of administrative responsibility in the interests of efficiency and economy. For each insured person there will be a single weekly contribution, in respect of all his benefits. There will be in each locality a Security Office able to deal with claims of every kind and all sides of security. The methods of paying different kinds of cash benefit will be different and will take account of the circumstances of insured persons, providing for payment at the home or elsewhere, as is necessary. All contributions will be paid into a single Social Insurance Fund and all benefits and other insurance payments will be paid from that fund.

307. *Adequacy of Benefit*: The fourth fundamental principle is adequacy of benefit in amount and in time. The flat rate of benefit proposed is intended in itself to be sufficient without further resources to provide the minimum income needed for subsistence in all normal cases. It gives room and a basis for additional voluntary provision, but does not assume that in any case. The benefits are adequate also in time, that is to say except for contingencies of a temporary nature, they will continue indefinitely without means test, so long as the need continues, though subject to any change of conditions and treatment required by prolongation of the interruption in earning and occupation.

308. *Comprehensiveness*: The fifth fundamental principle is that social insurance should be comprehensive, in respect both of the persons covered and of their needs. It should not leave either to national assistance or to voluntary insurance any risk so general or so uniform that social insurance can be justified. For national assistance involves a means test which may discourage voluntary insurance or personal saving. And voluntary insurance can never be sure of covering the ground. For any need moreover which, like direct funeral expenses, is so general and so uniform as to be a fit subject for insurance by compulsion, social insurance is much cheaper to

administer than voluntary insurance.

309. *Classification*: The sixth fundamental principle is that social
insurance, while unified and comprehensive, must take account of the
different ways of life of different sections of the community: of those
dependent on earnings by employment under contract of service, of
those earning in other ways, of those rendering vital unpaid service as
housewives, of those not yet of age to earn and of those past earning.
The term 'classification' is used here to denote adjustment of
insurance to the differing circumstances of each of these classes and to
many varieties of need and circumstance within each insurance class.
But the insurance classes are not economic or social classes in the
ordinary sense; the insurance scheme is one for all citizens irrespective
of their means.

From: Sir W. Beveridge, *Social Insurance and Allied Services*, Cmd.
6404, HMSO (1942), pp. 121–2.

Document six
ABANDONING CHILD BENEFIT

After the 4 May cabinet meeting, the new Prime Minister began working behind the scenes. At the cabinet meeting of 6 May, he reported receiving an 'excellent report' from the Whips Office which had created fresh doubts in his own mind about the political implications of introducing child benefit. The new Chief Whip, Michael Cocks, reported to the cabinet that, after surveying opinion (though the minutes do not recall whose opinion was canvassed), the introduction in April 1977 of child benefit would have grave political consequences which had not been foreseen when the bill went through the House of Commons. In the ensuing discussions cabinet ministers expressed the belief that the distribution effects of child benefit could not be 'sold' to the public before this scheme was brought in in April 1977. In summing up, the Prime Minister commented that to defer the scheme would *also* require careful public presentation. The two cabinet meetings of 4 and 6 May had scuttled the child benefit policy.

Under the guise of how best to present publicly the immediate abandonment of introducing child benefits, DHSS officials later put forward a number of policy alternatives. Shirley Williams as Paymaster-General and Secretary of State for Prices and Consumer Protection, and David Ennals, argued in an attached memorandum for those proposals which were aimed at salvaging something for families. Their view was that the government would gain respect for introducing the child benefits scheme in a modest form rather than by making a U-turn on a major commitment on which the government had fought two general elections and had enshrined in subsequent legislation.

The cabinet discussed this on 20 May. But it was now having to make its decision on child benefit in the knowledge that much of the cabinet discussion was being leaked to two major national newspapers. As a result of these leaks, those trade union leaders who were committed to child benefit insisted on inserting the crucial phrase into the statement agreed by the TUC/Labour Party Liaison Committee at their meeting on the 24 May. The statement read: 'It is of the utmost importance that the new child benefit scheme, to be introduced next year, provides benefit generous enough to represent a determined and concerted attack on the problem [of poverty].'

The full trade union delegation at that meeting did not know that a small group of union leaders – those who lead the trade union side on the National Economic Development Council (Neddy) – had arranged to see the Chancellor of the Exchequer and other senior ministers later in the day. At the cabinet meeting on the following day (25 May), the Prime Minister asked the Chancellor to report on this meeting with TUC chiefs to discuss the proposals put forward at the cabinet meeting on 6 May. The TUC were asked to agree to a postponement of the child benefit scheme for three years because of the effect the loss of child tax allowances would have on take-home pay. The cabinet minutes record: 'On being informed of the reduction in take-home pay, which the child benefits scheme would involve, the TUC representatives had reacted immediately and violently against its implementation, irrespective of the level of benefits which would accompany the reduction in take-home pay.' Both TUC and cabinet ministers were agreed in opposing any cut in child tax allowances, on the ground that this would appear to reverse part of the budget strategy underlying stage two of the incomes policy.

In order to prevent any further leaks finding their way into the national press, the cabinet then proposed that the announcement on the effective postponement of child benefits scheme should be made in the House of Commons that afternoon. At 3.30 pm on 25 May, David Ennals therefore rose and made the best he could of the government's abandonment of its plan to tackle family poverty.

From: CPAG, 'Killing a commitment: the Cabinet v. the Children (1976)', in F. Field, *Poverty and Politics: The Inside Story of the CPAG's Campaigns in the 1970s*, Heinemann EB (1982), pp. 111–12.

1.1 The Secretary of State for Social Services gave us in September 1976 a general remit to conduct a comprehensive review of the supplementary benefits scheme. We set ourselves the following objectives:

    a. to examine the scope and purpose of the scheme and its method of operation, including its relationships with other central and local services;

    b. to produce a simpler scheme which would be more readily comprehensible to claimants and staff, with rules capable of being published, whether in the form of regulations or otherwise;

    c. to deploy more effectively the financial resources likely to be available over the next few years;

    d. to reduce the rising demands on staff, having regard to available financial resources;

    e. to devise arrangements which, in the light of the Bell Report, would lead to a more effective appeals system;

    f. to examine the role of the Supplementary Benefits Commission (SBC), including its agency and other duties not directly connected with supplementary benefit.

1.2 We have engaged in many consultations, but we have not sought formal views from interested organisations or the public. We have regarded it as our task at this stage to analyse the main structure of the scheme and to identify options for change. The Secretary of State has undertaken to publish these, so that all interested people and organisations can express considered views before any decisions are taken on the future shape of the scheme. While this second stage of public consultation is in progress we shall be studying other more detailed aspects of the scheme. Some of these arise and are mentioned in our discussion of major issues; others have been put to us by organisations as points requiring review. Some examples of both are in Annex 1.

From: *Social Assistance: A Review of the Supplementary Benefits Scheme in Great Britain*, DHSS (1978) p. 1.

THE 1984 REVIEW TEAMS

Review Teams.

Supplementary Benefit review

Tony Newton MP, Minister for Social Security (Chair)
Robin Wendt, Chief Executive Cheshire County Council, Member Social Security Advisory Committee
Basil Collins, Chair Nabisco Brands, Member Institute of Directors

Benefits for children and young persons review

Rhodes Boyson MP, Minister for Social Security (Chair), replaced by Norman Fowler after Cabinet reshuffle
Barbara Shenfield, Chair WRVS, Member Adam Smith Institute
TG Parry Rogers, Director of Personnel Plesseys, Member Institute of Directors

Housing Benefit review

Jeremy Rowe, Chair Peterborough Development Corporation, Deputy Abbey National Building Society (Chair)
Alan Blakemore, Former Chief Executive London Borough of Croydon
Rhea Martin, Lecturer Hatfield Polytechnic, Vice-Chair National Association of Citizens' Advice Bureaux

Pensions review

Norman Fowler MP, Secretary of State (Chair)
Tony Newton MP, Minister for Social Security

Barney Hayhoe MP, Treasury Minister
Peter Morrison MP, Minister in Department of Employment
Alex Fletcher MP, Undersecretary for Social Security
Ray Whitney MP, Undersecretary for Social Security
Alan Peacock, Former Vice-Chancellor (Private) University of Buckingham
Marshall Field, General manager Phoenix Assurance Company
Stewart Lyon, Legal & General Insurance, President Institute of Actuaries
Edward Johnson, Government Actuary

From: P. Alcock 'The Fowler Reviews: Social Policy on the Political Agenda', *Critical Social Policy*, Issue 14 pp. 101–2.

1.1 To be blunt the British social security system has lost its way. There is no question that it has helped to raise the living standards of the poorest people; that it has provided a safety net against urgent need; and that it has improved the position of some of the most vulnerable groups in society like the retired, poor families with children and sick and disabled people. Yet those achievements have to be weighed against a number of other factors.

1.2 The cost of social security will this year be over £40 billion. Since the Second World War, it has grown five times faster than prices, twice as fast as the economy as a whole; and it is set to rise steeply for the next forty years. Despite mounting costs, resources have not always been directed to those most in need and under present plans will not be so in the future. The piecemeal development of the system has resulted in a multitude of benefits with overlapping purposes and differing entitlement conditions. The complexity in benefit rules has meant that social security is difficult to administer and at times impossible for the public to understand. While the overlap between social security and income tax means that significant numbers of people are paying income tax and receiving means-tested benefits at the same time.

1.3 Each new development in social security since the War has been made for the best of motives. All too often, however, the effect has been to confuse and to complicate. Worse still our understanding of what the social security system should be seeking to achieve has been obscured. Our responsibilities as individuals and collectively through the state have become ill-defined.

1.4 This Green Paper aims to define a system which is founded on public understanding of the purposes and the workings of social security; which is more relevant to the needs of today; and which is capable of meeting the demands into the next century. It sets out a new approach to social security – but it recognises and seeks to build on what has been achieved over the past forty years.

From: Green Paper, *Reform of Social Security*, Vol. 1, Cmnd. 9517, HMSO (1985), p. 1.

Document ten
THE CONTRIBUTION PRINCIPLE

Extract from *Minutes of Evidence*, Subcommittee of the House of Commons Treasury and Civil Service Committee, Session 1982–3, 'The Structure of Personal Income Taxation and Income Support', paras 838–41.

[Mr Wainwright]

838. As to the benefits, could we explore the rationale nowadays, bearing in mind all the other non-contributory benefits which are available, of the contribution record system?

(*Mr Regan*) I think there are two points, and I am not sure which one you are after. If you are asking whether there is a rationale for a contribution record, I think the answer is simply that if you did not have a contribution record as a basis for entitlement to benefit you would have to have some other test. I do not think you would simply be able to accept that anybody, including anybody who had just arrived in the country, who had made no contributions should get a retirement pension or short-term benefit, so you have to have some test, and it seems to us probable that the contribution test is as good a one as any. Otherwise people like married women and widows who have opted out of National Insurance contributions would be eligible for benefits without any test at all and you would have a very large increase in benefit expenditure. I am not sure whether you were directing your remarks to the question whether there was a justification for a contributory principle?

839. Yes, and also what justification there is for the particular contribution requirement which to my mind bears very little relationship to the benefits received. It seems to be an extraordinarily arbitrary system because in no way is a certain level of contribution paid for an average benefit.

(*Mr Regan*) I think one could certainly accept it as true that there are very easy tests for short-term benefits – though not for benefits where a lifetime average has to be maintained. There is a certain justification for this in the relative ease administratively with which it is done now that these records are computerised. If the computers are working all right we can do it easily and do not have to go to employers. You have a record on the basis of which short-term benefits are calculated. Whether it is too easy a test is a matter of judgment. One issue which enters into it is the question whether, if you made it more difficult, you would have to pay out more in supplementary benefit, if entitlement to supplementary benefit was increased. That is probably in itself not a desirable thing to do. On the question of the contributory principle, I am a National Insurance man born and bred and for over 30 years I have firmly believed that it is a principle which is worth maintaining and has a rationale in its acceptance even now despite all that has happened. You have quoted non-contributory benefits. The great majority of our fellow citizens believe there is a direct relationship between what they pay and what eventually they get out of it at the end of the day as of right without the proof required for means-tested benefits, and that is something which people value.

Mr Howell
840. Do you agree that that is mumbo-jumbo?
   (*Mr Regan*) I can only give you my view, which I have just expressed.
   Mr. Howell: It sounds like mumbo-jumbo to me.

Mr Wainwright
841. You have not answered the second part of my question. How on earth are the contribution requirements fixed and what relationship do they bear to the marvellous benefits they unlock?
   (*Mr Regan*) They are not fixed on any particularly rational basis but on the basis that you want a reasonable test and do not want to make it too hard for people to get the benefits, because, after all, the contingencies are there and you do not want resort to means-tested benefits. But all the benefits in some sense are based on a pay as you go system, which is what the National Insurance system is. If you like, all the benefits are too easy. None of us has ever paid, or will ever pay, because even on the pension side it is not actuarially calculated, the full value of our benefits. This is a function of the inter-generation apportionment process whereby the working generation today basically pays for the pensions of the generation which has now retired and we go forward in the hope that each successive generation will, in return for something which is much less than full value, go on doing so. I do not think there is a particular sort of logic to any particular figure.

Mr. C. M. Regan is an Under Secretary in the Family Support and Supplementary Benefit Division of the DHSS.

From: A. Dilnot, J. Kay & C. Morris, *The Reform of Social Security*, Oxford UP (1984) App. B. pp. 33–4.

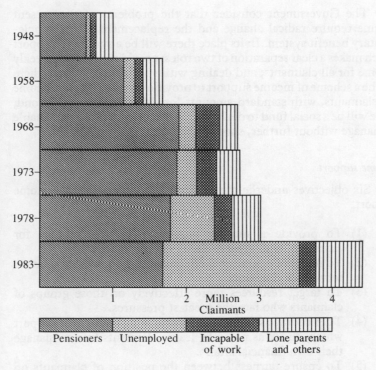

Figure 2.1. Number of Supplementary Benefit Claimants by Client Group

From: Green Paper, *Reform of Social Security: Programme for Change,* Vol. 2, Cmnd. 9518, HMSO (1985).

THE AIMS AND STRUCTURE OF INCOME SUPPORT

PROPOSALS FOR REFORM

2.69 The Government consider that the problems of the present scheme require radical change and the replacement of the supplementary benefit system. In its place there will be a system of support which makes a clear separation of two roles: providing a regular weekly income for all claimants; and dealing with special needs. First, there will be a scheme of income support to provide a regular weekly income for claimants, with standard amounts for different groups. Second, there will be a social fund to deal with the minority of claimants unable to manage without further, specialist support.

Income support

2.70 Six objectives underlie the Government's proposals on income support.

(1) To provide a simpler system of income support for claimants, with greater clarity of entitlement.
(2) To improve operational effectiveness and provide a better service for claimants.
(3) To target resources more effectively on those groups of claimants who face the greatest pressures.
(4) To encourage self-reliance by providing a system of support which, so far as possible, leaves claimants free to manage their own financial affairs.
(5) To ensure fairness between the position of claimants on benefit and those with similar levels of income in work.
(6) To provide a better base on which provisions in other income-related benefits can be aligned.

The structure of income support

2.71 The Government believe that the new income support structure should be simpler than the present arrangements. The aim will be to give claimants a reasonable level of help rather than to provide in detail for every variation in individual circumstances. The proposals base income support on the following elements – age and marital status; family responsibilities; and client group.

From: Green Paper, *Reform of Social Security: Programme for Change*, Vol. 2, Cmnd. 9518, HMSO (1985), p. 23.

OFFICIAL OPPOSITION TO UNIFIED HOUSING
BENEFIT

Discussions continued interminably in an interdepartmental working party of officials. The DOE resisted action: they opposed DHSS proposals, responded reluctantly to Treasury requests for counter-proposals, sent representatives to the meetings who were more junior than the spokesmen sent by other Departments, and dragged their feet all the way. If it had not been for Geoffrey Beltram, our under secretary working on the problem, the whole idea would probably have died at this stage.

The DOE had one very good reason for opposing reform. The means tests for supplementary benefits, rate rebates and rent rebates were different. That was why they were such an incomprehensible mess. The 'tapers' – that is to say, the speed at which the benefits are withdrawn as incomes rise – were much more gentle for rent rebates, and particularly for rate rebates, than they were for supplementary benefits. The poorest of the people not on supplementary benefits were treated less generously than people with similar incomes who were on supplementary benefit. But other less poor people, with incomes well above supplementary benefit levels, were getting quite a lot of help: these were mainly pensioners with rate rebates. Therefore any reform which was to treat equal needs equally would probably cost a good deal of money in order to increase benefits for the poorest people outside the supplementary benefit scheme; otherwise it would not be 'saleable' to politicians. The only other way of increasing benefits for these people would be to scrape some money down to them from slightly less poor people getting rate rebates. That could be done by making the 'taper' applied to a new, unified benefit a good deal steeper than the present tapers for rebates. But there was no point in asking a government which was already losing its nerve to take money away from a lot of elderly ratepayers. Thus a single, comprehensive scheme of housing benefits for people with low incomes would either be expensive, or there would be too many 'losers' and not enough 'gainers' to make the idea politically saleable. Either way, the DOE and its Ministers would get the backwash that followed. No wonder they opposed reform.

From: D. Donnison, *The Politics of Poverty*, Martin Robertson (1982), pp. 187–8.

The types of abuse

129. The principal abuses which are known to the Department are described below.

(a) Earnings offences

These offences concern the deliberate concealment or under-statement of earnings by claimants to benefit or of their dependants for whom they are claiming dependency increases. They affect unemployment, sickness, invalidity, injury, maternity and supplementary benefits and retirement pensions. We discuss the problems involved at Chapter 12.

(b) Sickness and injury benefit offences

This includes falsely claiming to be incapable of work and, as regards injury benefit, falsely claiming that incapacity is due to an industrial accident. The problems affecting sickness benefit, particularly medical certification, are described in Chapter 9 and of injury benefit in Chapter 10.

(c) Voluntary unemployment

Claimants who continue to draw unemployment and/or supplementary benefit without making reasonable efforts to obtain employment. We discuss the general control measures and the particular measures for the reduction or refusal of benefit in Chapter 11.

(d) Cohabitation and fictitious desertion

This affects supplementary benefit and widows' benefit. There is an offence when a woman who is drawing benefit conceals the fact that she is cohabiting with a man as his wife (see also paragraph 159(a)). In the case of fictitious desertion the woman falsely claims supplementary benefit on the grounds that she has been deserted by her husband, when that is not in fact the case. The problems involved in both situations are basically the same and are described in Chapter 13.

(e) Itinerant fraud

This is peculiar to supplementary benefit. Persons claiming to be in immediate need, move from office to office giving false information about their circumstances. This problem is described in more detail at Chapter 16.

(f) Family, guardians and child's special allowance offences

The principal form of abuse is failure to report changes of circumstances affecting the constitution of the family. This is described at Chapter 14.

From: Fisher Committee, *Report of the Committee on Abuse of Social Security Benefits*, Cmnd. 5228, HMSO (1973), p. 44.

THE CHANGING BURDEN OF TAXATION

2.2 We noted in paragraph 1.5 that there is, at the present time, a considerable range of incomes over which people both pay tax and receive benefits. Thirty years ago, an enquiry into personal income taxation and income support would have implied two separate enquiries rather than one. An income support system, based on national insurance benefits supplemented by means-tested assistance, applied to those not in employment. People in work were liable to personal income taxation, but low income households were exempt. Family allowances (now replaced by child benefit) were payable to both groups. The interactions between the tax and social security systems were limited, unimportant and transparent. Subsequent developments have altered this situation and helped make our subject far more complex.

2.3 Many more of the lowest incomes have been brought into tax. The thresholds above which tax starts to be paid have risen in line with prices,[2] but failed to keep pace with incomes, most markedly in the 1950s and 1960s when incomes were pushing ahead of prices. So incomes at the bottom end of the distribution have been increasingly drawn into the tax net. Figures from the Government's evidence[3] are:

TABLE 1

Tax threshold as percentage of average male earnings

	single persons	*married couples without children*	*married couples with 2 children under 11*
1949–50	39	63	123
1959–60	27	46	104
1969–70	25	37	68
1982–83	22	34	60

In 1949 tax started to be paid at a rate of 12 per cent and in 1959 at 7 per cent.[4] It now starts at 30 per cent. During the last 30 years the whole tax burden has doubled, creating a powerful pressure to tax the lowest incomes more heavily.

[2]Evidence, p. 214.
[3]Evidence, p. 214. Child benefits have been taken into account as an equivalent tax allowance.
[4]Evidence, p. 6.

From: Meacher Committee, *Third Special Report of the House of Commons Treasury and Civil Service Committee*, HMSO (1983), p. xi.

Document sixteen
THE POVERTY TRAP

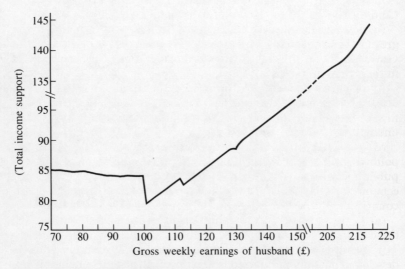

Source: DHSS, Tax/benefit model tables (1982)

Figure 1. The relationship between total income support and gross earnings of the husband for a married couple with three children aged 3, 8 and 11, with the wife not earning (as at November 1982)

From: A. Deacon & J. Bradshaw, *Reserved for the Poor: The Means Test in British Social Policy,* Blackwell/Martin Robertson (1983) p. 157.

190

Document seventeen
LOCAL AUTHORITY CAMPAIGN POLICY

'This Council (a) notes that the Social Security Bill is now in the Committee stage of the House of Commons;

(b) notes the fact that the vast majority (over 90%) of responses to the green paper were highly critical of the Government's proposals yet the Government has shown virtually no consideration of these responses in their final proposals;

(c) reaffirms its policy as expressed at the Council meeting on the 3rd July, 1985 that it "believes that the clear intention of the review is to save money at the expense of the old, the young, the poor and the unemployed";

(d) recognises that these proposals together with Government policy in other areas (e.g. wage councils, anti-trade union legislation, public spending cuts) are aimed at creating and reinforcing a low wage economy that is of "benefit" only to those who hold the wealth of the country;

(e) expresses grave concern and anger at the potential effects of these proposals on the people of Sheffield and on the City Council;

(f) believes that an alternative to the present system needs to be developed but only through consideration of all benefits (including tax benefits) and redistribution of wealth;

(g) reaffirms its intention to use its powers to campaign, with other organisations, against these proposals and in so doing to assist in the development of alternative proposals which allow for adequate standards of living without loss of dignity; and

(h) directs that copies of this resolution be sent to the Prime Minister, the Secretary of State for Social Services, the Rt Honourable Neil Kinnock M.P., Mr Michael Meacher M.P., the Sheffield Members of Parliament and the local office of the Department of Health and Social Security.'

From: Sheffield City Council, Motion, 5 March 1986.

Document eighteen
THE OBJECTIVES OF SOCIAL SECURITY POLICY

1.12 In developing this approach the Government believe that three main objectives should underlie the reform of social security.

First, the social security system must be capable of meeting genuine need. This is a basic responsibility of any government. No individual should be left in a position where through no fault of his own he is unable to sustain himself or his family. Supplementary benefit is based on that principle and – while it has many faults – it is more effective than many equivalent schemes overseas. At the same time the overall system must be flexible enough to recognise that what constitutes need changes and that those groups most in need also change. In the 1930s working-age families were seen as the main group in poverty: the main causes being unemployment and low earnings among men with large families. By the 1950s and 1960s pensioners were the major cause for concern. Now the position has changed again and in 1985 it is families with children who face the most difficult problems.

Second, the social security system must be consistent with the Government's overall objectives for the economy. Social security is already by far the largest government programme – more than twice defence spending and larger than health, social services, education and housing put together. It is responsible for a major share of the current heavy tax burden on individuals and companies. As many other countries recognise, continued growth of this burden could severely damage the prospects for economic growth. Yet in the longer term, the scope for sustaining and improving social security provision depends on the performance of the economy. But there are other issues. While it is one of the functions of the social security system to help those who are unemployed, it is self-defeating if it creates barriers to the creation of jobs, to job mobility or to people rejoining the labour force. Clearly such obstacles exist if people believe themselves better off out of work than in work; or if employers regard the burden of national insurance as a substantial discouragement to providing new jobs. Equally restrictions in areas like pensions can discourage people from changing jobs. If we wish to encourage individuals to provide for themselves then the social security system – public and private – must not stand in the way.

Third, the social security system must be simpler to understand and easier to administer. Forty years of tinkering have resulted in complexity and confusion. Nobody can be happy with the system as it stands today. The supplementary benefit system alone requires some 38,000 staff to administer it. The rules of entitlement are so complex that the manual of guidance to staff runs to two volumes and 16,000 paragraphs. Nor is it only the rules which cause confusion. All the main income-related benefits – supplementary benefit, housing benefit and family income supplement – use different measures of income and capital. Not surprisingly, therefore, some benefits are shrouded in an obscurity which at times is virtually total. As for administration, much of the social security system is run from local offices which largely lack the kind of aids which modern computer science can provide. The result is that the service for the public too often fails as the staff hunt for files in a Dickensian paper-chase.

From: Green Paper, *Reform of Social Security*, Vol. 1, Cmnd. 9517, HMSO (1985), pp. 2–3.

Document nineteen
PROPOSALS FOR NEGATIVE INCOME TAX

It is our view that all these benefits should be replaced by a single system combining the payment of income tax and the distribution of benefit based on a single assessment of need or ability to pay. In broad terms, such a system would assess an individual's or a family's needs and make payments to them if they were below the determined level or deduct taxes from them if they were above, with a sliding scale provision in the detailed arrangements at the margin to ensure that there was some incentive in favour of taking up employment and working towards higher wages.

The purpose of any such reform must be to ensure that no one falls below an agreed standard of living. Any minimum income guarantee that is proposed would therefore have to take into account local and even seasonal variations in housing, food, transport, and so on. To set the appropriate figures and keep them updated would probably be the work of an independent panel.

Revisions would reflect changes (upward or downward) in the costs of the commodities that are thought essential to provide a minimum standard of living, rather than general movements in prices or incomes, and from time to time new 'essentials' would enter the equation and outmoded items would drop out.

Above the level of zero earnings, benefits would still be payable, but their size would be gradually reduced. This would mean that there was always an incentive for individuals to seek employment, or better-paid employment, although nobody would fall below the minimum living standard. (See Fig. 1)

Rationalizing tax payments. A number of unified tax and benefit schemes have been suggested in the past, from modest ones covering limited measures of income support to fully fledged systems of negative income tax that would incorporate virtually all social security support. It is the latter comprehensive approach that we are proposing.

Instead of collecting income from those above the poverty line (and some below it too) by means of national insurance at 9% and income tax at 30%, we recommend a single income tax structure. Increasing the basic rate of income tax to 40% would produce roughly the same income as is currently produced from employees. Those with higher incomes would be a little worse off, most would be very little affected, but those on lower incomes would gain. A single person earning less than £2,000 and a married man earning less than £3,150 would pay nothing under the new scheme, whereas they currently have to pay 9% of their earnings if they receive more than around £1,800. We also suggest the abolition of the employers' element of the national insurance contribution, which is not in fact an insurance contribution in any meaningful sense, but merely a tax on jobs and an administrative headache for the very people – small businesses – that are most likely to generate new jobs if given the opportunity and incentive.

From: Adam Smith Institute, *Omega Report: Social Security Policy*, ASI (1984), pp. 6–7.

THE PRINCIPLES OF SOCIAL DIVIDENDS

The main principle of the social dividend is disarmingly simple: that every citizen should be paid a weekly income, sufficient for subsistence, by the state, on no conditions except proof of citizenship. Income from work would therefore be over and above this minimum for all. A supplement would be paid to people, like the disabled, frail elderly, who were unfit to work at all. The system would be paid for by a unified tax on incomes. Since the social dividend would take the place not only of all social security benefits, child benefits and student grants, but also of all tax allowances. All earnings would be taxed.

A single agency would collect and redistribute about 50 per cent of national income. The system would be so simple that it could be readily computerised and would, in fact, involve large savings of administrative costs.

Up till recently, such a proposal would have seemed utopian and absurd – indeed, people like myself who have been advocating it for over a decade were treated with the caution usually reserved for lunatics. Two things have changed this. First, the state now redistributes very large proportions of national income, and according to principles and methods which are for many people repugnant. For instance, a third of all tenants now qualify for means-tested housing benefits, and the state effectively determines the income levels (through the tax-benefit system) of most people below average earnings, snaring millions in poverty traps of one kind or another.

A more important contributory factor is mass unemployment, which is likely to continue at the present rates or above until the end of the decade, not merely in Britain but also in much of western Europe. Market-oriented politicians and economists can neither deny the probability of this enduring problem, nor suggest any credible solutions to it. Unemployment remains a costly and politically embarrassing fact of life. It is a drain on national resources in itself. It leads to inflexibility in working practices, and defensiveness by trade unions, holding onto jobs, which restrain the potential for productivity growth.

From: B. Jordan 'The social wage: a right for all', *New Society*, 26 April 1984, p. 143.

PROPOSALS FOR TAX AND BENEFIT CREDITS

Tax credits and benefit credits

At present, the information provided in a tax return allows the Inland Revenue to compute the allowances due to any taxpayer. A coding, based on these allowances, is then used to determine the amount deducted from his pay each week or month. With tax allowances replaced by tax credits, precisely the same administrative procedures could be used to calculate the credits due to a taxpayer, and this is what would have happened under the Cockfield scheme. We also envisage that these administrative procedures would be used to compute benefit credits. It is these benefit credits, which would replace the major social security benefits (such as housing benefit and FIS) given to the working poor, which are at the centre of our proposed reforms.

How would a benefit credit work? Both tax credits and benefit credits are lump-sum payments which depend on the particular circumstances of the household – marital and working status, number of children, housing costs, etc. Both of them are reduced in amount as income increases, under a schedule which is prescribed for that group of taxes or benefits: by a tax schedule for income tax, by a withdrawal rate of benefits. The difference between a tax credit and a benefit credit is a simple one. A tax credit can reduce your tax liability, but the most it can do is to extinguish it. If your income is very low, the tax you pay will fall correspondingly; but however high your tax credit and low your income, the smallest amount you can pay in tax is zero. A benefit credit works in just the opposite way. However high your income is, the most it can do is to extinguish your benefit credit. The minimum you can receive is zero, regardless of how low your benefit credit may be and how high your income.

The following example may help to clarify the scheme. Suppose the marginal rate of tax is 30 per cent, and a household is entitled to a tax credit of £24. If its income is less than £80 its tax liability (30 per cent of £80) will be extinguished by its tax credit. Suppose that the benefit credit is £24 with a marginal rate of withdrawal of 30 per cent: the effect is that someone with no other income would get £24; someone earning £30 would be paid £15 (£24 less 30 per cent of £30). Someone on £80 would neither pay nor receive: the tax liability would be eliminated by the tax credit, and the benefit credit would be eliminated by his income.

Clearly, there is no special reason why the tax and benefit credits have to be structured in the same way. If the benefit credit were £40, with a marginal withdrawal rate of 50 per cent, then everyone with an income above £80 – in the paying rather than the receiving range – would be unaffected. Everyone below this would be better off than in the earlier example, but the price would be a higher effective rate of tax on people in this range.

From: A. Dilnot, J. Kay & C. Morris, *The Reform of Social Security*, Oxford UP (1984), pp. 80-1.

The case for social insurance

545. The key arguments commonly used in the case against the principle of social insurance are that:

(a) *The contributory system effectively excludes major groups – for example, women, part-time workers, the young and the disabled – from coverage by national insurance benefits.*

(b) *Entitlement to benefit should be based upon the criterion of present need alone – such as unemployment, sickness or disability – rather than on a past contribution record.*

(c) *National insurance contributions are in reality a tax rather than an insurance premium. Contributions are not worked out on the usual insurance principles of risk. Benefits are not paid out of a fund only paid for by those people who get them.*

(d) *The current system of national insurance is not even as progressive as the income tax system. The upper earnings limit makes it positively regressive and the lower earnings limit produces its own poverty trap and acts as a disincentive to increase earnings to low paid workers, especially part-timers.*

546. As we have acknowledged, there are very substantial problems with the national insurance system as it currently operates. However, we do not see these as insurmountable. As well as the crediting-in of claimant groups we would also seek a reform of contributions. We would want an abolition of both the upper and lower earnings limits, which (on the one hand) produce marginal tax rates of several hundred per cent as income crosses the lower threshold, and (on the other), actually leads to a fall in the marginal rate from 39 per cent to 30 per cent for those whose earnings rise above the upper limit. With the reforms we suggest, social insurance would be able to provide a level of benefit which is substantially above any likely rate of universal benefit in our present social and economic system.

547.   However national insurance operates in practice, the principle of social insurance has wide popular support. This was found in the poll conducted for the Civil Service unions by MORI, where a majority of those interviewed favoured a social security system to which all contributed and from which all could claim benefits.

548.   Social insurance is a system which involves people across a range of incomes and occupations. Rather than being mainly of interest only to those who are low paid or unwaged, it enables all those contributing to have insurance against a range of contingencies such as unemployment and sickness. As such it can be expected to elicit a wide spectrum of political support.

549.   The removal of the principle of social insurance would increase divisions in our society between those on lower and those on higher wages and increase resistance to the redistribution of wealth which social security can potentially achieve.

550.   Finally, social insurance is relatively cheap and simple to administer and there is a high take-up rate on national insurance benefits, demonstrating the popularity and relative lack of stigma attached to them.

From: SCPS, *Social Security for All the People: An Alternative to the 'New Poor Law'*, SCPS (1985), p. 70.

We favour two categories of benefits to replace the whole of the present benefit system. The first category is that of 'positional benefits' paid to the various groups of people who are not in full-time work and so cannot rely on a wage as an adequate source of income. We call these 'positional benefits' because they relate to an individual's 'position' when s/he claims benefit – as an unemployed person, a carer, someone who is sick, a part-time worker, etc. The second category is that of 'cost-related benefits', for those people who have a need to incur extra expenditure, whether in work or not, for example, those with high housing costs. This approach would avoid the use of means tests and make contributions tests unnecessary. Moreover, it would relate benefit payments directly to the social causes of need. Thus, for example, the unemployed, the sick, the elderly and those engaged in child-care (whether as single parents or in couples) would receive a flat-rate positional benefit, irrespective of income or contributions. Disabled people would receive a cost-related benefit to help with mobility, care and other needs. Despite its universalist character, such a system could be made to be strongly progressive through a comprehensive taxation system. In order to overcome the current obstacles to part-time work, we propose that it should be possible to claim benefit as unemployed on a part-time basis.

The principle of relating benefits to needs would be extended to those in full-time work, in that they should be able to receive benefits for additional needs on the same basis as those people not working. As at present, parents would be able to claim child benefit when working, but the level should be increased substantially to approach the full costs of supporting a child. Similarly, disabled people would be able to receive additional benefits whether or not they are working. We do not, however, believe that the benefit system should meet the basic needs of those in full-time work, by some form of 'social credit', as has been proposed, for example, by the National Federation of Claimants' Unions. Such needs would be the responsibility of employers to meet through the wages system, and that responsibility would be enforceable through a minimum wage. Nevertheless we recognize that in the medium term it is impossible for wages or a flat-rate benefit to cover the wide variation in housing costs which presently exists: we therefore propose a taxable housing allowance which would vary according to the level of housing costs. Benefits, taxation and entitlement to minimum wages should be assessed on an individual basis. Living relationships should be a matter of choice. At the moment they are not: many women suffer an enforced financial dependency on men, because of the use of the family unit as the basis of income maintenance assessment and because of the obstacles to women (especially mothers) obtaining genuine financial independence through work. All adults should be given financial independence with dignity. We also propose a uniform system which would not discriminate on grounds of sex, race or locality. In turn, that entails guaranteeing the confidentiality of treatment under the income maintenance system, particulary in order to safeguard the rights of black claimants.

From: P. Esam, R. Good & C. Middleton, *Who's to Benefit: A Radical Review of the Social Security System*, Verso (1985), pp. 20–1.

REFERENCES

ABEL SMITH, B. (1963) 'Beveridge II: another viewpoint', *New Society*, 28 February.

ABEL SMITH, B. (1983) 'Sex equality and social security', in Lewis, J. (ed.), *Women's Welfare/Women's Rights*, Croom Helm.

ABEL SMITH, B. & TOWNSEND, P. (1965) *The Poor and the Poorest*, G. Bell & Sons.

ABBOT, E. & BOMPAS, K. (1943) *The Woman Citizen and Social Security*, K. Bompas.

ADAM SMITH INSTITUTE (1984) *Omega Report: Social Security Policy*.

ALCOCK, P. (1985a) 'Socialist security: where should we be going and why', *Critical Social Policy*, Issue 13.

ALCOCK, P. (1985b) 'The Fowler reviews: social policy on the political agenda', *Critical Social Policy*, Issue 14.

ALCOCK, P. (1986) 'Poverty, welfare and the local state', in Lawless, P. & Raban, C. (eds), *The Contemporary British City*, Harper & Row.

ALLBESON, J. & SMITH, R. (1984) *We Don't Give Clothing Grants Any More: the 1980 Supplementary Benefit Scheme*, CPAG.

ANDERSON, P. (1974) *Lineages of the Absolutist State*, New Left Books.

ASHBY, P. (1984) *Social Security after Beveridge: What Next?*, NCVO.

ATKINSON, A. (1969) *Poverty in Britain and the Reform of Social Security*, Cambridge University Press.

ATKINSON, A. (1984) 'A guide to the reform of social security', *New Society*, 13 December.

BARRETT, M. (1980) *Women's Oppression Today: Problems in Marxist Feminist Analysis*, Verso.

BARRETT, M. & MCINTOSH, M. (1981) 'The "Family wage": some problems for socialists and feminists', *Capital and Class*, No. 11.

BARRETT, M. & MCINTOSH, M. (1982) *The Anti-Social Family*, Verso.

BEECHEY, V. (1977) 'Some notes on female wage labour in capitalist production', *Capital and Class*, No. 3.

BELFAST COMMUNITY INFORMATION SERVICE (1985) *Computerised Welfare Rights.*

BELTRAM, G. (1984) *Testing the Safety Net: an Enquiry into the Reformed Supplementary Benefit Scheme,* Bedford Square Press/ NCVO.

BENNETT, F. (1983) 'The state, welfare and women's dependence', in Segal, L. (ed.), *What Is To Be Done About the Family?,* Penguin.

BERTHOUD, R. (1984) *The PSI Study: the Reform of Social Security – Working Papers,* Policy Studies Institute.

BERTHOUD, R. (1985) *The Examination of Social Security,* Policy Studies Institute.

BERTHOUD, R. (1986) *Selective Social Security: an Analysis of the Government's Plan,* Policy Studies Institute.

BERTHOUD, R., BROWN, J. & COOPER, S. (1981) *Poverty and the Development of Anti-Poverty Policy in the UK,* Heinemann.

BEVERIDGE, SIR. W. (1942) *Report on Social Insurance and Allied Services,* Cmd. 6404, HMSO.

BINNEY, V., HARKELL, G. & NIXON, J. (1981) *Leaving Violent Men: a Study of Refuges and Housing for Battered Women,* Women's Aid Federation.

BISSETT, L. & COUSSINS, J. (1982) *Badge of Poverty: a New Look at the Stigma Attached to Free School Meals,* CPAG.

BOOTH, C. (1889) *The Life and Labour of the People, Vol. I,* Williams & Norgate.

BRADSHAW, J. (1982) 'Public expenditure on social security', in Walker, A. (ed.), *Public Expenditure and Social Policy: an Examination of Social Spending and Social Priorities,* Heinemann EB.

BRADSHAW, J. (1985) 'Tried and found wanting: the take-up of means-tested benefits', in Ward, S. (cd.), *DHSS in Crisis: Social Security – under Pressure and under Review,* CPAG.

BROWN BOOK (1976) *The Law Relating to Social Security and Family Allowances,* HMSO.

BROWN, C. (1984) *Black and White Britain: the Third PSI Survey,* Heinemann EB.

BULL, D. & WILDING, P. (eds), (1983) *Thatcherism and the Poor,* CPAG.

BURGHES, L. & STAGLES, R. (1983) *No Choice at Sixteen: a Study of Educational Maintenance Allowances,* CPAG.

CANNAN, C. (1975) 'Welfare rights and wrongs', in Bailey, R. & Brake, M. (eds), *Radical Social Work,* Edward Arnold.

CHILD POVERTY ACTION GROUP *National Welfare Benefits Handbook*, CPAG.

CHILD POVERTY ACTION GROUP *Rights Guide to Non-means-tested Social Security Benefits*, CPAG.

CHILD POVERTY ACTION GROUP (1984) *Poverty*, No. 57.

CHILD POVERTY ACTION GROUP (1985) *Burying Beveridge: a Detailed Response to the Green Paper – Reform of Social Security*, CPAG.

COHEN, R. & RUSHTON, A. (1982) *Welfare Rights*, Heinemann EB.

COLLARD, D. (1980) 'Social dividend and negative income tax', in Sandford, C., Pond, C. & Walker, R. (eds), *Taxation and Social Policy*, Heinemann EB.

COOPER, S. (1985) *The Education and Training Benefits*, Policy Studies Institute.

CREEDY, J. & DISNEY, R. (1985) *Social Insurance in Transition: an Economic Analysis*, Oxford University Press.

CROSLAND, C. (1956) *The Future of Socialism*, Jonathan Cape.

DALE, J. & FOSTER, P. (1986) *Feminists and State Welfare*, RKP.

DEACON, A. & BRADSHAW, J. (1983) *Reserved for the Poor: the Means Test in British Social Policy*, Basil Blackwell & Martin Robertson.

DELPHY, C. (1984) *Close to Home: a Materialist Analysis of Women's Oppression*, Hutchinson.

DHSS (1978) *Social Assistance: a Review of the Supplementary Benefits Scheme in Great Britain*.

DILNOT, A., KAY, J. & MORRIS, C. (1984) *The Reform of Social Security*, Oxford UP.

DONNISON, D. (1979) 'Benefit of simplicity', *Roof*, March/April.

DONNISON, D. (1982) *The Politics of Poverty*, Martin Robertson.

ENGELS, F. (1970) 'The origin of the family, private property and the state', in Marx, K. & Engels, F., *Selected Works*, Lawrence & Wishart.

EQUAL OPPORTUNITIES COMMISSION (1981) *Behind Closed Doors*, EOC.

ESAM, P., GOOD, R. & MIDDLETON, C. (1985) *Who's to Benefit: a Radical Review of the Social Security System*, Verso.

FEDERATION OF CLAIMANT'S UNIONS (1984) *A Guaranteed Minimum Income*.

FIELD, F. (1982) *Poverty and Politics: the Inside Story of the CPAG's Campaigns in the 1970s*, Heinemann EB.

FIELD, F., MEACHER, M. & POND, C. (1977) *To Him Who Hath: a Study of Poverty and Taxation*, Penguin.

FIELD, F. & PIACHAUD, D. (1971) 'The poverty trap', *New Statesman*, 3 December.

FIMISTER, G. (1986) *Welfare Rights Work in Social Services*, Macmillan.

FINER COMMITTEE (1974) *Report of the Committee on One-Parent Families, Cmnd. 5629, HMSO.*

FISHER COMMITTEE (1973) *Report of the Committee on Abuse of Social Security Benefits*, Cmnd. 5228, HMSO.

FITCH, M. & REID, P. (1983) 'Take-up campaigns', unpublished paper.

FRANEY, R. (1983) *Poor Law: the Mass Arrest of Homeless Claimants in Oxford*, CHAR/CPAG/CDC/NAPO/NCCL.

FRIEDMAN, M. (1962) *Capitalism and Freedom*, University of Chicago Press.

GILBERT, B. (1966) *The Origins of National Insurance*, Michael Joseph.

GILMOUR, I. (1978) *Inside Right*, Quartet Books.

GINSBURG, N. (1979) *Class, Capital and Social Policy*, Macmillan.

GOLDING, P. & MIDDLETON, S. (1982) *Images of Welfare: Press and Public Attitudes to Welfare*, Basil Blackwell & Martin Robertson.

GORDON, P. (1983) 'Medicine, racism and immigration control', *Critical Social Policy*, Issue 7.

GORDON, P. & NEWNHAM, A. (1985) *Passport to Benefits: Racism in Social Security*, CPAG/Runnymede Trust.

GOUGH, I. (1979) *The Political Economy of the Welfare State*, Macmillan.

GREEN PAPER (1985) *Reform of Social Security*, Vols 1, 2 & 3, Cmnd. 9517, 9518 & 9519, HMSO.

GROVES, D. (1983) 'Members and survivors: women and retirement-pensions legislation', in Lewis, J. (ed.), *Women's Welfare/Women's Rights*, Croom Helm.

HALL, P., LAND, H., PARKER, R. & WEBB, A. (1975) *Change, Choice and Conflict in Social Policy*, Heinemann EB.

HENWOOD, M. & WICKS, M. (1986) *Benefit or Burden? The Objectives and Impact of Child Support*, Family Policy Studies Centre.

HIGGINS, J. (1978) *The Poverty Business: Britain and America*, Blackwell/Martin Robertson.

HIGGINS, J., DEAKIN, N., EDWARDS, J. & WICKS, M. (1983) *Government and Urban Poverty*, Blackwell.

HILL, M. & LAING, P. (1979) *Social Work and Money*, George Allen & Unwin.

HOLMAN, R. (1978) *Poverty: Explanations of Deprivation*, Allen Lane.

HOWE, L. (1985) 'The "deserving" and the "undeserving": practice in an urban, local social security office', *Journal of Social Policy*, Vol. 14.

HUMPHRIES, J. (1977) 'Class struggle and the persistence of the working-class family', *Cambridge Journal of Economics*, Vol. 1.

JESSOP, R. (1982) *The Capitalist State: Marxist Theories and Methods,* Martin Robertson.

JORDAN, B. (1984) 'The social wage: a right for all', *New Society,* 26 April.

JOSEPH, K. (1972) Speech to Preschool Playgroups Association, 29 June.

KEMP, P. (1984) *The Cost of Chaos: a Survey of the Housing Benefit Scheme,* SHAC.

KINCAID, J. (1964) *Poverty and Equality in Britain: a Study of Social Security and Taxation,* Penguin.

LABOUR PARTY (1963) *New Frontiers for Social Security,* Labour Party.

LAND, H. (1976) 'Women: supporters or supported?', in Barker, D. & Allen, S. (eds), *Sexual Divisions and Society: Process and Change,* Tavistock.

LANSLEY, S. (1982) *Alternatives to Housing Benefit,* CPAG.

LEE, P. & RABAN, C. (1987) *Marxism, Fabianism and Welfare,* Forthcoming.

LEES, D. (1967) 'Poor families and fiscal reform', *Lloyds bank Review,* No. 86.

LE GRAND, J. (1981) *The Strategy of Equality,* George Allen & Unwin.

LEWIS, O. (1968) *La Vida,* Panther.

LISTER, R. (1975) *The Case for Reform,* CPAG.

LISTER, R. (1978) *Social Assistance – the Real Challenge,* CPAG.

LISTER, R. & FIMISTER, G. (1980) *The Case Against Contribution Tests,* CPAG.

LISTER, R., ROLL, J. & SMITH, R. (1985) *What Future for Social Security? A Preliminary Commentary on the Green Paper on the Reform of Social Security,* CPAG.

LONEY, M. (1983) *Community Against Government: the British Community Development Project 1968–1978,* Heinemann.

LONEY, M. (1986) *The Politics of Greed: the New Right and the Welfare State,* Pluto Press.

LONSDALE, S. (1985) *Work and Inequality,* Longman.

MCCARTHY, M. (1986) *Campaigning for the Poor: CPAG and the Politics of Welfare,* Croom Helm.

MCCLELLAND, J. (1982) *A Little Pride and Dignity: the Importance of Child Benefit,* CPAG.

MACGREGOR, S. (1981) *The Politics of Poverty,* Longman.

MCGURK, P. & RAYNSFORD, N. (1982) *A Guide to Housing Benefits,* Institute of Housing/SHAC.

MCINTOSH, M. (1981) 'Feminism and social policy', *Critical Social Policy*, Vol. 1, No. 1.

MACK, J. & LANSLEY, S. (1985) *Poor Britain*, George Allen & Unwin.

MCKNIGHT, J. (1985) 'Pressure points: the crisis in management', in Ward, S. (ed.), *DHSS in Crisis: Social Security – under Pressure and under Review*, CPAG.

MACMILLAN, H. (1938) *The Middle Way*, Macmillan.

MACNICOL, J. (1980) *The Movement for Family Allowances 1918–45*, Heinemann EB.

MANN, K. (1986) 'The making of a claiming class: the neglect of agency in analysis of the welfare state', *Critical Social Policy*, Issue 15.

MANWARING, T. & SIGLER, N. (eds) (1985) *Breaking the Nation: a Guide to Thatcher's Britain*, Pluto Press/New Socialist.

MARX, K. (1970) 'The Eighteenth Brumaire of Louis Bonaparte', in Marx, K. & Engels, F., *Selected Works*, Lawrence & Wishart.

MASSON, J. (1985) 'Women's pensions', *Journal of Social Welfare Law*, November.

MEACHER COMMITTEE (1983) *Third Special Report of the House of Commons Treasury and Civil Service Select Committee*, HMSO.

MEACHER, MICHAEL (1985) 'The good society', *New Socialist*, June.

MEACHER, MOLLY (1974) *Scrounging on the Welfare: the Four Week Rule*, Penguin.

MEADE, J. (1978) *The Structure and Reform of Direct Taxation*, IFS/George Allen & Unwin.

MESHER, J. (1985) *Supplementary Benefit and Family Income Supplement: the Legislation*, second edition, Sweet & Maxwell.

MILTON KEYNES WELFARE RIGHTS GROUP (1985) *How the Millions Were Claimed!*

MINFORD, P. (1984) *Economic Affairs*, April/June.

NATIONAL ASSOCIATION OF CITIZENS' ADVICE BUREAUX (1985) *Reform of Social Security: Programme for Change*, NACAB.

NATIONAL CONSUMER COUNCIL (1976) *Means-tested Benefits: a Discussion Paper*, NCC.

NATIONAL CONSUMER COUNCIL (1984) *Of Benefit to All: a Consumer Review of Social Security*, NCC.

NATIONAL CONSUMER COUNCIL (1985) *Of Benefit to Whom? A Response to the Government's Green Paper, Reform of Social Security*, NCC.

OGUS, A. & BARENDT, E. (1982) *The Law of Social Security*, second edition, plus supplements, Butterworths.

OUTER CIRCLE POLICY UNIT (1978) *Beyond Beveridge*.

PAHL, J. (1980) 'Patterns of money management within marriage', *Journal of Social Policy*, Vol. 9.

PARKER, H. (1984) *Action on Welfare: Reform of Personal Income and Taxation*, Social Affairs Unit.

PARSONS, T. (1949) *The Structure of Social Action*, Glencoe.

PIACHAUD, D. (1979) *The Cost of a Child*, CPAG.

PINKER, R. (1974) 'Social policy and social justice', *Journal of Social Policy*, Vol. 3.

PIVEN, F. & CLOWARD, R. (1972) *Regulating the Poor: the Functions of Public Welfare*, Tavistock.

POND, C. & WINYARD, S. (1983) *The Case for a National Minimum Wage*, Low Pay Unit, Pamphlet No. 23.

PRICE, S. (1979) 'Ideologies of female dependence in the welfare state – women's response to the Beveridge Report', unpublished paper.

PROSSER, T. (1983) *Test Cases for the Poor: Legal Techniques in the Politics of Social Welfare*, CPAG.

RABAN, C. (1986) 'The welfare state – from consensus to crisis', in Lawless, P. & Raban, C. (eds), *The Contemporary British City*, Harper & Row.

RAYNOR REPORT (1981) *Payment of Benefits to Unemployed People*, DOE/DHSS.

REDDIN, M. (1968) 'Local authority means tested services', in *Social Services for All?*, Fabian Society.

RHYS WILLIAMS, J. (1943) *Something to Look Forward to*, McDonald.

ROUTH, G. (1980) *Occupation and Pay in Great Britain 1906-1979*, Macmillan.

ROWE REPORT (1985) *Housing Benefit Review*, Cmnd. 9520, HMSO.

ROWNTREE, B. (1901) *Poverty: a Study of Town Life*, Macmillan.

ROWNTREE, B. (1941) *Poverty and Progress: a Second Social Survey of York*, Longman.

ROWNTREE, B. & LAVERS, G. (1951) *Poverty and the Welfare State*, Longman.

RUNCIMAN, W. (1966) *Relative Deprivation and Social Justice*, RKP.

RUTTER, M. & MADGE, N. (1976) *Cycles of Disadvantage*, Heinemann EB.

SHEFFIELD ADVICE CENTRES GROUP (1985) *The Case for Advice Centres*.

SIMPSON, T. (1978) *Advocacy and Social Change: a Study of Welfare Rights Workers*, National Institute for Social Work.

SMAIL, R. (1984) 'A taxing time for the poor', in *Setting the Record on Taxes Straight*, Low Pay Review No. 17.

SMITH, R. (1985) 'Whose fiddling? Fraud and abuse', in Ward, S. (ed.), *DHSS in Crisis: Social Security – under Pressure and under Review*, CPAG.

SOCIETY OF CIVIL AND PUBLIC SERVANTS (1985) *Social Security for All the People: an Alternative to the 'New Poor Law'*, SCPS.

SOUTH TYNESIDE WELFARE RIGHTS SERVICE (1985) *Welfare Benefits Take-up Campaign: a Report*.

STEDMAN JONES, G. (1971) *Outcast London*, Oxford UP.

STRATHCLYDE REGIONAL COUNCIL (1981) *The Post Card Campaign*.

STUDY COMMISSION ON THE FAMILY (1983) *Families in the Future*.

SUPPLEMENTARY BENEFITS COMMISSION (1978) *Annual Report*, HMSO.

SUPPLEMENTARY BENEFITS COMMISSION (1979) *Response of the SBC to 'Social Assistance: a Review of the Supplementary Benefits Scheme in Great Britain'*, HMSO.

TAYLOR GOOBY, P. (1976) 'Rent benefits and tenants' attitudes: the Batley rent rebate and allowance study', *Journal of Social Policy*, Vol. 5.

TAYLOR GOOBY, P. & DALE, J. (1981) *Social Theory and Social Welfare*, Edward Arnold.

THANE, P. (1982) *The Foundations of the Welfare State*, Longman.

TITMUS, R. (1958) 'The social division of welfare', in Titmus, R. *Essays on the 'Welfare State'*, Allen & Unwin.

TOPLISS, E. (1982) *Social Responses to Handicap*, Longman.

TOWNSEND, P. (1979) *Poverty in the United Kingdom*, Penguin.

TOWNSEND, P. (1984) *Why Are the Many Poor?*, Fabian Tract 500.

TOWNSEND, P. & DAVIDSON, N. (1982) *Inequalities in Health: the Black Report*, Penguin.

TUNNARD, J. (1977) *Battle Royal*, CPAG.

VINCE, P. (1983) *Tax Credit*, Women's Liberal Federation.

WALKER, C. (1983) *Changing Social Policy: the Case of the Supplementary Benefits Review*, Occasional Papers on Social Administration 70, Bedford Square Press.

WALKER, R., LAWSON, R. & TOWNSEND, P. (eds) (1984) *Responses to Poverty: Lessons from Europe*, Heinemann EB.

WALSH, A. & LISTER, R. (1985) *Mother's Lifeline: a Survey of how Women Use and Value Child Benefit*, CPAG.

WARD, S. (1985) 'The financial crisis facing pensioners', *Critical Social Policy*, Issue 14.

WHITELEY, P. & WINYARD, S. (1983) 'Influencing social policy: the effectiveness of the poverty lobby in Britain', *Journal of Social Policy*, Vol. 12.

WHITE PAPER (1944) *Social Insurance,* Cmd. 6550, HMSO.
WHITE PAPER (1985) *Reform of Social Security: Programme for Action,* Cmnd. 9691, HMSO.
YELLOW BOOK (1983) *The Law Relating to Supplementary Benefits and Family Income Supplements,* HMSO.

INDEX